THE
CIGAR
COMPANION

THE CIGAR COMPANION

The Connoisseur's Guide

Third Edition

Anwer Bati

chartwell
books

Brimming with creative inspiration, how-to projects, and useful information to enrich your everyday life, Quarto Knows is a favorite destination for those pursuing their interests and passions. Visit our site and dig deeper with our books into your area of interest: Quarto Creates, Quarto Cooks, Quarto Homes, Quarto Lives, Quarto Drives, Quarto Explores, Quarto Gifts, or Quarto Kids.

© 1997 Quarto Publishing plc

This edition published in 2020 by Chartwell Books,
an imprint of The Quarto Group,
142 West 36th Street, 4th Floor
New York, NY 10018, USA
T (212) 779-4972 F (212) 779-6058
www.QuartoKnows.com

Chartwell titles are also available at discount for retail, wholesale, promotional, and bulk purchase. For details, contact the Special Sales Manager by email at special-sales@quarto.com or by mail at The Quarto Group, Attn: Special Sales Manager, 100 Cummings Center Suite 265D, Beverly, MA 01915 USA.

10 9 8 7 6 5 4 3

ISBN: 978-0-7858-3842-5

Library of Congress Control Number: 2019956406

Originally published as The Cigar Companion in 1997
Conceived, designed, and produced by
The Bright Press, an imprint of The Quarto Group
6, Blundell Street
London N7 9BH

Cover Design: Greg Stalley
Layout Design: Ian Hunt
Photographers: Ian Howes & Pail Forrester

Printed in China TT032021

Cigar smoking can cause cancer of the mouth and throat, even if you do not inhale and cigars contain nicotine which is an addictive substance. Cigar smoking can cause lung cancer and heart disease. Cigars are not a safe alternative to cigarettes. Tobacco smoke increases the risk of lung cancer and heart disease, even in non-smokers. This book provides general information. It should not be relied upon as recommending or promoting cigar smoking against medical advice.

CONTENTS

ACKNOWLEDGMENTS

It wouldn't have been possible to update this book without the help and support of a number of people in the cigar trade, so the Publisher would like to thank the following for the help they have given:

Philip Thompson, C.A.O. International; Felipe Gregorio, Cigars of Honduras; Jean Clement; Janelle Rosenfeld, Consolidated Cigar Corporation; Christine Brandt and Raymond Scheurer, Davidoff; Oscar Rodriguez, Dominican Cigar Imports; Carlos Fuente Jr; Paul Garmirian; Eddie Panners, Gold Leaf Tobacco Co.; Alan Edwards, Hollco Rohr; Liz Facchiano, J.R. Cigars; Stanley Kolker; Brian G. Dewey, Lane Limited; Robert Newman, M & N Cigar Mfrs, Inc.; Oscar Boruchin, Mike's Cigars; Bill Sherman, Nat Sherman Incorporated; Jorge L. Padron, Padron Cigars; Chris Boon, Rothman's International; Patrick Clayeux, Seita; Mark Segal, Segal Worldwide; Dorette Meyer, Suerdieck; Ralph Montero, Tropical Tobacco; Sherwin Seltzer, Villazon & Co., Inc.

PUBLISHER'S FOREWORD

$\mathscr{C}$igar culture has expanded on an unprecedented scale since this book was first published in 1993. In England and the United States in particular cigar-smoking has become a prestigious public pastime, and a hobby of the rich and famous. One rarely sees a movie or rock star without a cigar, and over the last 12 months alone the world has witnessed countless magazine covers sporting glamorous cigar-smoking women.

This boom in cigar culture has naturally had a tremendous effect on demand and while researching this edition, it was not uncommon to hear manufacturers admit to large back-orders in supplies—sometimes as high as six months worth. At the same time, there has been great scope for expansion, and several companies have taken advantage of this; new cigar brands have hit the market as fast as existing ones have been increasing their lines, and, with few exceptions, every brand has new sizes and many have a new look. There is a deliberate retrospective edge to current trends, and the *figuardo* shape, properly popular for the first time since the nineteenth century, has made a welcome comeback.

Despite the change of pace forced by the great boom in their industry, cigar manufacturers have contributed generously to this book for the third time. Their continued enthusiasm and praise for *The Cigar Companion* was evident at many levels within the trade; some brands use their entry as a basis for their own sales pitch, while others regard the book as their most reliable source. Whatever the reason, the book has played a major role in the cigar world over the last four years, and there is a definite indication that it will continue to do so for the foreseeable future.

MARCH 1997

INTRODUCTION

*T*he cigar has always had a very strong image in a way that the cigarette, despite its popularity, has never had. True, some cigarette brands evoke strong associations – the Marlboro cowboy, for instance – but only through advertising. Cigars, on the other hand, have acquired their image not only through the people who smoke them – one need only mention Winston Churchill, Edward VII, and any number of Hollywood film directors and producers such as Darryl F. Zanuck – but also through the occasions on which they are smoked. This applies to cigars in general, but handmade cigars, the subject of this book, in particular.

The aim of this book, whether you are a regular or occasional smoker of handmade cigars, is to tell you as much about them as possible and help you to understand the subject better. Above all, however, this book has been written to enhance your enjoyment of fine cigars and to encourage your interest in them.

ANWER BATI
AUTHOR
MARCH 1993

*M*y eighteen years in the cigar trade have been spent mainly in the company of Havana. You should know that they pay my salary, so watch out in these pages for self-serving bias. Having said that, we are all biased by our own taste in cigars. Mine is unlikely to match yours and, in the end, the choice is personal.

Cigars have seen heady days since the first appearance of this book. The "Cigar Boom," "The Renaissance of the Cigar," call it what you will, started for me at Cuba's El Corojo plantation in February 1992. Anwer Bati, Marvin Shanken, and I stood watching the massive wrapper leaves inching their way to maturity under the muslin cover. Not even Marvin could have foreseen quite what was to follow.

In revising and updating *The Cigar Companion*, I hope to do justice to Anwer's original work and, like him, to augment the pleasure you obtain from your cigars.

SIMON CHASE
AUTHOR, 2ND EDITION
MAY 1995

1

THE STORY
OF
CIGARS

THE CIGAR WORLD

*N*obody knows for sure *when* the tobacco plant was first cultivated, but there is little doubt about *where*. The native peoples of the American continent were undoubtedly the first not only to grow, but to smoke the plant, which probably first came from the Yucatán peninsula, Mexico. It was certainly used by the Maya of Central America, and when the Maya civilization was broken up, the scattered tribes carried tobacco both southward into South America, and to North America, where it was probably first used in the rites of the Mississippi Indians. It didn't come to the attention of the rest of the world until Christopher Columbus's momentous voyage of 1492.

Columbus himself was not particularly impressed by the custom, but soon Spanish and other European sailors fell for the habit, followed by the conquistadores and colonists. In due course the

THE AMERICAN INDIANS WERE ALMOST CERTAINLY THE FIRST PEOPLE TO SMOKE CIGARS.

LEFT: CHRISTOPHER COLUMBUS. HIS MEN WERE THE FIRST FROM EUROPE TO ENCOUNTER THE NORTH AMERICAN HABIT OF SMOKING.

returning conquistadores introduced tobacco smoking to Spain and Portugal. The habit, a sign of wealth, then spread to France, through the French ambassador to Portugal, Jean Nicot (who eventually gave his name to nicotine, and *Nicotiana tabacum*, the Latin name for tobacco), and to Italy. In Britain, as every school-child knows, Sir Walter Raleigh was probably responsible for intro-ducing tobacco and the new fashion for smoking.

The word tobacco, some say, was a corruption of Tobago, the name of the Caribbean island. Others claim it comes from the Tabasco province of Mexico. Cohiba, a word used by the Taino Indians of Cuba was thought to mean tobacco, but now is con-sidered to have referred to cigars. The word cigar originated from *sikar*, the Mayan word for smoking.

Although the first tobacco plantations were set up in Virginia in 1612, and Maryland in 1631, tobacco was smoked only in pipes in the American colonies. The cigar itself is thought not to have arrived until after 1762, when Israel Putnam, later an American general in the Revolutionary War, returned from Cuba, where he had been an officer in the British army. He came back to his home in Connecticut—an area where tobacco had been grown by settlers since the 17th century (and before them by the Indians)—with a selection of Havana cigars, and large amounts of Cuban tobacco. Before long, cigar factories were set up in the Hartford area, and the attempt was made to grow tobacco from Cuban seed. Produc-tion of the leaves started in the 1820s, and Connecticut tobacco today provides among the best wrapper leaves to be found outside Cuba. By the early 19th century, not only were Cuban cigars being imported into the United States, but domestic production was also taking off.

The habit of smoking cigars (as opposed to using tobacco in other forms) spread out to the rest of Europe from Spain where cigars, using Cuban tobacco, were made in Seville from 1717 on-ward. By 1790, cigar manufacture had spread north of the Pyrenees, with small factories being set up in France and Germany. But cigar smoking didn't really take off in France and Britain until after the Peninsular War (1806–12) against Napoleon, when returning British and French veterans spread the habit they had learned while serving in Spain. By this time the pipe had been replaced by snuff as the main way of taking tobacco, and cigars now became the fashionable way of smoking it. Production of segars, as they were known, began in Britain in 1820, and in 1821 an Act of Parliament was needed to set out regulations governing production. Because

FERDINAND VII KING OF SPAIN. HE VIGOROUSLY PROMOTED THE PRODUCTION OF CUBAN CIGARS.

of a new import tax, foreign cigars in Britain were already regarded as a luxury item.

Soon there was a demand for higher-quality cigars in Europe, and the Sevillas, as Spanish cigars were called, were superseded by those from Cuba (then a Spanish colony), not least as the result of a decree by King Ferdinand VII of Spain in 1821, encouraging the production of Cuban cigars, a Spanish state monopoly. Cigar smoking became such a widespread custom in Britain and France that smoking cars became a feature of European trains, and the smoking room was introduced in clubs and hotels. The habit even influenced clothing—with the introduction of the smoking jacket. In France, tuxedos are still referred to as *le smoking*. By the end of the 19th century, the after-dinner cigar, with port or brandy, was a firmly established tradition. It was given an added boost by the fact that the Prince of Wales (the future Edward VII), a leader of fashion, was a devotee, much to the chagrin of his mother, Queen Victoria, who was not amused by the habit.

Cigar smoking didn't really take off in the United States until the time of the Civil War (although John Quincy Adams, 6th President of the United States, was a confirmed cigar smoker at the beginning of the century; later, President Ulysses Grant was also to become a devotee) with the most expensive domestic cigars,

ILLUSTRATION OF A MID-19TH-CENTURY CIGAR FACTORY IN ENGLAND.

made with Cuban tobacco, called clear Havanas. The name Havana, by now, had become a generic term. Some of the best-known domestic cigars came from the factory at Conestoga, Pennsylvania, where the long "stogie" cigar was made. By the late 19th century, the cigar had become a status symbol in the United States, and branding became important. Thus, there was Henry Clay, for instance, named after the Senator. A tax reduction in the 1870s made the cigar even more popular and widely available, and encouraged domestic production. By 1919, Thomas Marshall, Woodrow Wilson's Vice President was able to say in the Senate: "What this country really needs is a good five-cent cigar," an ambition not to be achieved until almost 40 years later when new methods of cigar production allowed truly cheap cigars to be made by machine. Cigar sales in the United States have, however, declined over the last 20 years—from 9 billion cigars (of all types) in 1970, to 2 billion today.

Machine production of cigars wasn't introduced until the 1920s (in Cuba, the Por Larranaga firm was the first to attempt it, and handmade production in the United States fell from 90 percent in 1924, to a mere 2 percent by the end of the 1950s.

It was a different story in Cuba, where the cigar became a national symbol. Cuban peasants started becoming *vegueros*, tobacco growers, from the 16th century onward, waging a constant

NOTE THE WOMEN SMOKING CIGARS AS THEY LEAVE A CIGAR
FACTORY IN MANILA.

battle against the big landowners as exports of the crop grew. Some of them became tenant farmers or sharecroppers; others were forced to find new land to farm, opening up areas such as Pinar del Rio and Oriente.

By the mid-19th century, by which time there was free trade in tobacco, there were 9,500 plantations, and factories in Havana and other cities sprang up (at one stage, there were as many as 1,300, though there were only around 120 by the beginning of the 20th century), and cigar production became a fully fledged industry. Export was mainly to the United States until tariff barriers were put up in 1857. During the same period, brand and size differentiation began, and the cigar box and band were introduced.

As the industry grew, the cigar makers became the core of the Cuban industrial working class, and a unique institution was set up in 1865, which lasts to this day: the reading of literary, political, and other texts, including the works of Zola, Dumas, and Victor Hugo, to the rollers by fellow workers. This was to alleviate the boredom, and help the cause of worker education. During the last quarter of the 19th century, faced with the growing political upheaval caused by the struggle for independence from Spain, many cigar makers emigrated to the United States or nearby islands like Jamaica, where they set up cigar industries in towns like Tampa, Key West, and Kingston.

SUPERLATIVE CUBAN CIGARS ARE STILL MADE EXCLUSIVELY FOR FIDEL CASTRO, THE CUBAN LEADER, TO PRESENT TO STATE VISITORS AND DIPLOMATS.

These Cubans abroad were instrumental in funding the revolt against Spain, led in 1895 by José Martí, the Cuban national hero, and later the increasingly politicized cigar workers in Cuba were to take an important part in national life. Martí's order for the uprising was, symbolically, sent from Key West to Cuba inside a cigar. Cigar workers continued at the center of political consciousness after Fidel Castro's revolution against General Batista in 1959. After Castro started to nationalize Cuban and foreign assets, the United States embargo on Cuba, imposed in 1962, meant that Havana cigars could no longer be legally imported into the United States, except in small quantities for personal use. The cigar industry—much of which had been American-owned—was nationalized along with everything else and put under the control of the state monopoly, Cubatabaco.

Many of the dispossessed cigar factory owners such as the Palicio, Cifuentes, and Menendez families fled abroad, determined to start production up again, often using the same brand names they had owned in Cuba. As a result, cigars called Romeo Y Julieta, H. Upmann, and Partagas are made in the Dominican Republic; La Gloria Cubana in Miami; Punch and Hoyo de Monterrey in Honduras; and Sancho Panza in Mexico. In the case of Montecruz cigars, the name was slightly changed from the original Montecristo, and they were originally made in the Canary Islands, though they are now manufactured in the Dominican Republic. These brands using Cuban names usually bear no relation in terms of flavor to their Havana counterparts, however well made they may be. Entirely new brands, too, such as Don Miguel, Don Diego, and Montesino were also set up. After two decades of investment by both local and American companies, the Dominican Republic has seen rapid growth in its cigar industry during the 1990s. More than any other country, it has benefitted from the explosion of American consumer enthusiasm for handmade cigars touched off by the launch of *Cigar Aficionado* magazine in September 1992.

At the start of the decade, sales from the Dominican Republic to the United States had been expanding at a rate of around 5 percent per year. This leapt to 18 percent in 1993 when 55 million handmade cigars were shipped, accounting for just over half of all the handmade cigars imported into the United States. In 1994 growth continued, adding another 20 percent overall, with some factories claiming increases of nearly 40 percent. The greatest problem facing the Dominican Republican manufacturers today appears to be finding enough tobaccos of quality for handmade cigars.

The early 1990s have been less kind to Cuba. In the two years following the collapse of the Soviet Union, half of the island's gross domestic product evaporated. The cigar industry suffered less than most because its essential raw material—tobacco—is all grown on the island. Nonetheless, shortages of fertilizers, packaging materials, and even such mundane items as string, all of which had come from the former Eastern bloc, took their toll.

The weather played its part, too. Unseasonal rains in the Vuelta Abajo constrained the 1991 and 1992 harvests. Then the great storm of March 1993, which ended up depositing ten feet of snow on New York City, started life wreaking havoc in the Partido wrapper-growing region. Production of Havanas, which had topped 80 million in 1990, fell to around 50 million by 1994. If cigar enthusiasts around the world have been forced to search hard for their preferred Havana, their difficulties pale into insignificance alongside the trials of their Cuban counterparts. Domestic cigar production tumbled by well over half from a remarkable figure of 280 million in 1990, and stringent rationing was introduced as a result of this.

Such changes of fortune are nothing new to Cuba's hardy population. Just after the revolution, cigar exports dropped to 30 million.

THE ARCHETYPAL VIEW OF THE CIGAR SMOKER: GOOD WINE,
GOOD TOBACCO.

Havanos SA, the company which recently took over most of the marketing responsibilities for Havanas from the state-owned Cubatabaco, arranged hard currency deals with its international partners to supply materials for the crops from 1995 onward.

There can be few symbols of capitalism and plutocracy more potent than the cigar. Tycoons rarely seem happier, or more prosperous, than when pictured puffing a large Havana. It says: power, privilege, prestige—and, above all, expense. But the irony, of course, is that Havana cigars are produced in one of the world's few remaining bastions of communism.

It would be quite wrong to give the impression that the growing of cigar tobacco and the production of cigars is limited to Cuba and the Dominican Republic. Nearby Jamaica has had its own industry for over a century, and several Central American countries like Mexico, Honduras, and Nicaragua enjoy traditions of cigar making that go back much further. Ecuador now produces a good-quality wrapper, oddly known as Ecuador/Connecticut, and Brazil brings its own unique flavor and style to the creation of cigars. Further afield, the Indonesian islands of Java and Sumatra have time-honored links with the cigar makers of the Netherlands, Germany, and Switzerland, as do the Philippines with Spain. Africa's contribution comes from Cameroon, in the form of some of the most sought-after, rich, dark wrappers in the world.

THE DOMINICAN REPUBLIC

The Dominican Republic, east of Cuba, has a similar climate and very good tobacco-growing conditions, particularly in the Cibao River valley. It has, over the last 15 years or so, become a major exporter of top quality handmade cigars, particularly to the United States, which imports over 60 million cigars a year from there. This accounts for half of the American handmade cigar market. It has attracted major cigar manufacturers such as General Cigar (with brands like Partagas) and Consolidated Cigar (brand names such as Don Diego and Primo del Rey). Consolidated moved its operations to the Dominican Republic from the Canary Islands. Most of the tobacco grown in the Dominican Republic is for fillers only. Virtually all the wrappers and many of the binders for cigars made there are imported from countries like the U.S. (Connecticut), Cameroon (for Partagas, for instance), Brazil, Honduras, Mexico, and Ecuador. Some fillers, too are brought in from abroad. Major efforts, led by the Fuente family, are now being made to extend the variety of tobaccos grown in the country. Wrappers, always the toughest challenge, are now to be seen on the Fuente's plantations … and, increasingly, on their cigars.

CONNECTICUT VALLEY

The sandy loam of the Connecticut valley (where conditions suitable for growing top-quality cigar tobacco are created under huge, 10-foot high tents), and the use of the Hazelwood strain of Cuban seed produces some of the world's best wrapper leaves, called Connecticut Shade. The leaves are very expensive to produce and sell for as much as $40 a pound, adding between 50 cents and a dollar to the price of a cigar. The growing cycle begins in March, with the harvest taking place in August. The drying process, though essentially the same as in Cuba, is helped, in Connecticut, by the use of careful heating from below using gas burners. Connecticut wrappers are used for cigars such as Macanudo, and the Dominican-made Davidoffs.

PINAR DEL RIO *and*

T*here are those who disagree (the leaf producers of Connecticut, the Dominican Republic, and Honduras foremost among them), but it is still generally acknowledged that the finest cigar tobacco in the world comes from Cuba, and in particular from the Vuelta Abajo area of the Pinar del Rio province.*

Pinar del Rio is the region at the western end of Cuba, situated between mountains and the coast, the island's third largest province. The area, which points toward the Mexican Yucatán peninsula, is undulating, green, and lush (it was under the sea in prehistoric times), rather resembling southeast Asia or parts of southern Louisiana and Florida. Life and living conditions there are primitive for the 600,000 inhabitants, with none of the sophistication or development to be found near Havana. But the agricultural conditions—climate, rainfall, and soil (a reddish sandy loam)—are perfect for tobacco production, by far the main industry. Tobacco is grown on smallholdings (many of them privately owned, but selling tobacco to the government at a fixed

price), totaling about 100,000 acres. They create a patchwork effect across the plains. Before the revolution, large tracts of land were owned by the main tobacco companies, but today, although vegueros *can own up to 150 acres, most cultivate from five to ten acres. Outside the tobacco season, maize is often grown on the same land. Vuelta Abajo takes up most of the 160 square miles of Pinar del Rio. Tobacco grows freely here, but the finest,*

VUELTA ABAJO, CUBA

destined for cigars to be known as Havanas or Habanos, comes from a surprisingly small area centered around the two towns of San Juan y Martinez and San Luis. Not much more than 2,500 acres are devoted to wrappers and 5,000 acres to fillers and binders. Amongst the best known plantations are El Corojo, where the Corojo wrapper plant was developed, and Hoyo de Monterrey, famous for its fillers.

The rainfall in Pinar del Rio is among the highest in Cuba, with 65 inches a year, although significant for tobacco growth, only 8 inches or so of rain—over an average of 26 days—falls during the main growing months from November to February. They come in the middle of La Seca, the dry season, by which time the soil has had plenty of rain from storms in the period from May to October. Temperatures during the growing season reach average highs of 80°F, with around 8 hours a day of sunshine, and average humidity of 64 percent. The Semivuelta area is the second tobacco-growing area of Pinar del Rio, and produces thicker leaves, with a stronger aroma than those of Vuelta Abajo. This tobacco was once exported to the United States, but is now used for the domestic cigar industry.

The Partido area, near Havana, also grows high-quality wrappers for handmade Havanas. Remedios in the island's center, and Oriente at its eastern end produce tobacco, too, but not for top-quality cigars.

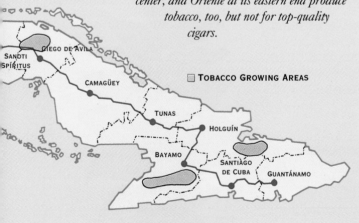

■ **TOBACCO GROWING AREAS**

GROWING CIGAR TOBACCO

The following passage is specifically for Havana cigars, but the process is, broadly speaking, similar elsewhere.

Cigars are a natural product, often compared to wine (though the comparison sometimes tends to get out of hand), and the quality of a cigar is directly related to the type and quality of leaves used in its construction, just as the quality of wine depends on the type and quality of grapes used.

Tobacco seedbeds have to be in flat fields, so that the seeds aren't washed away. After being planted, the seeds are covered with cloth or straw to shade them from the sun. This covering is gradually removed as they begin to germinate, and after around 35 days (during which the seed will be sprayed with pesticides), they are transplanted—usually in the second half of October—into the tobacco fields proper. The leaves are watered both by rain and the morning dew, and irrigated from below.

The tobacco plant is considered in three parts: the top, or corona, the middle, and the bottom. As the leaves develop, buds appear. These have to be removed by hand to prevent them from stunting leaf and plant growth. The quality of wrapper leaf is crucial in any

CUBAN TOBACCO PLANT

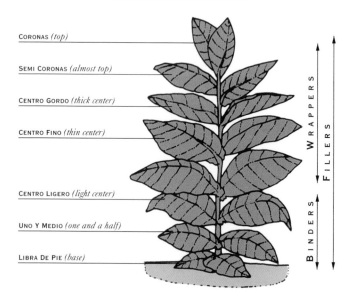

CORONAS *(top)*

SEMI CORONAS *(almost top)*

CENTRO GORDO *(thick center)*

CENTRO FINO *(thin center)*

CENTRO LIGERO *(light center)*

UNO Y MEDIO *(one and a half)*

LIBRA DE PIE *(base)*

WRAPPERS

FILLERS

BINDERS

cigar. Plants called Corojos, specifically designated to provide wrapper leaves for the very best cigars, are always grown under gauze sheets held up by tall wooden poles. They prevent the leaves from becoming too thick in a protective response to sunlight. The technique, called *tapado* (covering), also helps them to remain smooth.

When harvesting time arrives, leaves are removed by hand, using a single movement. Those selected as wrappers are put in bundles of five, a manojo, or hand. The leaves are picked in six phases: *libra de pie* (at the base), *uno y medio* (one-and-a-half), *centro ligero* (light center), *centro fino* (thin center), *centro gordo* (thick center), and *corona* (crown). The *libra de pie* section isn't used for wrappers. A week passes between each phase. The finest leaves found in the middle of the plant; the top leaves (*corona*) are usually too oily to be used for wrappers, except for domestic consumption, and are often used as binder leaves. The whole cycle, from transplanted seedlings to the end of harvesting takes some 120 days, with each plant being visited an average of 170 times—making it a very labor-intensive process.

Wrapper leaves grown under cover are classified by color as *ligero* (light), *seco* (dry), *viso* (glossy), *amarillo* (yellow), *medio tiempo* (half texture), and *quebrado* (broken), while those grown under the sun are divided into *volado*, *seco*, *ligero*, and *medio tiempo*. The ligero leaves from the top of the plant have a very strong flavor, the seco

EL COROJO WRAPPER PLANTATION IN SAN LUÌS ONE WEEK AFTER PLANTING.

HARVESTED WRAPPER LEAVES ARRIVE AT CURING BARN,
LA GUIRA, CUBA.

from the middle are much lighter, and the volado leaves from the bottom are used to add bulk and for their burning qualities. The art of making a good cigar is to blend these, along with a suitable wrapper leaf, in such proportions as to give the eventual cigar a mild, medium, or full flavor, and to ensure that it burns well. The leaves are also classified by size (large, average, small) and by physical condition (unhealthy or broken leaves are used for cigarettes or machine-made cigars). If all the leaves are good, each wrapper plant can wrap 32 cigars. The condition and quality of the wrapper leaf is crucial to the attractive appearance of a cigar, as well as its aroma.

The bundles of leaves are then taken to a tobacco barn on the *vega*, or plantation, to be cured. The barns face west so that the sun heats one end in the morning, and the other in the late afternoon. The temperature and humidity in the barns is carefully controlled, if necessary by opening and closing the doors at both ends (usually kept shut) to take account of changes of temperature or rainfall.

Once the leaves reach the barn, they are strung up on poles, or *cujes*, using needle and thread. The poles, each holding around 100 leaves, are hoisted up horizontally (their position high in the barn allows air to circulate), and the leaves left to dry for between 45 and 60 days, depending on the weather. During this time, the green chlorophyll in the leaves turns to brown carotene, giving them their characteristic color. The poles are then taken down, the threads cut, and the leaves stacked into bundles according to type.

The bundles are then taken to the fermentation houses and placed in piles about three feet high, covered with jute. Enough moisture remains in the leaves to spark the first fermentation, a process like composting. Heat develops, but the temperature must be watched carefully so that it does not exceed 92°F during the 35 to 40 days that the piles are left intact. The leaves assume a uniform color.

The piles are then broken up and the leaves cooled. The next stop in their journey is at the *escogida*, or sorting house, where they will be graded according to color, size, and texture and where the fillers will have part of their stems stripped out. In preparation for handling, they are moistened either under a spray of pure water for wrappers or a mixture of water and the juices from tobacco stems for fillers.

THREADING THE WRAPPER LEAVES TOGETHER. THEY ARE HUNG
UP IN BATCHES OF 50.

CIGAR TOBACCO PRODUCTION

1 WRAPPER LEAF CURING BARN. THE LEAVES TURN BROWN AS CHLOROPHYLL TURNS TO CAROTENE.

2 SORTING HOUSE. UNPACKING "TERICOS" PRIOR TO MOISTENING AND GRADING.

3 INSPECTING WRAPPER LEAVES DURING PRIMARY FERMENTATION.

4 WRAPPER LEAVES BEING SORTED BY SIZE, COLOR, AND TEXTURE.

BACKGROUND PHOTOGRAPH: WRAPPER LEAVES GROWING UNDER CHEESE GAUZE "TAPADOS" TO SHADE THEM FROM THE SUN.

3

Traditionally, women perform the tasks of sorting and stripping. Each leaf is tenderly examined and graded. Broken leaves are set aside for use in cigarettes.

Flattened onto boards (*planchas*), the leaves return to the fermentation area. In dark rooms, they are built into stacks called *burros* up to 6 feet high. The second, more powerful fermentation begins within the damp leaves. A perforated wooden casing has been buried in the *burro*, into which a sword-like thermometer is thrust. The temperature inside must not exceed 110°F for around 60 days, longer for some leaf types, shorter for others. If it does, the bulk is broken down and the leaves cooled before it s rebuilt. Ammonia is released as the leaves shed their impurities.

Because of the fermentation process, cigar tobacco is much lower in acidity, tar, and nicotine than cigarette tobacco, making it much more palatable.

It is now time for the leaves to be sent to the factories or warehouses in *tercios*, square bales wrapped with palm bark, which helps to keep the tobacco at a constant humidity, and slowly mature until it is needed—sometimes for as long as two years.

These long and complicated processes of selection and fermentation have to be carefully supervised and are crucial to the final flavor of handmade cigars.

WRAPPER LEAVES FOR **C**OHIBA CIGARS MOISTENED
BEFORE GOING TO CIGAR ROLLER.

THE STRUCTURE OF A CIGAR

Handmade cigars have three constituent parts—the filler, the binder, and the wrapper. Each of the parts has a different function when the cigar is actually smoked.

The outside wrapper (or *capa*) dictates the cigar's appearance. As described, it is always grown under gauze and fermented separately from other leaves to ensure that is smooth, not too oily, and has a subtle bouquet. It also has to be soft and pliable so that it is easy for the roller to handle.

Wrapper leaves from different plantations have varying colors (and thus subtly different flavors, more sugary if they are darker, for instance) and are used for different brands. Good wrapper leaves have to be elastic and must have no protruding veins. They have to be matured for between one year and 18 months, the longer the better. Wrappers of handmade non-Cuban cigars might come from Connecticut, Cameroon, Sumatra, Ecuador, Honduras, Mexico, Costa Rica, or Nicaragua. The wrapper is the most expensive part of the cigar.

The binder leaf (capote) holds the cigar together and is usually two halves of coarse sun-grown leaf from the upper part of the plant, chosen because of its good tensile strength.

The filler is made of separate leaves folded by hand along their length, to allow a passage through which smoke can be drawn when the cigar is lit. The fold can only be properly achieved by hand and is the primary reason why machine-made cigars are less satisfactory. This style of arranging the filler is sometimes called the "book" style—which means that if you were to cut the cigar down its length with a razor, the filler leaves would resemble the pages of a book. In the past, the filler was sometimes arranged using the "entubar" method—with up to eight narrow tubes of tobacco leaf rolled into the binder—making the cigar very slow-burning.

Three different types of leaf are normally used for the filler (in fatter sizes, like Montecristo No. 2, a fourth type is also used).

Ligero leaves from the top of the plant are dark and full in flavor as a result of oils produced by exposure to sunlight. They have to be matured for at least two years before they can be used in cigar making. Ligero tobacco is always placed in the middle of the cigar, because it burns slowly.

Seco leaves, from the middle of the plant, are much lighter in color and flavor. They are usually used after maturing for around 18 months.

Volado leaves, from the bottom of the plant, have little or no flavor, but they have good burning qualities. They are matured for about nine months before use.

The precise blend of these different leaves in the filler dictates the flavor of each brand and size. A full-bodied cigar like Ramon Allones will, for instance, have a higher proportion of ligero in its filler, than a mild cigar such as H. Upmann, where seco and volado will predominate. Small, thin cigars will very often have no ligero leaf in them at all. The consistency of a blend is achieved by using tobacco from different harvest and farms, so a large stock of matured tobacco is essential to the process.

ROLLING A CIGAR

In making a handmade cigar, two to four filler leaves (depending on the size and strength of the cigar) are laid end to end and rolled into the two halves of the binder leaves—making up what is called the "bunch." Great skill is required to make sure that the filler is evenly distributed so that the cigar will draw properly. Wooden molds are used into which the filler blend (rolled into the binder) is pressed by the "bunchers," with a mechanical press than used to complete the process. In the Havana factory, the bunching is done by the same person who eventually adds the wrapper. The practice is slightly different in, for instance, the factories of the Dominican Republic, where specialist bunchers work in teams with specialist wrapper rollers. In both systems, the result is that each roller has a supply of ready molded fillers, prepared for what is being made on that day, at his or her work bench.

GATHERING THE BLEND OF FILLER LEAVES.

ROLLING A CIGAR

AFTER PRESSING, THE "BUNCHES" ARE READY TO HAVE WRAPPER LEAVES ROLLED AROUND THEM.

ROLLING COHIBA LANCERO CIGARS AT EL LAGUITO FACTORY, HAVANA.

THE "CHAVETA" IS USED TO TRIM SURPLUS TOBACCO.

THE FRAGILE WRAPPER IS GENTLY STRETCHED BEFORE ROLLING.

Surplus filler is trimmed from the end to form a round top. A wrapper leaf is then selected, the remaining stalk is stripped off the binder, and the wrapper is trimmed to the right size (using the central part of the leaf, placed upside-down, to avoid having any veins showing) with an oval steel blade called a chaveta. The cylinder of tobacco in its binder (the "bunch") is now laid at an angle across the wrapper, which is then stretched as necessary and wound carefully around the binder, overlapping at each turn, until it is stuck down using a tiny drop of colorless and flavorless tragacanth vegetable gum. The cigar is then rolled, applying gentle pressure, with the flat part of the steel blade to make sure its construction is even. Next, a small round piece of wrapper (about the size of a small coin) is cut out from the trimmings on hand to form the cap, which is stuck in place. In the case of cigars such as the Montecristo Especial, the closed end is sealed by twisting the end of the wrapper. This is a version of what is known as the "flag" method of capping a cigar—a highly skilled process in which the wrapper itself is smoothed down to form the cap. The flag method is only used on the best handmade cigars. Finally, the open end is guillotined to the correct length.

The construction of a cigar is a crucial factor in how well you enjoy it. If it is under-filled, it will draw easily, but burn fast, and get hot and harsh as a result. If it is over-filled, it will be difficult to draw on, or "plugged." Good cigars have to be consistent. That relies on skill, quality control, and the resources (reserves of suitable leaf, essentially) to guarantee that this year's cigars are the same as last year's, even if there is a bad harvest.

FITTING THE CAP

A SEPARATE PIECE OF WRAPPER IS
USUALLY USED TO CAP THE CIGAR.

THE LEGENDARY PARTAGAS FACTORY, HAVANA.

THE HAVANA CIGAR FACTORY

The Havana cigar factory today is much as it was when the art of cigar making was standardized in the mid-19th century and the production of cigars became industrialized. There are only eight factories making handmade cigars in Cuba today (compared with 120 at the beginning of the century). The names of the factories were all officially changed after the revolution to what were considered more ideologically sound titles, but most of them are still commonly referred to by their pre-revolutionary names, and still display their old signs outside. The best known are H. Upmann (now called José Marti), Partagas (Francisco Perez German), Romeo Y Julieta (Briones Montoto), La Corona (Fernando Roig), and the elite El Laguito, which originally opened in the mid-1960s as a training school. Each factory specializes in a number of brands of a particular flavor. The Partagas factory, for instance, specializes in full-bodied cigars, producing six brands including Bolivar, Ramon Allones, Gloria Cubana and, of course, Partagas. Factories also often specialize in making a particular range of sizes.

The procedures in the various factories are essentially the same, though the size and atmosphere of each factory differs. The grand El Laguito, for instance, is an Italianate mansion (built in 1910) and former home of the Marquez de Pinar del Rio. It is located in three buildings in a swanky residential suburb. The rather gloomy three-story Partagas factory, on the other hand, which was built in downtown Havana in 1845, is rather more down to earth. Laguito was the first factory to use female rollers, and even today the majority of the 94 rollers there are women. The 200 rollers at the

THE MANUFACTURING PROCESS
OF HAVANA CIGARS

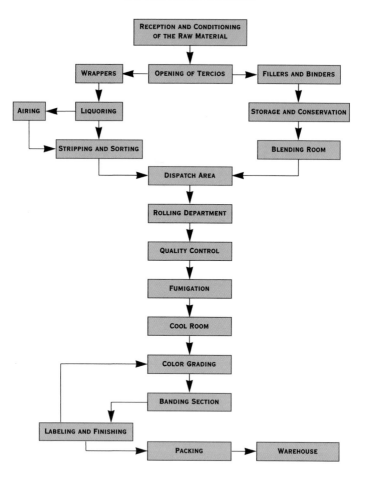

Partagas factory, the biggest for export production, turn out 5 million cigars a year. No matter which factory you go to, the walls of all of them display revolutionary slogans and portraits of Castro, Che Guevara, and others. Other slogans announced "La calidades el respeto al pueblo" (Quality is respect for people) or "Tu tambien haces calidad" (You have to care about quality).

It has been estimated that a handmade Havana cigar goes through no fewer than 222 different stages from seedling to the finished product, before being ready for distribution. And the care and expertise shown at the factory is not only crucial to the final

CIGAR ROLLER, HAVANA.

appearance of the cigar, but also affects how well it burns and what it actually tastes like. Not surprisingly, apprenticeship for the task of roller is a lengthy and competitive process, taking nine months. Even then, many fail, and those who succeed are confined to making small-sized cigars before being allowed to graduate to the larger, generally fuller-flavored, sizes.

The cigar rollers, or *torcedores*, work in large rooms where the old custom, dating from 1864, of reading aloud from books and newspapers continues to this day. The radio is also switched on, from time to time, to bring the news and important announcements. The worker who acts as reader (lector), selected by his peers for his expressive voice and literacy, is compensated by a small payment from each of the rollers, all of whom are paid piece work, according to the number of cigars they produce. Each roller is

TYPICAL WORKPLACE OF A CIGAR ROLLER.

responsible for seeing a cigar through from the bunching stage until it is finally trimmed to size. The ready-blended combination of filler leaves and binder are prepared in advance by each roller and pressed in wooden molds of the appropriate size. The use of molds started in around 1958, before the Cuban revolution. As a result, the cigar rollers—sitting at benches rather like old-fashioned school desks—each start with a quota of filler appropriate to the size and brand of cigar being made that day. All is concentration: errors are costly. But the atmosphere is cheerful, the torcedores taking great pride in their work. If a visitor enters the room, the rollers greet him by tapping their chavetas in unison on their tables.

There are as many as 42 handmade cigar sizes made today, and a good cigar maker can usually roll around 120 medium-sized cigars (though exceptionally skilled rollers can make as many as 150) a day—an average of four to five minutes for a cigar. But the average for the Montecristo A size is only 56 cigars a day. Some star rollers, such as Jesus Ortiz at the H. Upmann factory, can do much better: he can produce a staggering 200 Montecristo As a day.

The torcedores work an eight-hour day, usually six days a week, for around 350–400 pesos ($350–400 at the official exchange rate) a month. They are allowed to take home five cigars a day and can smoke as many as they wish while they work.

There are seven grades of worker in the Havana factory, the least experienced rollers (in grade 4) making only cigars up to and including the petit corona size; those in grade 5 making corona size and above, and those in grades 6 and 7 (the latter consists of a handful of star rollers) making the difficult specialist sizes such as

QUALITY CONTROL

QUALITY CONTROL. CHECKING THE GIRTH AND LENGTH OF A COHIBA LANCERO.

MIRIAM LOPEZ, EL LAGUITO'S ONLY FEMALE TASTER, ASSESSES A COHIBA LANCERO.

pyramides. The skill of the roller is reflected in the eventual cost per inch of the cigar. The smaller sizes are, in other words, cheaper than the larger ones.

Using colored ribbon, each roller ties his or her cigars into bundles (all of the same size and brand) of 50. Most of these bundles (*media ruedas*, or "half wheels") go into a vacuum fumigation chamber, where the cigars are treated against potential pests. A proportion of each roller's output is also taken to be checked for quality.

The man in charge of quality control at El Laguito, Fernando Valdez, tests a fifth of each roller's daily output (though only 10 percent of cigars are checked at the Partagas factory) according to no fewer than eight different criteria such as length, weight, firmness, smoothness of the wrappers, and whether or not the ends are well cut. Later, cigars from different batches are actually blind tasted by a team of six catadores, or professional smokers—themselves rigorously examined every six months—who must assess qualities such as a cigar's aroma, how well it burns, and how easily it draws. The important of each category varies according to the type of cigar. When testing a fat robusto, for instance, the flavor is paramount, but in the slim panatela size, draw is more important. There is a standard for each type of cigar. The catadores do their tasting in the morning only, smoking about an inch of each cigar, and refreshing their palates with sugarless tea. By the end of any given week, every roller's work will have been tasted.

After being removed from the vacuum chamber, cigars are held in special cool cabinets (*escaparates*) for three weeks, in order to shed any excess moisture acquired in the factory and settle down any fermentation that is taking place. A cabinet might hold up to 18,000 cigars, all kept under careful supervision.

When they are ready, batches of 1,000 cigars from a particular brand and size are sent in wooden boxes to be graded according to appearance. The cigars are classified into as many as 65 different shades—and each selector must be familiar with all of them. First the selector takes into account the basic color of the cigar (hues given names such as sangre de toro, encendido, colorado encendido, colorado, colorado pajizo, and clarisimo), and then the shade within that particular color category. The color grader then puts the cigars into transit boxes, making sure that all the cigars in a particular box are the same color. The darkest cigar is placed on the left of the box, and the cigars arranged according to nuances of shade so that the lightest is on the right.

FINISHING AND PACKAGING

CIGARS SORTED INTO DIFFERENT COLOR SHADES.

THE BAND IS ADDED.

CIGARS ARE BOXED ACCORDING TO COLOR.

Once the cigars are color-graded, they go to the packing department, where bands are put on. The cigars are then put in the familiar cedar boxes in which they will be sold. The packers also watch out for cigars which have escaped the quality control department. Once the final box is filled, the cigars are checked again, and then a thin leaf of cedar wood is laid on top of them.

The box is then sealed with the essential label guaranteeing that it is a genuine box of Havanas or Habanos. The word "Habanos" in red on a chevron has been added to boxes since 1994.

The practice of making handmade cigars is essentially the same wherever they're made, but in the Dominican Republic, for instance, the arrangement between bunchers and rollers is sometimes different (the jobs usually being separated). The large, modern American-owned factories of the Dominican Republic have state-of-the-art quality-control methods, using machines (at the bunch stage, as well as later) to check suction, and thus how well a cigar will draw. Despite this, other manufacturers still prefer to do everything by hand, particularly checking for gaps in the bunch, which will make a cigar overheat. In the Philippines, there is a method of rolling in which leaves are spiraled around two thin wooden sticks, which are removed when the cigar is wrapped.

HANDMADE VERSUS MACHINE-MADE CIGARS

The essential difference between handmade and machine-made cigars lies in the fact that, on the whole, most machine-made cigars aren't made with long fillers—fillers, that is, which run the whole length of the cigar—thus making the drawing and burning qualities (they burn faster and become hotter) of the machine-mades significantly inferior. Some machine-made brands, Bering for instance, use long fillers, making them better but still inferior to handmade cigars. The quality of wrappers on machine-made cigars is also usually inferior to those used on the best handmades.

For cheap, mass market, machine-made brands, blended filler is fed into rod-making machines—a process similar to cigarette making—and covered by a continuous sheet of binder. This creates a tube which is sealed at each end to the appropriate length. The wrapper is then added and the cigars trimmed.

In the case of more expensive machine-made, an operator sitting in front of a cigar-making machine feeds a mixture of filler tobacco (usually shredded leaves or scraps) into a hopper, and places two

THE DIFFERENCE
BETWEEN CIGAR TYPES

MACHINE-MADE: THE FILLER IS MADE OF SCRAPS OF LEAF.

HANDMADE: FILLER, BINDER, WRAPPER. NOTE THE
LONG FILLER WHICH RUNS THE LENGTH OF THE CIGAR.

binder leaves on a plate where they are cut. The two leaves are then positioned, overlapping, on a moving belt which feeds them into the rolling machine. This wraps the measured amount of filler and feeds out the cigar, which is then trimmed.

It is reasonably easy to tell the difference between handmade cigars and all but the best machine-mades: the caps on machine-mades are often very much more pointed; the cigars tend to be much less smooth to the touch; and the wrapper is likely to be much coarser, quite often with protruding veins. If a cigar doesn't have a cap, you can be certain that it is one of the cheaper machine-mades. Cellophane wrapping can also be a giveaway, particularly with Cuban cigars, but many very good non-Cuban handmade brands come wrapped in cellophane, so this is by no means an infallible way of telling whether the cigars are machine-made or not.

The Cubans recently introduced the concept of "hand-finished" machine-bunched cigars, with the Quintero brand for instance. These cigars have caps similar to handmades, long filler, and decent-quality wrappers. They can approach the experience of smoking a handmade cigar in flavor, though they wouldn't fool an experienced smoker.

Handmade cigars are so much more expensive than machine-mades quite simply because they take much longer to make, are labor-intensive, and use much more expensively produced and matured leaves. The handmaking process also leads to wastage.

THE CIGAR BOX

Cigars were originally sold in bundles covered with pigs' bladders (with a pod or two of vanilla to improve the smell); then came the use of the large cedar chests, holding up to 10,000 cigars.

But in 1830, the banking firm of H. Upmann started shipping back cigars, for the use of its directors in London, in sealed cedar boxes stamped with the bank's emblem. When the bank decided to go, full-scale, into the cigar business, the cedar box took off as a form of packaging for all the major Havana brands, and all hand-made cigars (though small quantities today are sometimes packaged in cardboard cartons, and single cigars of many brands come in aluminum tubes lined with cedar). Cedar helps to prevent cigars from drying out and furthers the maturing process.

The idea of using colorful lithographic labels, now used for all handmade brands, wherever they come from, started when Ramon Allones, a Galician immigrant to Cuba, initiated it for the brand he started in 1837. As the industry grew in the mid-19th century, so

H. UPMANN WAS AMONG THE FIRST USERS OF THE
CEDAR BOXES TO PACKAGE CIGARS.

did the need for clear brand identification. Labels or other illustrations also appear on the inside of the lids of many Havana and other brands. Boxes also usually have colorful decorative borders. The cedar box is sometimes referred to as a "boîte nature." Paper, usually colored, is normally glued to the interior of the box and is used to cover the cigars it contains.

Finally, after being filled and checked, the box is nailed shut and tightly sealed with a green and white label (a custom dating from 1912) to guarantee that the cigars are genuine Havanas. The practice of using a label, usually printed in similar colors and with similar wording, to seal the box continues today for most handmade brands, Cuban or not.

The Havana seal reads: "Cuban Government's warranty for cigars exported from Havana. Republica de Cuba. Sello de garantia nacional de procedencia."

Most sizes of the élite Cohiba brand come in varnished boxes, as do one or two of the larger sizes of a handful of other Cuban brands. The H. Upmann Sir Winston size, for instance, is available in a polished dark green box. These polished boxes are usually stamped with the brand symbol, rather than carrying any sort of label other than the government seal.

The form of packaging called 8–9–8 is used for some cigars in the Partagas and Ramon Allones brands. These boxes are polished, have curved edges, and contain 25 cigars, arranged in three layers with eight at the bottom, mine in the middle, and eight on top. Cigars with this sort of packaging are relatively expensive.

CIGAR BOX STAMPS

THE HAVANA SEAL.

THE STAMP TELLING YOU THE CIGARS ARE HANDMADE.

A PREREVOLUTIONARY HAVANA BOX.

Hecho en Cuba has been stamped on the underside of Cuban boxes since 1961, when it replaced the English inscription "Made in Havana—Cuba." Since 1985, they have also carried a factory code and Cubatabaco's logo, the latter being replaced with Habanos SA from late 1994.

In 1989 the words "Totalmente a Mano" were added. Meaning "Totally by Hand," they provide the only cast-iron clue that the cigars are genuinely handmade in the traditional Cuban manner. "Hecho a Mano" or "Made by Hand" can cover a multitude of sins (European Union law permits cigars that are hand finished but machine bunched to be described as made by hand)—so the situation can be confusing.

Unless you have complete trust in your cigar merchant when buying older cigars, the only way to play safe is to buy post-1989 cigars with the "Totalmente a Mano" legend. If the box says: "Made in Havana, Cuba," it is almost certainly pre-revolutionary.

The factory code, on Havana cigars, is stamped in blue—using post-revolutionary factory designations. Thus, for instance:

JM stands for José Martí, formerly H. Upmann.
FPG stands for Francisco Perez German, formerly Partagas.
BM stands for Briones Montoto, formerly Romeo Y Julieta.
FR stands for Fernando Roig, formerly La Corona.
EL stands for El Laguito.
HM stands for Heroes del Moncada, formerly El Rey del Mundo.

Havana boxes also used to be stamped with the color of the cigars contained in them, but this practice has stopped, for the time being at least. Boxes, in the past, often read "claro," but this color classification was frequently inaccurate.

On non-Havana boxes, you might read "Envuelto a mano"—which only means hand-*packed*, but could deceive the unwary. "Hand rolled" means simply (as with Cuban "hand-finished" cigars) that the *wrapper* is put on by hand, the rest of the cigar is machine-made.

Underneath the boxes of American-produced cigars, there is normally a code: the letters TP, followed by a number identifying the manufacturer. Cigars imported into the United States don't show this code. Some cigars (Dominican Dunhills and the most expensive Macanudos, for instance) refer to a "vintage" on the box. This refers to the year of the tobacco crop, not the year of manufacture. Dunhills currently on sale, for example, are 1989 vintage—made from the Dominican 1989 harvest.

THE CIGAR BAND

The cigar band was introduced by the Dutchman, Gustave Bock, one of the first Europeans to get involved in the Havana cigar industry, somewhat after the introduction of the cigar box and labels, and for the same reason: to distinguish his brand from the many others on the market. His lead was soon followed by all the other brands, and cigar bands are still used by almost all handmade brands. When bands were originally introduced, other manufacturers followed Bock's example and had them made in Holland. Some cigars, sold in "Cabinet Selection" packaging—usually a deep cedar box containing a bundle of 50 loosely packed cigars tied together with silk ribbon—are sold without bands. This "half-wheel," as it is called, of 50 cigars is the way cigars were normally presented before the band was introduced. Some Honduran handmades are also often sold in Europe without bands (and usually singly), primarily for trademark reasons.

The band also has other minor functions, such as protecting the smoker's fingers from becoming stained (this was important when gentlemen wore white evening gloves) and, some claim, holding the wrapper together—though no decent wrapper should need help.

The cigar bands of older brands tend to be much fancier (with gold leaf in abundance) than those of modern brands. Those aimed at the very top of the market in particular—Cohiba, Dunhill, Montecristo, and Davidoff, for instance—are all simple and elegant.

The bands on non-Havana cigars with Cuban brand names tend to be similar to the Cuban originals, although they vary in small details (a typical one being that they bear the date of origin of the brand in the space where the Cuban version says "Habana").

Some Cuban brands use more than one band design, Hoyo de Monterrey, for instance, or Tomeo Y Julieta, where the Churchill sizes have a simple, slim gold band, but other sizes have red ones.

The question of whether to smoke a cigar with the band on or off is purely a matter of personal choice. In Britain, it has traditionally been considered a matter of "bad form" to advertise the brand you are smoking, an inhibition which doesn't apply elsewhere.

If you insist on removing the band, it is best to wait until you have smoked the cigar for a few minutes. The heat of the smoke will help to loosen the band from the wrapper and will make the gum on the band less adhesive and easier to remove. If you try to take the band off the cigar before starting to smoke it, you will risk damaging the wrapper.

CIGAR SIZES

There are countless cigar sizes. Cuba alone produces 69, 2 of which are for handmade Havanas. Each has a factory name, which usually bears no relationship to the name by which we know them, like Prominente (Double Corona), Julieta 2 (Churchill), Mareva (Petit Corona), Franciscano, Carolina, and so on. Some brands, Partagas for example, have 40 sizes, though several are machine-made. This is a throwback to the past when many selections were even larger. More modern brands such as Cohiba and Montecristo have just 11 sizes. Non-Havana brands tend to offer more manageable lines, although many, like Davidoff, which now boasts 19 sizes, have started to grow.

Sadly for the novice, there is no such thing as a standard size or a comprehensive list of sizes. Even the common Petit Corona can be found with different girths, and the name of Churchill covers a variety of alternative, albeit substantial, cigars. Listed below are the 25 most popular Havana sizes under their factory names. This may serve to indicate just how wide a selection is available, but it merely scratches the surface of the full panoply of choice offered by Cuba, let alone the Dominican Republic, Honduras, Mexico, and others.

The girth of a cigar is customarily expressed in terms of its ring gauge in 1/64ths of an inch. Thus, if a cigar has a ring gauge of 49, it is 49/64ths of an inch thick. Similarly, if a cigar had a ring gauge of 64, it would be an inch thick. Only a couple of cigars come into

CIGARS COME IN A BEWILDERING ARRAY OF SIZES AND SHAPES RANGING FROM THE 9¼-INCH GRAN CORONA TO THE 4-INCH ENTREACTO.

BASIC HAVANA SIZES

NAME	LENGTH: INCHES	RING GAUGE
HEAVY RING GAUGE		
Gran Coron	9¼ inches	47
Prominente	7⅝ inches	49
Julieta 2	7 inches	47
Piramide*	6⅛ inches	52
Corona Gorda	5⅝ inches	46
Campana*	5½ inches	52
Hermoso No. 4	5 inches	48
Robusto	47/8 inches	50
STANDARD RING GAUGE		
Dalia	6¾ inches	43
Cervante	6½ inches	42
Corona Grande	6⅛ inches	42
Corona	5½ inches	42
Mareva	5 inches	42
Londres	5 inches	40
Minuto	4⅜ inches	42
Perla	4 inches	40
SLENDER RING GAUGE		
Laguito No. 1	7½ inches	38
Ninfas	7 inches	33
Laguito No. 2	6 inches	38
Seoane	5 inches	36
Carolina	4¾ inches	26
Franciscano	4½ inches	40
Laguito No. 3	4½ inches	26
Cadete	4½ inches	36
Entreacto	3⅞ inches	30

These sizes, having pointed heads, are often referred to as "torpedoes." This name suggests, incorrectly, that they should be pointed at both ends. Cigars which are pointed at both ends are termed "Figuerados."

this size today, the 9-inch long Royal Jamaica Goliath, and the same length José Benito Magnum from the Dominican Republic. The Casa Blanca Jeroboam and Half Jeroboam come with a whopping 66 ring gauge.

The largest properly smokable cigar made was Koh-i-Noor, made before World War II by Henry Clay for a maharaja. The same size, called the Visible Inmenso (18 inches long, 47 ring gauge) was made for King Farouk of Egypt. There was also once a panatela measuring 19½ inches. At the Partagas factory in Havana, they keep a collector's item: a cigar measuring almost 50 inches. You can also see a cigar a yard long with a ring gauge of 96 kept at the Davidoff store in London.

The smallest regularly made cigar was the Bolivar Delgado— measuring under 1½ inches.

There are plenty of variations to be found within a particular brand, particularly if the choice is large. Different brands, on the whole, tend to be expert at making different sizes. So, while the large ring gauge cigars in a certain brand might be excellent, you shouldn't assume that the smaller ones will either taste similar or be as well made. It comes down to actually trying the cigars.

SELECTING A CIGAR

As a general rules, cigars with larger ring gauges tend to be fuller flavored (there is normally more *ligero* and less *volado* in the blend), smoke more smoothly and slowly, and heat up less fast than those with small ring gauges. They also tend to be better made than the smaller ones (which are the sizes recently qualified apprentices start on). Cigars with small ring gauges often have little or no *ligero* tobacco in the filler blend. Large ring gauge cigars are almost always the preferred choice—if there is no hurry—of connoisseurs or experienced cigar smokers.

The beginner, however, is advised to choose a relatively small cigar, say a minuto or carolina, and then move up to the bigger sizes of a mild brand (see The Cigar Directory). Jamaican cigars, such as Macanudo (also made in the Dominican Republic), tend to be mild, or try H. Upmann among Havanas. A cervante is probably the best cigar above the corona size to move up to when you feel you have gone beyond the beginner stage.

A number of cigar experts, including the legendary Zino Davidoff, have pontificated about a person's physical appearance related to cigar size, and the Cubans have a saying, "As you approach 30, you have a 30 ring gauge; as you approach 50, you have a 50 ring gauge." This is, on the whole, so much hogwash. What size of cigar you smoke is entirely up to you and your pocket. Having said that, smoking a fat cigar, if you are very small or thin, can sometimes look rather comic or pretentious. But there is a case to be made about what sort of cigar to smoke at what time of day. Most smokers prefer milder, smaller cigars in the morning, or after a light lunch. The seasoned smoker, however, might go for something like a robusto after a heavy lunch—a lot of flavor packed into a reasonably short smoke. Certainly, most experienced smokers prefer a big, full-bodied cigar after a heavy meal or late at night, partly because a thin cigar will not last very long, and a mild one isn't so satisfying on a full stomach. So they will select a belicoso, Churchill, or double corona. By the same token, smoking a heavy cigar before dinner is likely to spoil your appetite and play havoc with your taste buds. Much the same consideration applies when people have strong drinks like port or brandy after dinner, rather than something lighter, which they will take before or during dinner. If you want to compare cigars, it is best to smoke them at similar times of day, taking meals and location into account, too.

When you choose a cigar, you should first make sure that the wrapper is intact (if not, reject it) and has a healthy sheen. You should also make sure that it isn't too dry or brittle (otherwise it will taste harsh) and that there is a noticeable bouquet (if not, the cigar has probably been badly stored). A good cigar should be neither too firm nor too soft. If the wrapper is heavily veined, the cigar should be rejected: quality control went wrong somewhere.

The color of a cigar's wrapper (and that part of the filler that you can see) will give you some clues, though it is not infallible since the filler blend is the key, as to its flavor. As a rule of thumb, the darker a cigar, the more full-bodied and (since darker wrappers contain more sugar) sweeter it is likely to be. Cigars, if properly stored, continued to mature and ferment in their cedar boxes. This aging process, during which a cigar loses acidity, is not unlike the maturing of good wine. Fuller-bodied cigars, particularly those with big ring gauges, tend to age better than milder ones. But it should be said that some full-bodied brands, such as Cohiba and Montecristo (apart, perhaps from the very largest sizes) don't age particularly well because the tobacco is fermented for longer—a complete extra fermentation in the case of Cohiba—in the factory, thus leaving little room for further maturation. There are even those who argue that if tobacco has been properly fermented, it is very unlikely to mature further (and if it has been fermented too little, it can't mature at all).

Milder cigars, particularly those with pale wrappers, will merely lose their bouquet if kept too long. In general, you should smoke lighter cigars before darker ones. Wrappers which are destined to age well start off oily, and get slightly darker and oilier as they mature.

Most importers of fine handmade cigars take care to age them a little before releasing them to the public (about two years for Havana cigars taken into Britain). There is not hard and fast rule about how long cigars should be left to mature (it can often be a matter of luck), but some experts state that cigars aged for six to ten years will be in the peak of condition. Others warn, quite rightly, that even if they are stored under ideal conditions, most cigars will lose their bouquet. If storage conditions are less good, they will also become dry. Even if well stored, it's probably sensible not to keep cigars for more than 10 years—by that time, they're unlikely to get any better, and will almost certainly have lost some of their bouquet.

Cigars should be smoked either within three months of manufacture or, failing that, not for at least a year after they are made. The intervening "period of sickness" as it is known—when the maturing process starts—is the worst time to smoke a cigar.

WRAPPER COLORS

Cigar wrappers can be classified into seven basic colors, although there are dozens of possible shades:

THE BASIC COLORS OF WRAPPERS RANGE FROM CLARO (PALE BROWN) TO OSCURO (BLACK).

DOUBLE CLARO (also called AMS, American Market Selection, or candela)—greenish brown (for instance, as in Macanudo "jade.") The color is achieved by picking the leaf before it reaches maturity and then drying it rapidly. Very mild, almost bland, with very little oil. Cigars with this color have traditionally been popular in the United States, but are very much less so today.

CLARO—pale brown, like milky coffee. (For example, Havana brands like H. Upmann, or brands using Connecticut Shade wrappers.) The classic mild cigar color. The color is also called "natural," as is colorado claro.

COLORADO CLARO—mid-brown, tawny. (For example, brands, such as Dominican Partagas, using Cameroon wrappers.)

COLORADO—reddish dark brown, aromatic. This color is associated with well-matured cigars.

COLORADO MADURO—dark brown, medium strength, rather more aromatic than maduro. Usually gives a rich flavor, as found in many of the best Honduran cigars.

MADURO—very dark brown, like black coffee. (For example, full-bodied Havana brands such as Bolivar; cigars made with Mexican wrappers.) A color for seasoned smokers. Sometimes thought of as the traditional Cuban color.

OSCURO—more or less black. Very strong with little bouquet. Wrappers of this color, though once popular, are rarely produced today. If they are produced these wrappers tend to be from Nicaragua, Brazil, Mexico, or the Connecticut Broadleaf (as opposed to Shade) type.

The darker the color, the sweeter and stronger the flavor is likely to be, and the greater the oil and sugar content of the wrapper. Darker wrappers will normally have spent longer on the tobacco plant or will come from higher altitudes: the extra exposure to sunlight produces both oil (as protection) and sugar (through photosynthesis). They will also have been fermented for longer.

The term EMS or English Market Selection is a broad one, which refers to brown cigars—anything other than double claro (AMS) essentially.

All handmade cigars need to be cut at the closed end before they can be smoked. Just how you do this is up to you. There are a number of cutters on the market ranging from small, cheap, easily portable guillotines (which come in single or double blade versions, the latter being the best), to fancy cigar scissors—which need some skill to use properly. You can use a sharp (that's essential) knife. If you use your fingernails, just pinch off the very top of the cap. The important thing is that the cut should be clean and level; otherwise, you will have difficulties with draw and risk damaging the wrapper. You should cut the cigar so that you leave about ⅛ inch of the cap. Piercing the cap isn't recommended: it interferes with the passage of smoke by compressing the filler, and will make the cigar overheat, leading to an unpleasant flavor. Cutters which make a wedge shape in the cap aren't recommended for the same reason. You should never cut a cigar on or below cap level: it is a certain way of ruining the wrapper. The idea is to take off just enough of the cap to expose the filler leaves. Whatever you use, make sure it is sharp.

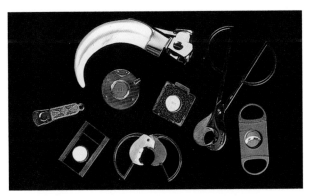

CUTTERS. THE GUILLOTINE TYPE IS THE SIMPLEST, CHEAPEST, AND BEST.

When you light a cigar you can use a butane lighter (though not a gasoline lighter, which will impair the flavor) or a match. There are special long slow-burning matches designed for cigar smokers available from high quality shops such as Dunhill or Davidoff, but a normal wooden match will do perfectly well. You should, however, avoid matches with a high sulfur or wax content. A properly lit cigar is always more enjoyable than one that isn't, so take it easy when you light one.

1 Hold the cigar horizontally, in direct contact with the flame, slowly revolving it until the end is charred evenly over its entire surface.

2 Only now do you put the cigar between your lips. Hold the flame about half an inch away from the end and draw slowly while turning it. The end of the cigar should now ignite. Make sure it is evenly lit; otherwise, one side will burn faster than the other.

3 Gently blow on the glowing end to make sure that it is burning evenly.

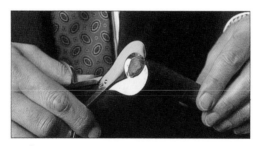

CUTTING A CIGAR. MAKE SURE IT'S NOT TOO NEAR THE BOTTOM OF THE CAP.

LIGHTING A CIGAR. DO IT CAREFULLY.

ALMOST READY TO SMOKE.

Older, well-matured cigars burn more easily than younger ones. If properly lit, the highest quality cigars have only a very narrow carbon rim at the lit end; mediocre cigars will have a thicker band.

To get the best out of them, cigars should be smoked slowly. They should not be dragged on or puffed too frequently. This will lead to overheating and spoil the flavor. Nor should the smoke—it hardly needs saying—be inhaled. The strong alkaline smoke and low nicotine content means that you will cough in reaction. A cigar like a corona will take about half an hour to smoke, with larger cigars taking an hour or more.

If your cigar goes out, don't worry: this is quite normal, particularly if you have already smoked half of it. Tap the cigar to remove any clinging ash. Then blow through the cigar to clear any stale smoke. Re-light as you would a new cigar. You should have a satisfactory smoke even if you leave the cigar for a couple of hours. Left much longer than that, it will taste stale, although a large ring gauge cigar smoked less than halfway down will still be smokeable, if not so enjoyable, the following day.

Cigars, unlike cigarettes, don't need to be tapped to remove the ash—it should fall off in due course. There is, on the other hand, no virtue in keeping a long cylinder of ash at the end of your cigar just because it is there: it impairs the passage of air and will make the cigar burn unevenly. The better the construction of the cigar, the longer and more "solid" will the ash cylinder be.

Once the cigar starts producing hot smoke and you get a strong aftertaste (usually when you are down to the last couple of inches), it is time to abandon it. As the French actor Sacha Guitry wrote: "If the birth of a genius resembles that of an idiot, the end of a Havana Corona resembles that of a five-cent cigar." It isn't necessary to stub out a cigar as you would a cigarette. Just leave it in the ashtray, and it will go out soon enough. Cigar stubs should be disposed of soon after they have gone out; otherwise, the room will acquire the lingering smell of stale smoke.

There are two things that really should not be done: first, don't roll a cigar near your ear. This is contemptuously known as "listening to the band" in the cigar trade. It tells you nothing at all about the cigar; second, you should never warm the length of the cigar before smoking it. This was originally done in order to burn off the rather unpleasant gum used to make some Seville cigars well over a hundred years ago. It is not necessary with today's high-quality handmade cigars, as they use a mere drop of flavorless, odorless vegetable gum.

2

THE
CIGAR
DIRECTORY

*T*he selected list of handmade cigars in this section doesn't claim to be totally comprehensive, but it should contain most of the brands you are likely to come across. Some of them are only available in the United States, others only in Europe: but these things change. The same applies to sizes within brands (always listed in descending order of length).

Notes on flavor and aroma are necessarily subjective, but construction, draw, and wrapper quality can be more objectively assessed. You might love the flavor of a cigar even though it is criticized in the directory. It is, after all, a matter of personal taste.

C The country of origin of the cigar is denoted as follows:
> Cuba, for example
> Honduras, for example

F The categories for flavor range through four strengths:
> Mild
> Mild to medium
> Medium to full-bodied
> Very full-bodied

As for quality, the assessment takes into account appearance, construction, and consistency—the latter being of particular importance in any brand. Even so, cigars being handmade, and cigar tobacco being subject to the vagaries of climate (not to mention politics in some countries), things have changed and will change from time to time even for the best-known brands. These entries, then, can only be a guide, good for the time being.

Q The four categories for quality are as follows:
> Could be better
> Good-quality leaf and construction
> Superior quality
> The very best quality available

AFTER BEING ROLLED, CIGARS REST FOR 15 DAYS TO LOSE SOME OF THEIR MOISTURE.

ARTURO FUENTE

*C*igar lore says that farmers raise tobacco and manufacturers make cigars. So, when the Fuente family, the largest producers of handmade cigars in the Dominican Republic, bought a plantation, eyebrows were raised on both sides of the divide. As word spread that the farm near el Caribe would grow wrappers, the same eyebrows arched. Virtually no one grew wrappers in the Dominican Republic and certainly not for premium cigars.

When a cigar wrapped with leaf from the El Caribe farm, now known as Chateau de la Fuente, topped *Cigar Aficionado's* fall 1994 tasting, beating several Havanas before it even went on sale, the eyebrows hit the roof.

1995 saw the creation of the Fuente Fuente OpusX® series which features the wrapper grown at the Chateau de la Fuente farm. Since then it has been a very popular line, but sadly limited in production. The Fuente family aim to remedy this, however, with 150 acres of newly purchased land adjacent to the Chateau de la Fuente farm. This land has not been worked previously so the top soil is very deep. The Fuentes believe it is as good, if not better than that of the Chateau de la Fuente for growing wrapper leaves, and eventually hope to double the production of this line.

There are plenty of other Fuente cigars to enjoy in both their standard range and their Hemingway series of big figurados. Rare Colorado Cameroon wrappers are Fuente's hallmark, although some sizes like Royal Salute come dressed in "natural" Connecticut shade. All these cigars are well-constructed and well-blended, giving a distinguished light to medium flavor which reflects the enthusiasm of their makers. The Double Corona and Rothschild enclosed in cedar-wood wraps are particular favorites.

FUENTE FUENTE OPUSX® SIZES

Name	Length: inches	Ring Gauge
Reserva A	9¼ inches	47
Double Corona	7⅝ inches	49
Reserva No. 1	6⅝ inches	44
Reserva No. 2	6¼ inches	52
Petit Lanceros	6¼ inches	38
Fuente Fuente	5⅝ inches	46
Robusto	5¼ inches	50

RESERVA A : LENGTH 9¼ INCHES, RING GAUGE 47

RESERVA No. 2 : LENGTH 6¼ INCHES, RING GAUGE 52

ROBUSTO : LENGTH 5¼ INCHES, RING GAUGE 50

SIZES

NAME	LENGTH: INCHES	RING GAUGE
Canones	8½ inches	52
Royal Salute	7⅝ inches	52
Churchill	7½ inches	48
Panetela Fina	7 inches	38
Double Corona	6¾ inches	48
Privada No. 1	6¾ inches	46
Lonsdale	6½ inches	42
Flor Fina	6 inches	46
Cuban Corona	5¼ inches	44
Petit Corona	5 inches	38
Chateau Fuente	4½ inches	50
HEMINGWAY SERIES		
Masterpiece	9 inches	52
Classic	6 inches	47
Signature	6 inches	47

"PETIT CORONA: LENGTH 5 INCHES, RING GAUGE 38

CHATEAU FUENTE : LENGTH 4½ INCHES, RING GAUGE 50

PRIVADA No. 1 : LENGTH 6¾ INCHES, RING GAUGE 46

C Dominican
Republic
F Light to
medium
Q Superior
quality

⚜ ASHTON

*O*wned by a Philadelphia enterprise but named after an English pipe-maker of high repute, these well-tailored cigars are made in the Dominican Republic. The come in three styles of flavor. One is known simply as Ashton. Then there is Ashton Cabinet Selection and Ashton Aged Maduro. All three are wrapped in Connecticut leaf, although the Aged Maduro is in broadleaf rather than shade, and is filled with a Dominican blend.

The mildest are the Cabinet Selection, owing to extra aging of the tobaccos (the Nos. 1, 2 & 3 are tapered at both ends). For a mild to medium smoke, go for the standard selection in a size like the Magnum, or if sweetness appeals, try a Maduro No. 10. The Ashton Crown series uses precious leaves from the Chateau de la Fuente farm.

SIZES

NAME	LENGTH: INCHES	RING GAUGE
Cabinet No. 1	9 inches	52
Churchill	7½ inches	52
Cabinet No. 10	7½ inches	52
No. 60 Maduro	7½ inches	52
Cabinet No. 8	7 inches	50
No. 50 Maduro	7 inches	48
Cabinet No. 2	7 inches	46
Prime Minister	6⅞ inches	48
No. 30 Maduro	6¼ inches	44
8–9–8	6½ inches	44
Elegante	6½ inches	35
Cabinet No. 7	6¼ inches	52
No. 40 Maduro	6 inches	50
Double "R"	6 inches	50
Cabinet No. 3	6 inches	46
Panetela	6 inches	36
Cabinet No. 6	5½ inches	50
Corona	5½ inches	44
No. 20 Maduro	5½ inches	44
No. 10 Maduro	5 inches	50
Magnum	5 inches	50
Cordial	5 inches	30

CABINET NO. 3 : LENGTH 6 INCHES, RING GAUGE 46

NO. 40 MADURO : LENGTH 6 INCHES, RING GAUGE 50

NO. 60 MADURO : LENGTH 7½ INCHES, RING GAUGE 52

CABINET No. 2 : LENGTH 7 INCHES, RING GAUGE 46

PRIME MINISTER : LENGTH 6⅞ INCHES, RING GAUGE 48

MAGNUM : LENGTH 5 INCHES, RING GAUGE 50

C Dominican Republic
F Mild to medium
Q Good-quality leaf and construction

*A*vo Uvezian, accomplished musician and composer of *Strangers in the Night*, brings a clear understanding of harmony to the cigars which bear his name. Both in his standard selection and the more recent "XO" Series, the balance of flavor achieved between golden Connecticut wrappers and Dominican fillers and binders is well struck.

The "XO" Series, which can be identified by the two discreet letters on the side of the band, owes its premium price (no Avo is cheap) to a unique aging and fermenting process, although it is not clear quite what this entails.

The cigars are well constructed. The Pyramid and Belicosos sizes, however, should not be compared to the Cuban Piramides and Campana (often called Belicosos) sizes to which they bear little or no resemblance.

Flavors tend to intensify with the increase in girth of the cigars and can vary from a medium to a fuller, richer taste.

SIZES

NAME	LENGTH: INCHES	RING GAUGE
No. 3	7½ inches	52
Pyramid	7 inches	36/54
XO Maestoso	7 inches	48
No. 4	7 inches	38
No. 5	6¾ inches	46
No. 1	6¾ inches	42
No. 6	6½ inches	36
No. 2	6 inches	50
Belicoso	6 inches	50
No. 7	6 inches	44
XO Preludo	6 inches	40
XO Intermezzo	5½ inches	50
No. 8	5½ inches	40
Petit Belicoso	4¾ inches	50
No. 9	4¾ inches	48

XO MAESTOSO : LENGTH 7 INCHES, RING GAUGE 48

NO. 2 : LENGTH 6 INCHES, RING GAUGE 50

PYRAMID : LENGTH 7 INCHES, RING GAUGE 54

C Dominican Republic
F Medium to full
Q Superior quality

BANCES

A brand which comes in both hand- and machine-made sizes. The handmade sizes are all produced in Honduras from a blend of local tobaccos. The wrappers tend to be rather coarse, and tight rolling can give problems with the draw. Overall, these cigars offer a distinct, sweetish, slightly peppery taste at a keen price.

SIZES

Name	Length: inches	Ring Gauge
President	8½ inches	52
Corona Inmensas	6¾ inches	48
No. 1	6½ inches	43
Cazadores	6¼ inches	44
Breva	5¼ inches	43

C Honduras
F Mild to full-medium
Q Could be better

2¾

CORONA IMMENSAS : LENGTH 6¼ INCHES, RING GAUGE 48

BAUZA

*E*choes of pre-revolution Havana are still to be found on Bauza boxes, although today the cigars are made in the Dominican Republic. The wrappers are rich Ecuador. The Mexican binder combines with a mixture of Nicaraguan and Dominican fillers to deliver a very pleasant, aromatic smoke with a mild to medium flavor. The cigars are well put together by hand, but watch out for the Presidente (not listed below) which is short filler and not to be compared to the rest. Prices are very reasonable.

SIZES

Name	Length: inches	Ring Gauge
Fabulosos	7½ inches	50
Medalla D'Oro		
No. 1	6⅞ inches	44
Florete	6⅞ inches	35
Casa Grande	6¾ inches	48
Jaguar	6½ inches	42
Robusto	5½ inches	50
Grecos	5½ inches	42
Petit Corona	5 inches	38

- **C** Dominican Republic
- **F** Mild to medium
- **Q** Superior quality

$\mathcal{T}$he famous Bolivar label and box featuring a portrait of the 19th-century Venezuelan revolutionary Simon Bolivar, liberator of much of South America from the Spanish empire, is one of the most instantly recognizable of all Havana cigar brands. At one time, the brand had the distinction of producing the smallest Havanas: the Delgado, measuring 1⅞ inches by 20 ring gauge, and even made a miniature box of cigars for a dollshouse in the royal nursery at Windsor Castle in England. It was founded in 1901 by the Rocha company.

There are some 20 cigars in the line, but many of the sizes come in machine-made versions, so be particularly careful if you think you've found a bargain. There are 19 handmade sizes, a selection of which is listed below. Bolivars are among the cheapest of handmade Cuban cigars and represent a good buy if—and this is a big if—their powerful flavor appeals to you, because as a brand, they are also among the strongest, fullest-bodied of Havanas. They are certainly not for the beginner, but appeal to many seasoned smokers. With their characteristic dark wrappers, they age well. Go for the larger sizes (Royal Corona upward)—which are well-constructed, draw and burn evenly, and have a strong aroma. The torpedo-shaped Belicosos Finos are a favorite with many, ideal after a heavy meal, whereas the mellow Royal Corona (robusto) is a very good post-lunch cigar. The Petit Corona is one of the fullest flavored available. The Palmas (panatela) which is produced in limited quantities should be avoided by those who expect a light smoke in this size. The distinctive Bolivar flavor comes not, as might be expected, because an unusually high proportion of ligero leaf is used, but because much more seco than volado is in the blend.

There are also Dominican versions of Bolivar on the market, not particularly noted, though good value, well made with Cameroon wrappers, and mild to medium in flavor. The Dominican line consists of only five sizes.

ROYAL CORONA : LENGTH 4⅞ INCHES, RING GAUGE 50

GOLD MEDAL : LENGTH 6⅜ INCHES, RING GAUGE 42

PETIT CORONA : LENGTH 5 INCHES, RING GAUGE 42

C Cuba
F Very full-bodied
Q Superior quality

C Dominican Republic
F Mild to medium
Q Good-quality leaf and construction

BELICOSOS FINOS : LENGTH 5½ INCHES, RING GAUGE 52

CUBAN SIZES

Name	Length: inches	Ring Gauge
Corona Gigantes	7 inches	47
Churchill	7 inches	47
Lonsdales	6⅝ inches	43
Gold Medal	6⅜ inches	42
Corona Extra	5⅝ inches	44
Belicosos Finos	5½ inches	52
Corona	5½ inches	42
Petit Corona	5 inches	42
Bonitas	5 inches	40
Royal Corona	4⅞ inches	50
Regentes	4⅞ inches	34
Corona Junior	4¼ inches	42

DOMINICAN SIZES

Name	Length: inches	Ring Gauge
Bolivares	7 inches	46
Corona Grand	6½ inches	42
Belicosos Finos	6½ inches	38
Panetelita	6 inches	31
Corona Extra	5½ inches	42

MADE IN HAVANA, CUBA

C.A.O.

irst introduced in 1995, C.A.O.'s Honduran cigars are made at Nestor Plasencia's Fabrica de Tabacos Oriente factory and are made of Nicaraguan and Mexican filler tobacco, with binders from Honduras, and Connecticut shade wrappers. They tend to be very well constructed and offer a mild smoke. A new, superior line, C.A.O. Gold was introduced in 1996, and was an immediate success—so much so that, at the time of writing, C.A.O. International were five months behind orders. They are available in five sizes, all with Nicaraguan filler and binder, and Ecuadoran wrapper.

C Nicaragua
F Mild to Medium
Q Superior quality

CORONA GORDA : LENGTH 6½ INCHES, RING GAUGE 50

SIZES

Name	Length: inches	Ring Gauge
Churchill	8 inches	50
Presidente	7½ inches	54
Triangulare	7 inches	36/54
Lonsdale	7 inches	44
Corona Gorda	6 inches	50
Corona	6 inches	42
Petit Corona	5 inches	40
Robusto	4½ inches	50

SIZES C.A.O. GOLD

Name	Length: inches	Ring Gauge
Double Corona	7½ inches	54
Churchill	7 inches	48
Corona Gorda	6½ inches	50
Corona	5½ inches	42
Robusto	5 inches	50

CHURCHILL : LENGTH 7 INCHES, RING GAUGE 48

CORONA MADURO : LENGTH 6 INCHES, RING GAUGE 42

PRESIDENTE : LENGTH 7½ INCHES, RING GAUGE 54

C Honduras
F Mild
Q Good-quality leaf
and construction

CASA BLANCA

*W*ell-made Dominican cigars with Claro Connecticut wrappers on all sizes and maduro on some. The filler is Dominican and the binder Mexican. Casa Blanca's specialty is gargantuan cigars. The 10-inch Jeroboam and 5-inch Half Jeroboam have ring gauges over 1-inch thick (66). In general, the cigars are well-built (they must have some rollers with big hands), mild, and smooth.

SIZES

NAME	LENGTH: INCHES	RING GAUGE
Jeroboam	10 inches	66
Presidente	7½ inches	50
Magnum	7 inches	60
Lonsdale	6½ inches	42
De Luxe	6 inches	50
Panetela	6 inches	35
Corona	5½ inches	42
Half Jeroboam	5 inches	66
Bonita	4 inches	36

MAGNUM XL : LENGTH 7 INCHES, RING GAUGE 60

HALF JEROBOAM : LENGTH 5 INCHES, RING GAUGE 66

LONSDALE : LENGTH 6½ INCHES, RING GAUGE 42

C Dominican
Republic
F Mild
Q Good-quality
leaf and
construction

V CENTENNIAL

he Roman five in V Centennial signifies that the brand was introduced to mark the passing of the five centuries since Columbus discovered tobacco. It also serves as a reminder that the cigars are made of tobaccos from five different countries. The wrapper is American (Connecticut), the binder Mexican, and the filler a mixture of Honduran for spice, Nicaraguan for aroma, and Dominican to round it off. The cigars are made in Honduras.

Creating and maintaining a successful blend of such diverse tobaccos is far from easy. Few attempt it. Creating a compatible and palatable balance is the problem, but when it is achieved, the resultant flavor can make a refreshing change. Overall V Centennial succeeds both in its claro form and particularly in its maduro, which is available in some sizes.

These cigars are handmade and well-constructed, although the wrappers can be grainy. The line, which tends toward larger sizes, is well-priced. Its Torpedo resembles a blunderbuss rather than the classic Piramide shape, but nonetheless it offers an interesting variation and smokes well.

SIZES

NAME	LENGTH: INCHES	RING GAUGE
Presidente	8 inches	50
Numero Uno	7½ inches	38
Torpedo	7 inches	36/54
Churchill	7 inches	48
Cetro	6¼ inches	44
Numero Dos	6 inches	50
Coronas	5½ inches	42
Robusto	5 inches	50

C Honduras
F Medium to full-bodied
Q Superior quality

TORPEDO : LENGTH 7 INCHES, RING GAUGE 36/54

CETRO : LENGTH 6¼ INCHES, RING GAUGE 44

CHURCHILL : LENGTH 7 INCHES, RING GAUGE 48

COHIBA

*F*or a brand so young (founded in 1968) in the annals of Havanas, it is remarkable how many myths surround Cohiba. One affects its very name, which was said to be the aboriginal Taino Indian word for "tobacco," but is now understood to have meant "cigar." Another centers on Che Guevara's role in its creation. His portrait may hang above the Director's desk at the El Laguito factory, but since he quit his post as Minister of Industry in 1965 and perished in October of the year before the brand was born, his association with it could at best be described as fleeting. A third is that all Cohibas are made at El Laguito, which, although it was the case for over twenty years, is no longer so.

La verdad—the truth—about Cohiba's origin is now offered by Emilia Tamayo, the Director at El Laguito since June 1994. This charming and highly capable woman confirms that it all began in the mid-1960s when one of President Fidel Castro's bodyguards enjoyed a private supply of cigars from a local artisan. They so pleased the president that their creator, Eduardo Ribera, was asked to make cigars of his blend exclusively for Castro, under strict security in an Italianate mansion in the Havana suburb of El Laguito.

At first, the brand had no name, then in 1968, under the name Cohiba, production began of three sizes, each a personal favorite of the President—the Lancero, the Corona Especiale, and the Panetela. All were originals, so they were given the new factory names of Laguito No. 1, No. 2, which had the unique feature of a tiny pigtail on their caps, and No. 3.

For 14 years these three Cohibas were reserved solely for government and diplomatic use. However, the same sizes, using different blends, were adopted first by Davidoff as the No. 1, the No. 2, and the Ambassadrice when he was granted his brand in 1969 and then by Montecristo in the early 1970s as the Especial, the Especial No. 2, and the Joyita.

The guiding hand over this period, and indeed for 26 years, belonged to Avelino Lara. (He took over from Ribera in 1968.) Affable and relaxed, Lara, the eldest of four top-grade cigar rolling brothers, laid down the three principles which have made Cohiba Havanas the premier brand and, arguably, the world's finest cigar.

The first he calls "the selection of the selection." The produce of the top ten vegas in the Vuelta Abajo is put at his disposal. In any year he picks the five best for his wrappers, binders, ligeros, secos, and volados. The next is a special third fermentation, unique among Havana brands, which is applied to just two of the leaf-types—the ligero and seco. Moisture is added to the leaves as they age in barrels to ferment out the last vestiges of harshness. And third, the making of Cohibas is confined to the ablest rollers in Cuba, all of whom at El Laguito are female.

By 1982 word of this fabled cigar was out, and the decision was made to offer it to lesser mortals than the King of Spain and other such heads of state. Seven years later, three more sizes were introduced: the Esplendido (a Churchill), the Robusto, and the Exquisito, another unique size measuring 5 inches by 36 ring gauge. Of these, only the Exquisito is produced at el Laguito. The other two are made at either H. Upmann or Partagas.

More recently, to celebrate the 500th Anniversary of Columbus's discovery of cigars in Cuba, five new sizes known as the Linea 1492 (the six former sizes are now called the Linea Clasica) were first revealed at a celebration in Havana in November 1992, then launched at a glittering dinner at Claridge's Hotel in London a year later. Named Siglo (meaning century) I, II, III, IV, and V, the five centuries since Columbus are commemorated in a selection which bears more than a passing resemblance to some of the Davidoffs no longer made in Cuba. Crafted at Partagas, they are said to offer a lighter flavor than the Linea Clasica, which notably in its heavier size boasts a rare richness.

Cohibas made in the Dominican Republic can be found in a few American cigar stores. These bear no resemblance to the cigars above, but reflect an adroit move by General Cigar to register the name in the United States early in the 1980s. When the day of the repeal of the U.S./Cuban trade embargo finally dawns, contrary to the belief of many, Cohibas and virtually all other Havana brands will not flood onto the shelves of American cigar merchants. Instead, lawyers will rub their hands with glee as the battle to untangle one of the world's most complex trademark issues begins.

SIZES

NAME	LENGTH: INCHES	RING GAUGE
Lancero	7½ inches	38
Esplendido	7 inches	47
Coronas Especial	6 inches	38
Exquisito	5 inches	36
Robusto	4⅞ inches	50
Panetela	4½ inches	26

PANETELA : LENGTH 4½ INCHES, RING GAUGE 26

EXQUISITO : LENGTH 5 INCHES, RING GAUGE 36

ESPENDIDO : LENGTH 7 INCHES, RING GAUGE 47

EDUARDO RIBERA,
CREATOR OF THE
ORIGINAL COHIBA BLEND.

ROBUSTO : LENGTH 4⅞ INCHES, RING GAUGE 50

CORONAS ESPECIAL : LENGTH 6 INCHES, RING GAUGE 38

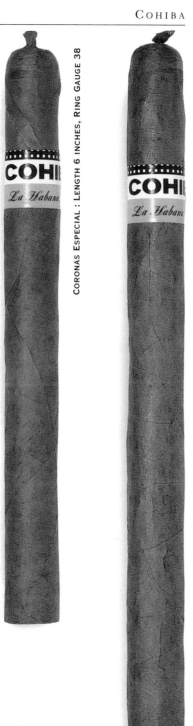

LANCERO : LENGTH 7½ INCHES, RING GAUGE 38

COHIBA

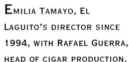

- **C** Cuba
- **F** Medium to full-bodied
- **Q** The very best quality available

SIGLO I : LENGTH 4 INCHES, RING GAUGE 40

SIGLO II : LENGTH 5 INCHES, RING GAUGE 42

EMILIA **T**AMAYO, **E**L **L**AGUITO'S DIRECTOR SINCE 1994, WITH **R**AFAEL **G**UERRA, HEAD OF CIGAR PRODUCTION.

SIGLO SERIES

NAME	LENGTH: INCHES	RING GAUGE
Siglo V	6⅞ inches	43
Siglo III	6⅛ inches	42
Siglo IV	5⅝ inches	46
Siglo II	5 inches	42
Siglo I	4 inches	40

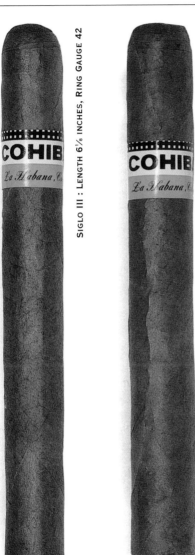

SIGLO III : LENGTH 6⅛ INCHES, RING GAUGE 42

SIGLO IV : LENGTH 5⅝ INCHES, RING GAUGE 46

SIGLO V : LENGTH 6⅝ INCHES, RING GAUGE 43

CUABA

*ℒ*aunched in the fall of 1996, this is the latest Havana to hit the cigar market and is produced by the Romeo Y Julieta factory in Cuba. Its name derives from an old Taino Indian word for a type of bush, that still grows on the island today. It was used for lighting cigars at religious ceremonies—chosen because it burned easily. *Quemar como una Cuaba*—to burn like a Cuaba—is an expression still used by Cuban farmers today.

Available in four sizes, this line is reminiscent of vintage cigars. Each cigar in the line has a tapered end, known as "figuardo," a shape very popular during the nineteenth century, which then lost its popularity to the straight-sided or "parejos" cigars that have dominated the twentieth century.

This mild to medium cigar offers a smoke of outstanding quality.

SIZES

NAME	LENGTH: INCHES	RING GAUGE
Exclusivos	5⅝ inches	46
Generosos	5¼ inches	42
Tradicionales	4¾ inches	42
Divinos	4 inches	43

DIVINOS : LENGTH 4 INCHES, RING GAUGE 43

A TYPICAL TOBACCO FARM IN CUBA, WITH THE THATCHED CURING HOUSE AMID THE CROP.

GENEROSOS : LENGTH 5¼ INCHES, RING GAUGE 42

TRADICIONALES : LENGTH 4¾ INCHES, RING GAUGE 42

EXCLUSIVOS : LENGTH 5⅝ INCHES, RING GAUGE 46

C Cuba
F Medium to full
Q The very best quality money can buy

CUBA ALIADOS

*T*he band on every Aliados cigar bears the word Cuba. But it doesn't come from Cuba. It comes from Honduras. No doubt the hands that made it are those of a Cuban émigré. No doubt its production is supervised by ex-patriate Cubans, and no doubt the seeds for its tobacco are émigré Cuban seeds, but that doesn't make it Cuban.

In some ways, this is a pity because the cigars are good. They reflect the tireless devotion of that island's people to make fine cigars anywhere, and they possess the quality to stand on their own, no matter where they are from. The Piramides and Diademas shapes are masterpieces of the cigar-maker's art.

Most sizes come with a choice of Claro, Colorado Claro, and Colorado wrappers, which add interesting flavor alternatives to what is a medium to full-bodied taste. The Colorado has a particular richness.

SIZES

NAME	LENGTH: INCHES	RING GAUGE
General	18 inches	66
Figurin	10 inches	60
Diademas	7½ inches	60
Piramides	7½ inches	60
Churchill	7⅛ inches	54
Valentino	7 inches	48
Cazadore	7 inches	45
Palma	7 inches	36
Corona Deluxe	6½ inches	45
Fuma	6½ inches	45
Lonsdale	6½ inches	42
Toro	6 inches	54
No. 4	5½ inches	45
Remedios	5½ inches	42
Rothschild	5 inches	51
Petit Cetro	5 inches	36

ROTHSCHILD : LENGTH 5 INCHES, RING GAUGE 51

CORONA DELUXE : LENGTH 6½ INCHES, RING GAUGE 45

LONSDALE : LENGTH 6½ INCHES, RING GAUGE 42

C Honduras
F Medium to full-bodied
Q Good-quality leaf and construction

CUESTA-REY

The name of Cuesta-Rey dates back to the time when Tampa, Florida, was the American capital of a flourishing cigar manufacturing industry. Founded in 1884 by Angel La Madrid Cuesta, who was soon joined by Peregrino Rey, "clear Havanas" (cigars made in the United States from Cuban tobaccos) were their trade.

These days, Cuesta-Rey is presided over by the Newman family, owners of the last of the great Tampa cigar houses. They, too, have a proud history dating back a century and recorded in a recent book by tobacco historian Glen Westfall.

There are two series: Cabinet Selection and Centennial Vintage Collection, celebrating the founding of the brand in 1884.

Cabinet and Centennial Vintage are all fully handmade in the Dominican Republic. Listed below is the Centennial Vintage Collection, a brand widely distributed throughout the world. These cigars are 100 percent handmade using Connecticut shade wrappers and Dominican binders. The filler is made from a blend of four types of long-filler tobacco.

SIZES

Name	Length: inches	Ring Gauge
Individual	8½ inches	52
Dominican #1	8½ inches	52
Dominican #2	7¼ inches	48
Aristocrat	7¼ inches	48
Dominican #3	7 inches	36
Riviera	7 inches	35
Dominican #4	6½ inches	42
Dominican No. 60	6 inches	50
Captiva	6³⁄₁₆ inches	42
Robusto	4½ inches	50
Dominican #5	5½ inches	43
Cameo	4¼ inches	32

DOMINICAN #1 : LENGTH 8½ INCHES, RING GAUGE 52

DOMINICAN #5 : LENGTH 5½ INCHES, RING GAUGE 43

CAPTIVA : LENGTH 6³/₁₆ INCHES, RING GAUGE 42

C Dominican Republic
F Mild
Q Superior quality

*D*avidoff is a byword for style and quality throughout the world. It encompasses men's fragrances, ties, glasses, cognac, humidors, and briefcases, but it is based upon cigars. To build such a multimillion dollar enterprise on a tobacco product in the late 20th century is a remarkable achievement, which owes its inspiration to Zino Davidoff and its present commercialisation to Ernst Schneider.

The life of Zino Davidoff, which ended in his 88th year on January 14, 1994, reads like a history of the 20th century. Born in Kiev, his family fled the pogroms to settle in Geneva and opened a tobacco shop where Lenin was a customer. Young Zino traveled the tobacco lands of Central and South America, ending up in Cuba, for which he formed a life-long affection. Amassing a hoard of Havanas from Vichy France, when World War II ended, he found himself with a rare stock of the finest cigars. His natural charm combined with a deep knowledge saw him first in 1947 create his Chateau selection based on Cuban Hoyo de Monterrey cabinets and then in 1969, aged 63, he was granted the accolade from the Cuban industry of a Havana brand.

His partnership with Ernst Schneider, one of several local Swiss importers at the time, dates from 1970. Schneider's Basel-based Oettinger Imex company saw the worldwide potential for the brand, and with Cubatabaco's expertise the cigar line was developed. There were three series of Davidoff Havanas, each with its own distinctive flavor. The fullest was the Chateau range, the lightest the Dom Perignon No. 1, No. 2, and Ambassadrice. In between there was the Thousand series.

THE EXTERIOR OF THE GENEVA BRANCH OF DAVIDOFF.

That these cigars should no longer be available is a tragedy born of a dispute between Oettinger and Cubatabaco, which resulted in the cessation of production of Davidoffs in Havana from March 1990 and the transfer of their manufacture to the Dominican Republic.

Much speculation has surrounded the reasons for the breakdown of what had been a highly successful marriage. It is perhaps best covered by Paul Garmirian in his book *The Gourmet Guide to Cigars.*

To their lasting credit, Davidoff and Schneider did not attempt to recreate the flavors of their former cigars. The sizes may be identical in many cases and the concept of different series with their own styles of taste is retained, but instead they have set out to create the very best of Dominican cigars. They accept that this will mean a lighter overall flavor, but believe that there are smokers who will be well pleased by it. Their success in several parts of the world suggests that they are right, but that is not to say that many previous devotees are not deeply disappointed.

DOMINICAN SIZES

NAME	LENGTH: INCHES	RING GAUGE
Aniversario No. 1	8⅔ inches	48
Double R	7½ inches	50
Tubo No. 1	7½ inches	38
Aniversatio No. 2	7 inches	48
3000	7 inches	33
Grand Cru No. 1	6³⁄₃₂ inches	42
4000	6³⁄₃₂ inches	42
Special T	6 inches	52
Tubo No. 2	6 inches	38
5000	5⅝ inches	46
Grand Cru No. 2	5⅝ inches	42
Tubo No. 3	5⅛ inches	30
Grand Cru No. 3	5 inches	42
2000	5 inches	42
Special R	4⅞ inches	50
Grand Cru No. 4	4⅝ inches	40
1000	4⅝ inches	34
Ambassadrice	4⅝ inches	26
Grand Cru No. 5	4 inches	40

Dominican Davidoffs, dressed in their claro Connecticut wrappers, are immaculately tailored. The "Grand Cru" range replaces the former Chateau range by offering the richest flavor. The No. 1, No. 2, No. 3, and Ambassadrice are as delicately mild as you can get, and the Thousand ("Mille") series are mild-flavored. There is a "Special" selection of heavier girth cigars, including the Special R (Robusto), the Special T (Piramides), the Double R (Double Corona) and the latest special "C" (Culebras).

Finally, there are two sizes of Aniversario (the name first used for a limited-edition Cuban cigar made to mark Zino's 80th birthday), which have a lightness remarkable in cigars of their size.

INSIDE THE DAVIDOFF SHOP, NEW YORK.

C Dominican
   Republic
F Mild to
   medium
Q Superior
   quality

DOUBLE R : LENGTH 7½ INCHES, RING GAUGE 50

SPECIAL T : LENGTH 6 INCHES, RING GAUGE 52

TUBO No 2 : LENGTH 6 INCHES, RING GAUGE 38

Made by Hand in the Dominican Republic

DIPLOMATICOS

*T*he Diplomaticos range was originally created for the French market in 1966. Although the brand's livery of a carriage and scrolls owes more to Walt Disney than to cigar tradition, it has been adopted recently by a Dominican Republic brand called Licenciados (also listed). The choice is limited, as is availability. They resemble Montecristos with a different label, and are cheaper.

Diplomaticos are very well-constructed, with a rich, but subtle flavor and excellent aroma. If you can find them, they are good value for the quality they represent. They are all good smokes, particularly No. 1, No. 2, and No. 3. The sizes, and numbering, are similiar to the Montecristo range—though the line itself is smaller.

SIZES

NAME	LENGTH: INCHES	RING GAUGE
No. 6	7½ inches	38
No. 1	6½ inches	42
No. 2	6⅛ inches	52
No. 7	6 inches	38
No. 3	5½ inches	42
No. 4	5 inches	42
No. 5	4 inches	40

DIPLOMATICOS NO. 2 : LENGTH 6⅛ INCHES, RING GAUGE 52

DIPLOMATICOS NO. 3 : LENGTH 5½ INCHES, RING GAUGE 42

DIPLOMATICOS NO. 5 : LENGTH 4 INCHES, RING GAUGE 40

C Cuba
F Medium to full-bodied
Q Superior quality

DON DIEGO

These mellow mild to medium cigars (not too different from their rival Macanudo) are made in the Dominican Republic with claro and colorado claro wrappers. They are well made, and come in tubes as well as boxes. The brand was originally made in the Canary Islands—until the mid-1970s—and then had different characteristics. Connecticut wrappers are generally used, though some (mostly smaller) sizes come with fuller-flavored, sweeter-tasting, Cameroon wrappers. Some sizes are available in a choice of double claro (AMS) or colorado (EMS).

The Monarch tubes are very good for their type, as are the Lonsdales. The Royal Palms and Corona Major are also tubed sizes. Generally, with this brand, flavor, aroma, and burning qualities are all high class. Don Diego Privadas are more fully matured.

SIZES

NAME	LENGTH: INCHES	RING GAUGE
Monarch (EMS)	7¼ inches	46
Lonsdales (EMS/AMS)	6⅝ inches	42
Coronas Bravas	6½ inches	48
Grecos (EMS)	6½ inches	38
Royal Palms	6⅛ inches	36
Coronas (EMS/AMS)	5⅝ inches	42
Petit Corona (EMS/AMS)	5⅛ inches	42
Corona Major (EMS)	5¹⁄₁₆ inches	42
Babies	5¼ inches	33
Preludes (EMS)	4 inches	28

LONSDALES : LENGTH 6⅝ INCHES, RING GAUGE 42

CORONA MAJOR : LENGTH 5¹¹⁄₁₆ INCHES, RING GAUGE 42

CORONAS : LENGTH 5⅝ INCHES, RING GAUGE 42

C Dominican
Republic
F Mild to
medium
Q Good-quality
leaf and
construction

DON LINO

First introduced in 1989, the Don Lino brand of handmade Honduran cigars has seen two new selections added in the last few years. The original blend covers fifteen very well-priced sizes wrapped in Connecticut shade and filled with a lightish mixture of Honduran tobaccos.

The seven sizes of the Habana Reserve line also come Connecticut wrapped and claim a special four-year aging before reaching the market. This mellows their flavor but adds to the price.

Darker Connecticut broadleaf wrappers are used for the four heavy gauge sizes in the Colorado series launched in 1994. These also show signs of aging and have a pleasing mild to medium taste. Each size is available in its own humidor, which can be refilled from standard cedar boxes.

If well-filled cigars appeal, any Don Lino is the cigar for you. However, they are sometimes too well-filled, which can impede the draw.

C Honduras
F Mild to medium
Q Good-quality leaf and construction

COLORADO LONSDALE : LENGTH 6½ INCHES, RING GAUGE 44

NAME	LENGTH: INCHES	RING GAUGE
Supremos	8½ inches	52
Churchill	7½ inches	50
Torpedo	7 inches	48
Panetelas	7 inches	36
No. 1	6½ inches	44
No. 5	6¼ inches	44
No. 3	6 inches	36
Corona	5½ inches	50
Robustos	5½ inches	50
Toros	5½ inches	46
Peticetro	5½ inches	42
No. 4	5 inches	42
Rothchild	4½ inches	50
Epicures	4½ inches	32

HABANA RESERVE SERIES

Churchills	7½ inches	50
Panetelas	7¹⁄₁₆ inches	36
Torpedo	7 inches	48
#1	6½ inches	44
Tubo	6½ inches	44
Toros	5½ inches	46
Robusto	5 inches	50
Rothschild	4½ inches	50

COLORADO SERIES

Presidente	7½ inches	50
Torpedos	7 inches	48
Lonsdale	6½ inches	44
Robustos	5½ inches	50

DON PEPE

*T*his brand was launched in Brazil in November 1994, and is the latest addition to the lines produced by Suerdieck. It is already a popular choice in the United States. They are a blend of *mata norte* and *mata fina* tobacco, wrapped in Brazilian-grown Sumatra leaf. Available in seven sizes these cigars offer a medium to full smoke that is rich and earthy.

SIZES

NAME	LENGTH: INCHES	RING GAUGE
Double Corona	7½ inches	52
Churchill	7 inches	48
Petit Lonsdale	6 inches	43
Slim Panatela	5¼ inches	26
Robusto	5 inches	52
Half Corona	4¼ inches	34

A TOBACCO CROP IN BRAZIL. THE BOTTOM LEAVES
ARE READY TO HARVEST.

CHURCHILL : LENGTH 7 INCHES, RING GAUGE 48

ROBUSTO : LENGTH 5 INCHES, RING GAUGE 52

DOUBLE CORONA : LENGTH 7½ INCHES, RING GAUGE 52

C Brazil
F Mild to
medium
Q Good-quality
leaf and
construction

DON RAMOS

*T*hese well-made, full-flavored, 100 percent Honduran cigars are made in San Pedro de Sula, mainly for the British market. There are a total of seven sizes, all available in bundles. Five come in tubes and four in boxes. The bundles are simply numbered; No. 11 is a Churchill, No. 14 a Corona, No. 19 a Rothschild, and so on, and offer good value for money. The heavy gauge sizes—6¾ inches, x 47 (Churchill/Gigantes/No. 11), 55/8 inches x 46 (No. 13) and 4½ inches x 50 (Epicures/No. 19) are substantial smokes. All sizes have a spicy richness. The list below gives the bundle numbers.

EPICURE : LENGTH 4½ INCHES, RING GAUGE 50

SIZES

Name	Length: inches	Ring Gauge
No. 11	6¾ inches	47
No. 13	5⅝ inches	46
No. 14	5½ inches	42
No. 16	5 inches	42
No. 19	4½ inches	50
No. 20	4½ inches	42
No. 17	4 inches	42

HONDURAS · HANDMADE

C Honduras
F Medium to full-bodied
Q Superior quality

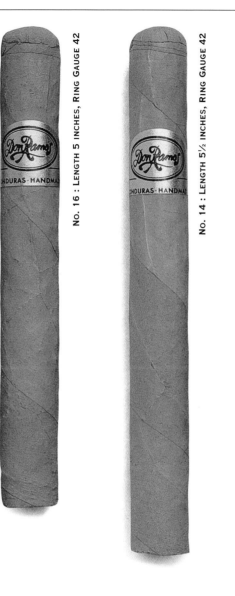

NO. 16 : LENGTH 5 INCHES, RING GAUGE 42

NO. 14 : LENGTH 5½ INCHES, RING GAUGE 42

NO. 11 : LENGTH 6¾ INCHES, RING GAUGE 47

HAND MADE

HECHO A MANO

Don Ramos

FLOR FINA

HONDURAS

DON TOMAS

*T*hese are very well-made Honduran cigars which come in three lines at differing price levels. Special Edition incorporates five super-premium priced sizes using Honduran, Dominican, and Connecticut seed tobaccos grown near Talanga, Honduras. The International series offers just four sizes, identified by a distinctive slanting band, using an all Cuban-seed blend at a premium price. The standard series gives a choice of natural or maduro wrappers on a wide choice of sizes, including a so-called Corona with an unusually large ring gauge for this size, but a good smoke nonetheless.

SIZES

Name	Length: inches	Ring Gauge
Gigante	8½ inches	52
Imperial	8 inches	44
President	7½ inches	50
Panatela Larga	7 inches	38
Cetro No. 2	6½ inches	44
Corona Grande	6½ inches	44
Supremo	6¼ inches	42
Panetela	6 inches	36
Corona	5½ inches	50
Toro	5½ inches	46
Matador	5½ inches	42
Blunt	5 inches	42
Rothschild	4½ inches	50
Epicure	4½ inches	32

CORONA GRANDE : LENGTH 6½ INCHES, RING GAUGE 44

IMPERIAL : LENGTH 8 INCHES, RING GAUGE 44

BLUNT : LENGTH 5 INCHES, RING GAUGE 42

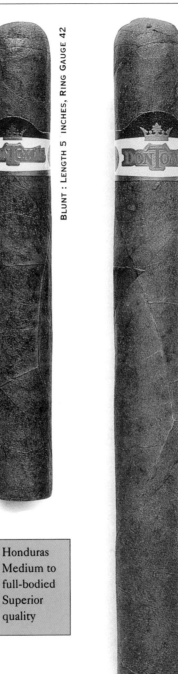

PRESIDENT : LENGTH 7½ INCHES, RING GAUGE 50

C Honduras
F Medium to full-bodied
Q Superior quality

[103]

The old English company of Alfred Dunhill can claim a long association with fine cigars. It was to Dunhill that the Menendez y Garcia company first took their infant Montecristo brand in 1935. There were house brands like Don Candido and Don Alfredo. The 1980s saw the brief creation of Dunhill's own brand of Havanas, sporting a red band bearing the company's elongated "d" logo on sizes like the Cabinetta, and Malecon.

Today Dunhill's accolade is reserved for two lines: one from the Dominican Republic—the Aged Cigar—which can be found throughout the United States, Europe, and the Middle East; and the other from the Canary Islands.

There are thirteen sizes of Aged Cigars each made from Dominican fillers and wrapped in U.S. Connecticut leaf. Aged for a minimum of three months before they are distributed, these mid-priced

CENTENAS : LENGTH 6 INCHES, RING GAUGE 50

DOMINICAN SIZES

Name	Length: inches	Ring Gauge
Peravias	7 inches	50
Caberas	7 inches	48
Fantinos	7 inches	28
Diamantes	6⅝ inches	42
Samanas	6½ inches	38
Centenas	6 inches	50
Condados	6 inches	48
Tabaras	5⁵⁄₁₆ inches	42
Valverdes	5⁵⁄₁₆ inches	42
Altamiras	5 inches	48
Romanas	4½ inches	50
Bavaros	4½ inches	28
Caletas	4 inches	42

CORONA EXTRA : LENGTH 5 INCHES, RING GAUGE 50

PERAVAIS : LENGTH 7 INCHES, RING GAUGE 50

ROMANAS : LENGTH 4½ INCHES, RING GAUGE 50

C Dominican
Republic
F Medium to
full-bodied
Q Superior
quality

cigars look good dressed with their blue bands and are well made and blended. They burn evenly and offer a distinctive, medium to full, but in no way heavy smoke, with a delicate aroma. Uniquely, a vintage is declared for this brand, based on the idea that its tobaccos are taken from a single year's harvest.

The Canary Islands selection is smaller, numbering just five sizes. Distinguished by their red bands, these cigars offer a mild to medium flavor with a touch of sweetness. They, too, are well constructed, but offer a somewhat rougher, less polished smoke.

CANARY ISLANDS SIZES

NAME	LENGTH: INCHES	RING GAUGE
Lonsdale Grandes	7½ inches	42
Corona Grandes	6½ inches	43
Panetelas	6 inches	30
Corona Extra	5½ inches	50
Coronas	5½ inches	43

PANETELA : LENGTH 6 INCHES, RING GAUGE 30

C Canary Islands
F Mild to medium
Q Good-quality leaf and construction

EL REY DEL MUNDO

*T*he name means "King of the World," a confident enough title for this brand, originally founded in 1882 by the Antonio Allones company. Many connoisseurs would rate it among their favorite brands. The selection is large, with some sizes available in machine-made versions. They are made in the Romeo Y Julieta factory along with other medium-flavored brands. There are also well-made (but much fuller-bodied) Honduran versions in 26 sizes (a selection is listed overleaf) from J.R. Tobacco with completely different names such as Flor de Llaneza, Imperiale, and Montecarlo, although they also list a Choix Supreme. Some contain a Dominican filler for a lighter flavor, aimed at the less-experienced smoker.

The El Rey del Mundo Corona was the favorite cigar of film producer Darryl F. Zanuck—former head of 20th Century-Fox—who once actually owned a plantation in Cuba. The British tycoon Sir Terence Conran is also a fan.

The Cuban are a well-constructed, high-quality line of cigars, with smooth, oily wrappers, particularly the larger sizes. Even the larger sizes are light and medium to mild (too mild for those for whom big cigars mean body), and the aroma is always subtle. These are good beginners' cigars, and very suitable for daytime smoking; even the larger sizes wouldn't be best appreciated after a heavy dinner.

CUBAN SIZES

Name	Length: Inches	Ring Gauge
Elegantes	6⅞ inches	28
Lonsdale	6⅜ inches	42
Corona De Luxe	5½ inches	42
Choix Supreme	5 inches	48
Petit Corona	5 inches	42
Tres Petit Coronas	4½ inches	40
Demi-Tasse	3⅞ inches	30

HONDURAN SIZES

Name	Length: inches	Ring Gauge
Coronation	8½ inches	52
Principale	8 inches	47
Flor del Mundo	7¼ inches	54
Robusto Suprema	7¼ inches	54
Imperiale	7¼ inches	54
Corona Inmensa	7¼ inches	47
Double Corona	7 inches	49
Cedar	7 inches	43
Flor de Llaneza	6½ inches	54
Flor de LaVonda	6½ inches	52
Plantation	6½ inches	30
Choix Supreme	6⅛ inches	49
Montecarlo	6⅛ inches	48
Robusto Larga	6 inches	54
Originale	5⅝ inches	45
Classic Corona	5⅝ inches	45
Corona	5⅝ inches	45
Rectangulare	5⅝ inches	45
Habana Club	5½ inches	42
*Tino	5½ inches	38
*Elegante	5⅜ inches	29
*Reynita	5 inches	38
Robusto	5 inches	54
Robusto Zavalla	5 inches	54
Rothschild	5 inches	50
*Petit Lonsdale	4⅝ inches	43
Cafe au Lait	4½ inches	35

*Lighter Dominican filler

C Cuba
F Mild to medium
Q Superior quality

CORONA : LENGTH 5⅝ INCHES, RING GAUGE 45

CAFE AU LAIT : LENGTH 4½ INCHES, RING GAUGE 35

FLOR DEL MUNDO : LENGTH 7¼ INCHES, RING GAUGE 54

C Honduras
F Medium to
full-bodied
Q Good-quality
leaf and
construction

EXCALIBUR

*E*xcaliburs are the very best of the Hoyo de Monterrey brand made by Villazon from Havana seed wrappers in Honduras (see also Hoyo de Monterrey entry). They are medium to full-bodied, rich, extremely well made, and among the best non-Cuban cigars on the market. They are sold with the Hoyo de Monterrey label in the United States (with the additional word Excalibur at the bottom of the band), but simply as Excalibur in Europe, for trademark reasons. Try the No. II.

NO. IV : LENGTH 5⅝ INCHES, RING GAUGE 46

S I Z E S

Name	Length: inches	Ring Gauge
No. I	7¼ inches	54
Banquet	6¾ inches	48
No. II	6¾ inches	47
No. III	6⅛ inches	48
No. V	6¼ inches	45
No. IV	5⅝ inches	46
No. VI	5½ inches	38
No. VII	5 inches	43
Miniatures	3 inches	22

C Honduras
F Medium to full-bodied
Q Superior quality

FELIPE GREGORIO

*F*elipe Gregorio is the flagship brand of Cigars of Honduras, founded in 1990. Named after the company's founder, it has enjoyed widespread success in the United States. The tobacco for filler, binder, and wrapper is all grown in the Jamastran valley of Honduras, and each cigar is made exclusively from tobacco grown in one *finca*, making each cigar a *puro*. Of particular interest is the fact that leaves of wrapper quality are used as binders. The cigars are available in six sizes and are very well constructed.

SIZES

NAME	LENGTH: INCHES	RING GAUGE
Glorioso	7¾ inches	50
Suntuoso	7 inches	48
Belicoso	6 inches	torpedo
Robusto	5 inches	52
Sereno	5¾ inches	42
Nino	4¼ inches	44

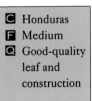

C	Honduras
F	Medium
Q	Good-quality leaf and construction

FONSECA

*B*oxes of Cuban Fonsecas feature both New York's Statue of Liberty and Havana's Morro Castle, indicating that the brand was born at a time when relations between these two great cities were easier than they are today.

Since 1965, the brand has also been made in the Dominican Republic, originally using Cameroon wrappers, but now preferring light Connecticut shade. Mexican binders combine with Dominican fillers in very well-made cigars for a truly mild smoke.

The small range of Cuban Fonsecas come uniquely encased in white tissue. They are Barcelona's favorite cigar, where prodigious quantities are consumed by people who know their smokes. The flavor is light to medium with a slight saltiness.

DOMINICAN SIZES

NAME	LENGTH: INCHES	RING GAUGE
#10–10	7 inches	50
#7–9–9	6½ inches	46
#8–9–9	6 inches	43
Triangular	5½ inches	56
#5–50	5 inches	50
#2–2	4¼ inches	40

CUBAN SIZES

NAME	LENGTH: INCHES	RING GAUGE
No. 1	6⅜ inches	44
Cosacos	5¼ inches	40
Invictos	5¼ inches	45
Delicias	4⅞ inches	40
K.D.T. Cadetes	4½ inches	36

K.D.T. CADETES : LENGTH 4½ INCHES, RING GAUGE 36

COSACOS : LENGTH 5¼ INCHES, RING GAUGE 40

NO. 1 : LENGTH 6⅜ INCHES, RING GAUGE 44

C Dominican
Republic
F Mild
Q Superior
quality

C Cuba
F Mild to
medium
Q Good-quality
leaf and
construction

GRIFFIN'S

*G*riffin is the brainchild of Geneva-based Bernard H. Grobet, an early disciple of Zino Davidoff. He was among the first Europeans who over a decade ago saw the potential for cigars made in the Dominican Republic. More recently, both the manufacture and marketing of the brand have come under the influence of his old mentor's organization —Davidoff & Cie. The cigars look good in their light Connecticut wrappers and are well-constructed. The flavor is as to be expected from Dominican filler in this presentation, and they are quite costly.

SIZES

Name	Length: inches	Ring Gauge
Prestige	7½ inches	50
No. 200	7 inches	43
No. 100	7 inches	38
No. 300	6¼ inches	43
No. 400	6 inches	38
No. 500	5⁹⁄₁₆ inches	43
Robusto	5 inches	50
Privilege	5 inches	32

C Dominican Republic
F Mild to medium
Q Superior quality

HECHO A MANO

H. UPMANN

*H*erman Upmann was a member of a European banking family and a lover of good cigars. It came as no surprise when, in around 1840, he volunteered to open a branch of the bank in Havana. The cigars he sent home proved so popular that, in 1844, he invested in a cigar factory. The company traded successfully as both bankers and cigar makers until 1922, when first the bank and then the cigar business failed. A British firm, J. Frankau & Co. saved the cigar brand and ran the factory until 1935 when it was sold to the newly founded Menendez y Garcia company.

In 1944 a new H. Upmann factory was opened in Old Havana's Calle Amistad to mark the centenary of Herman's enterprise. The brand is made there to this day, at present, under the direction of the talented Benito Molina.

Havana Upmanns are mild to medium-flavored, very smooth, subtle cigars. They are generally very satisfactory, although sometimes, particularly when they are machine-made, let down by construction and burning qualities, occasionally overheating and leaving a bitter aftertaste. They are, however, a good beginner's cigar, or one to be smoked after a light meal. Cuban Upmanns come in a bewildering choice of over 30 sizes, many of them similar to one another. A number of Upmann sizes (including machine-mades—so beware) are sold in tubes. Only handmade Upmanns are imported into Britain, however.

Handmade cigars bearing the Upmann name are also produced by the Consolidated Cigar Corporation in the Dominican Republic, with Cameroon wrappers and Latin American fillers. They are a very respectable, well-made, mild to medium smoke, usually in oily colorado wrappers. The 12 boxed sizes available include Corona Imperiales, Lonsdale, Corona, Petit Corona, and Churchill. There are also six tubed sizes. The label on non-Havana Upmanns reads: "H. Upmann 1844," whereas the Cuban version says: "H. Upmann Habana." The sizes given below are the standard Havana versions.

CUBAN SIZES

NAME	LENGTH: INCHES	RING GAUGE
Monarchs	7 inches	47
Monarcas (also called Sir Winston)	7 inches	47
Lonsdale (and No. 1)	6½ inches	42
Upmann No. 2	6⅛ inches	52
Grand Corona	5¾ inches	40
Magnum	5½ inches	46
Corona	5½ inches	42
Royal Corona	5½ inches	42
Corona Major	5 inches	42
Connoisseur No. 1	5 inches	48
Petit Corona (and No. 4)	5 inches	42
Corona Junior	4½ inches	36
Petit Upmann	4½ inches	36

UPMANN NO. 2 : LENGTH 6⅛ INCHES, RING GAUGE 52

CORONA MAJOR : LENGTH 5 INCHES, RING GAUGE 42

LONSDALE (AND NO. 1) : LENGTH 6½ INCHES, RING GAUGE 42

C Cuba
F Mild
Q Superior quality

PEQUENOS NO. 100 : LENGTH 4½ INCHES, RING GAUGE 50

CORONA : LENGTH 5⅞ INCHES, RING GAUGE 42

LONSDALE : LENGTH 6⅝ INCHES, RING GAUGE 42

C Dominican
Republic
F Mild to
medium
Q Good-quality
leaf and
construction

Habana Gold

vailable in eight sizes, these cigars come in three different bands, Black Label, White Label, and Sterling Vintage. Each type is different, with the Sterling Vintage coming highly recommended. All cigars are made in Honduras with Nicaraguan filler and binder, and it is the wrapper that gives each line its own distinctive flavor. The Black Label cigars have a natural Indonesian wrapper giving the cigars a smooth and spicy flavor. The White Label has a dark Nicaraguan wrapper, giving the cigars a rich chocolate flavor. Incidentally all of the tobacco for the White Label cigar is grown in one field making a "puro" cigar. The Sterling Vintage line has dark vintage wrappers from Ecuador, which give a mild to medium smoke of outstanding quality.

SIZES

Name	Length: inches	Ring Gauge
Presidente	8½ inches	52
Double Corona	7½ inches	46
Churchill	7 inches	52
No.2	6⅛ inches	52
Torpedo	6 inches	52
Corona	6 inches	44
Robusto	5 inches	50
Petite Corona	5 inches	42

C Honduras
F Mild to medium
Q (Sterling Vintage) Superior quality

CHURCHILL : LENGTH 7 INCHES, RING GAUGE 52

ROBUSTO : LENGTH 5 INCHES, RING GAUGE 50

CHURCHILL : LENGTH 7 INCHES, RING GAUGE 52

HABANICA

*F*elipe Gregorio launched this brand in Spring 1995, and it has yet to find the international acclaim enjoyed by fellow brand Petrus (also listed). Despite this it has been very well received and praised for its oily dark brown wrapper, and soft, slightly sweet flavors. All of the tobacco for these cigars is grown in the Jalapa valley of Nicaragua, and it offers an excellent mild to medium smoke.

SIZES

NAME	LENGTH: INCHES	RING GAUGE
Serie 747	7 inches	47
Serie 646	6 inches	46
Serie 638	6 inches	38
Serie 546	5¼ inches	46
Serie 550	5 inches	50

C Nicaragua
F Mild to medium
Q Good-quality leaf and construction

HENRY CLAY

*T*his was one of the most famous of the old Havana brands, dating back to the 19th century and named after an American senator with business interests in Cuba. In the 1930s, its manufacture was transferred from Havana to Trenton, New Jersey, to avoid the exuberance of the Cuban workforce. The brand is now made in the Dominican Republic. There are only three sizes, all medium to full-bodied with mid-brown wrappers.

SIZES

NAME	LENGTH: INCHES	RING GAUGE
Breva Fina	6½ inches	48
Breva Conserva	5⅝ inches	46
Breva	5½ inches	42

C Dominican Republic
F Medium to full-bodied
Q Good-quality leaf and construction

BREVA : LENGTH 5½ INCHES, RING GAUGE 42

BREVA CONSERVA : LENGTH 5⅝ INCHES, RING GAUGE 46

BREVA FINA : LENGTH 6½ INCHES, RING GAUGE 48

Hoyo De Monterrey

There is an old wrought-iron gate overlooking a square in the Vuelta Abajo village of San Juan y Martinez which bears the inscription "Hoyo de Monterrey: José Gener 1860." It leads to one of Cuba's most renowned "vegas finas," a plantation specializing in sun-grown tobaccos for binders and fillers. Here, José Gener started his career as a leaf grower on prime land (a "hoyo" is a dip in a field much favored by farmers for reasons of drainage) before founding the Hoyo de Monterrey brand in 1865.

Hoyo's flagship, the Double Corona, has become a unit of exchange among cigar lovers with a value far exceeding precious metals and usually only transacted as a token of close friendship. It has a delicacy of flavor combined with a richness of taste which is a credit to the blenders and rollers at the La Corona factory where it is made. It is felt that other Hoyo sizes, some of which are machine-made, do not live up to their champion. There is some truth in this, but the Epicure Nos. 1 & 2, particularly in 50 bundles, are clear exceptions. It should also be remembered that Zino Davidoff first created his Chateau range using cabinet selection Hoyos in standard sizes. Davidoff's early success in Switzerland inspired the creation in 1970, by a rival merchant, of the Le Hoyo series, which has a spicier, somewhat fuller flavor.

This pales into insignificance however alongside the brand of cigars bearing the same name made in Honduras. What these

CUBAN SIZES

Name	Length: inches	Ring Gauge
Double Corona	7⅝ inches	49
Le Hoyo du Gourmet	6⅝ inches	33
Le Hoyo des Dieux	6 inches	42
Le Hoyo du Dauphin	6 inches	38
Epicure No. 1	5⅝ inches	46
Jeanne D'Arc	5⅝ inches	35
Le Hoyo du Roi	5½ inches	42
Corona	5½ inches	42
Le Hoyo du Prince	5 inches	40
Epicure No. 2	4⅞ inches	50
Margarita	4¾ inches	26
Le Hoyo du Depute	4¼ inches	38
Le Hoyo du Maire	3⅞ inches	30

cigars lack in fine tailoring, they make up for in sheer flavor. They are an "espresso" of a cigar, particularly in the larger girth sizes like the Rothschild and Governors. They are made by men who clearly appreciate the taste of tobacco.

It is important not to confuse the standard Honduran Hoyo line with the Excalibur series (also listed). These are sold as Hoyo de Monterrey Excalibur in the United States, but for trademark reasons, the Hoyo connection is dropped in Europe. They are among the finest of cigars and have a different style of flavor.

HONDURAN SIZES

NAME	LENGTH: INCHES	RING GAUGE
Presidents	8½ inches	52
Sultans	7¼ inches	54
Cuban Largos	7¼ inches	47
Largo Elegantes	7¼ inches	34
Cetros	7 inches	43
Double Corona	6¾ inches	48
No. 1	6½ inches	43
Churchills	6¼ inches	45
Ambassadors	6¼ inches	44
Delights	6¼ inches	37
Governors	6⅛ inches	50
Culebras	6 inches	35
Coronas	5⅝ inches	46
Cafe Royales	5⅝ inches	43
Dreams	5¾ inches	46
Petit	5¾ inches	31
Super Hoyos	5½ inches	44
No. 55	5¼ inches	43
Margaritas	5¼ inches	29
Sabrosos	5 inches	40
Rothschild	4½ inches	50
Demitasse	4 inches	39

DOUBLE CORONA : LENGTH 7⅝ INCHES, RING GAUGE 49

CORONA : LENGTH 5½ INCHES, RING GAUGE 42

MARGARITA : LENGTH 4¾ INCHES, RING GAUGE 26

C Cuba
F Mild
Q Superior
quality

GOVERNOR : LENGTH 6⅛ INCHES, RING GAUGE 50

ROTHSCHILD : LENGTH 4½ INCHES, RING GAUGE 50

SULTAN : LENGTH 7¼ INCHES, RING GAUGE 54

C Honduras
F Medium to
full-bodied
Q Good-quality
leaf and
construction

J. R. CIGARS

*L*ew Rothman is a phenomenon. His J.R. Tobacco of America (J.R. stands for Jack Rothman, Lew's father) covers a mail-order, retail, and wholesale empire that handles 40 percent of all premium cigars sold in the United States.

He built it by playing Robin Hood to the manufacturers' Sheriff of Notthingham. He knows what a cigar costs and won't let his customers pay a cent more than they have to for it. The downside is that some manufacturers like to spend more time and money perfecting cigars to sell at prices Lew won't accept. His sales have

J. R. ULTIMATE

Name	Length: Inches	Ring Gauge
Estelo	8½ inches	52
Presidente	8½ inches	52
No. 10	8¼ inches	47
Super Cetro	8¼ inches	43
No. 1	7¼ inches	54
Cetro	7 inches	42
Palma Extra	6⅞ inches	38
Slims	6⅞ inches	36
Double Corona	6¾ inches	48
No. 5	6⅛ inches	44
Padron	6 inches	54
Toro	6 inches	50
Corona	5⅝ inches	45
Petit Cetro	5½ inches	38
Habenella	5 inches	28
Petit Corona	4⅝ inches	43
Rothschild	4½ inches	50

C Honduras
F Medium to full-bodied
Q Superior quality

INSIDE J.R.'S CIGAR STORE, THE LARGEST OF ITS KIND IN THE WORLD.

NO. 1 : LENGTH 7¼ INCHES, RING GAUGE 54

PETIT CORONA : LENGTH 4⅝ INCHES, RING GAUGE 43

CORONA : LENGTH 5⅝ INCHES, RING GAUGE 45

rocketed in the cigar boom, so this doesn't seem to matter much. Anyway, no one has to sell to him, and several don't.

If it's the best price you are after, look no further than your nearest J.R. store or catalog where you'll find his own brands of J.R. Ultimate, Special Coronas, and Special Jamaicans.

SPECIAL CORONAS

Name	Length: inches	Ring Gauge
Pyramides	7 inches	54
No. 754	7 inches	54
No. 2	6½ inches	45
No. 54	6 inches	54
No. 4	5½ inches	45

J. R. TOBACCO OF AMERICA'S LEW ROTHMAN WITH HIS WIFE AND PARTNER LAVONDA.

C Dominican Republic
F Mild to medium
Q Superior quality

NO. 754 : LENGTH 7 INCHES, RING GAUGE 54

In ascending order of flavor, Special Jamaicans, now made in the Dominican Republic and wrapped in claro Connecticut leaf, are true to their Jamaican origins and as mild as their price. J.R. Special Coronas are also made in the Dominican Republic from a four-country blend of tobaccos— Ecuadoran wrapper and binder matched with a Brazilian, Honduran, and Dominican filler. They are richer in flavor, but are still mild to medium.

J.R. Ultimate is the flagship, and six new sizes have been introduced since the second edition of this book. Made in San Pedro Sula, Honduras, from a local blend wrapped in oily Nicaraguan Colorado leaf, they aim to come close to the taste of Havanas. They offer a rich, full-bodied smoke and rate highly among Hondurans.

All these J.R. cigars are very well put to-gether by hand. Whether they are for you depends on how much you mind being seen with the same cigars as so many of the other chaps in Sherwood Forest.

SPECIAL JAMAICANS

Name	Length: inches	Ring Gauge
Rey del Rey	9 inches	60
Mayfair	7 inches	60
Pyramid	7 inches	52
Nobles	7 inches	50
Churchill	7 inches	50
A	6½ inches	44
Fancytale shape	6½ inches	43
Bonita Obsequio	6 inches	50
D	6 inches	50
B	6 inches	44
C	5½ inches	44
Pica	5 inches	32

SIZE D : LENGTH 6 IN / RING GAUGE 50

C Dominican Republic
F Mild
Q Superior quality

JOSE BENITO

These cigars, with their dark Cameroon wrappers, are made in the Dominican Republic. They are well constructed, and generally light to medium-bodied. They all come in attractive varnished cedar boxes (the huge Magnum, one of the biggest cigars on the market, is sold in a box by itself), and there are ten sizes.

SIZES

NAME	LENGTH: INCHES	RING GAUGE
Magnum	8¾ inches	60
Presidente	7¾ inches	50
Churchill	7 inches	50
Corona	6¾ inches	43
Panatela	6¾ inches	38
Palma	6 inches	43
Petite	5½ inches	38
Havanitos	5 inches	25
Rothschild	4¾ inches	50
Chico	4¼ inches	36

C Dominican Republic
F Mild to medium
Q Superior quality

CHURCHILL : LENGTH 7 INCHES, RING GAUGE 50

JOYA DE NICARAGUA

*B*ack in the 1970s Nicaraguan cigars were rated by many as the next best to Havanas. The war put an end to that when plantations were laid waste and tobacco barns used to billet Sandinista soldiers.

Since 1990 things have been on the mend, but to re-establish quality in tobacco takes time. The local economy still faces formidable problems, but as every year passes, there is a noticeable improvement in Joya de Nicaragua's standards. Gone is the sweaty aroma of the early 1990s' cigars as maturer tobaccos come into use. The more rounded medium flavor with a touch of spice is returning, and the cigars are better constructed and more reliable than they were.

Surprisingly the choice of sizes available in Britain is larger than it is in the United States.

SIZES

NAME	LENGTH: INCHES	RING GAUGE
Viajante	8½ inches	52
Presidente	8 inches	54
Churchill	6⅞ inches	49
No. 5	6⅞ inches	35
No. 1	6⅝ inches	44
No. 10	6½ inches	43
Elegante	6½ inches	38
No. 6	6 inches	52
Corona	5⅝ inches	48
National	5½ inches	44
Seleccion B	5½ inches	42
Petit Corona	5 inches	42
Consul	4½ inches	51
No. 2	4½ inches	41
Piccolino	4⅛ inches	30

PETIT CORONA : LENGTH 5 INCHES, RING GAUGE 42

ELEGANTE : LENGTH 6½ INCHES, RING GAUGE 38

CHURCHILL : LENGTH 7 INCHES, RING GAUGE 50

C Nicaragua
F Mild to
   medium
Q Good-quality
   leaf and
   construction

JUAN CLEMENTE

*F*renchman Jean Clement hispanicized his name for the Dominican Republic cigar brand he founded in 1982. Wrapped in a claro U.S. Connecticut shade leaf and filled with a blend of Dominican tobacco, it offers a mild, straightforward smoke with a pleasant aroma, best suited to the morning. They have been criticized for their draw, but this seems to be improving. The Club Selection, bearing a white band, carries a darker wrapper and is well-blended. Over the last two years six new sizes have been added to this line, including the huge 13 inch Gargantua, and No. 5 in the Club Selection, an *obelisco*. Uniquely, the band is placed at the foot of the cigar, securing a piece of silver paper which serves to protect its most vulnerable point. Logical, if unconventional.

SIZES

NAME	LENGTH: INCHES	RING GAUGE
Gargantua	13 inches	50
Gigante	9 inches	50
Especiales	7½ inches	38
Club Selection No. 3	7 inches	44
Churchill	6⅞ inches	46
Panatela	6½ inches	34
Club Selection No. 5	6 inches	52
Club Selection No. 1	6 inches	50
Grand Corona	6 inches	42
Especiales No. 2	5⅞ inches	38
Club Selection No. 4	5¼ inches	42
Corona	5 inches	42
No. 530	5 inches	30
Rothschild	4⅞ inches	50
Club Selection No. 2	4½ inches	46
Mini-Cigar	4⁵⁄₁₆ inches	22
Demi-Corona	4 inches	40
Demi-Tasse	3¹⁰⁄₁₆ inches	34

CLUB SELECTION No. 2 : LENGTH 4½ INCHES, RING GAUGE 46

CLUB SELECTION NO. 3 : LENGTH 7 INCHES, RING GAUGE 44

DEMI-CORONA : LENGTH 4 INCHES, RING GAUGE 40

ESPECIALES : LENGTH 7½ INCHES, RING GAUGE 38

C Dominican Republic
F Mild
Q Could be better

JUAN LOPEZ

(FLOR DE JUAN LOPEZ)

*T*his is an old Havana brand, no longer widely produced or distributed, but is a very light smoke, appealing to some European palates. There are only five sizes. They are fragrant, burn well, and good for daytime smoking. The cigars are only found in Spain, and the line will soon be reduced to only the Corona and Petit Corona sizes.

SIZES

NAME	LENGTH: INCHES	RING GAUGE
Corona	5⅝ inches	42
Petit Coronas	5 inches	42
Placeras	5 inches	34
Slimaranas	4¾ inches	32
Patricias	4½ inches	40

C	Cuba
F	Mild
Q	Good-quality leaf and construction

SLIMARANAS : LENGTH 4¾ INCHES, RING GAUGE 32

LA CORONA

ormerly one of the great Havana brands, although its production was transferred to Trenton, New Jersey, in the 1930s. At present, a small selection of well-made, mild to medium cigars are made in the Dominican Republic by the Consolidated Cigar Corporation. There are also some cigars made in Cuba under this name, but they are either machine-made or hand-finished. The La Corona factory remains in Havana as one of the most important production centers making Punch and Hoyo de Monterrey among others.

SIZES

Name	Length: inches	Ring Gauge
Directors	6½ inches	46
Aristocrats	6⅛ inches	36
Long Corona	6 inches	43
Corona Chicas	5½ inches	42

- **C** Dominican Republic
- **F** Mild to medium
- **Q** Good-quality leaf and construction

La Flor De Cano

This is a relatively rare Cuban brand, not widely produced or easily available. Rumor has it that Habanos SA has decided to discontinue the handmade sizes like the much-vaunted Short Churchill (a Robusto). Should this prove correct, a group of British fans are considering a campaign to bring them back into production. They are cigars of undoubted quality and interest for those who look for something easy to handle. The Short Churchill, the Punch-Punch sized Gran Corona, and the Diademas are all worth trying, the latter particularly suitable for those who were once Davidoff Dom Perignon fans but don't want to move up to the fuller flavor of the Cohiba Esplendido. Watch out for the many machine-made cigars with names like Preferidos and Selectos that are also available.

C	Cuba
F	Mild
Q	Superior quality

SIZES

Name	Length: inches	Ring Gauge
Diademas	7 inches	47
Corona	5 inches	42
Gran Corona	5⅝ inches	46
Short Churchill	4⅞ inches	50

LA GLORIA CUBANA

*P*roduced by the Partagas factory, which specializes in full bodied cigars, this is an old brand which disappeared until it was revived a couple of decades ago to extend the factory's selection of different types of cigar. The Medaille D'Or brand comes in varnished 8–9–8 boxes and the others in labeled boxes.

These are very spicy, rather peppery, strongly aromatic cigars which sometimes fall down (the Lonsdale size, for instance) in construction. They are lighter (more refined, some would say) than the Partagas brand made in the same factory, though still a rich smoke. The line is small, almost all long sizes.

There is also the Gloria Cubana range made in the United States by Miami's Ernesto Carillo. Ernesto is a man of great integrity whose aim is simply to make the best cigars he can with the best tobaccos he can find. In the main his wrappers are darkish Ecuadoran leaves and his fillers and binders Dominican, Nicaraguan, or Ecuadoran. He blends with his Cuban ancestors in mind to produce full-bodied cigars. The Wavell is strongly recommended if you can find it.

CUBAN SIZES

Name	Length: inches	Ring Gauge
Medaille d'Or 1	7⁵⁄₁₆ inches	36
Tainos	7 inches	47
Medaille d'Or 3	6⅞ inches	28
Medaille d'Or 2	6¹¹⁄₁₆ inches	43
Cetros	6½ inches	42
Sabrosas	6⅛ inches	42
Medaille d'Or 4	6 inches	32
Tapados	5⁵⁄₁₆ inches	42
Minutos	4½ inches	40

C Cuba
F Medium to full
Q Superior quality

U.S. SIZES

Name	Length: inches	Ring Gauge
Soberano	8 inches	52
Charlemagne	7¼ inches	54
Churchill	7 inches	50
Torpedo	6½ inches	52
Wavell	5 inches	50

- **C** United States
- **F** Medium to full
- **Q** The very best quality available

MEDAILLE D'OR 3 : LENGTH 6⅞ INCHES, RING GAUGE 28

MEDAILLE D'OR 4 : LENGTH 6 INCHES, RING GAUGE 32

MEDAILLE D'OR 1 : LENGTH 7⁵/₁₆ INCHES, RING GAUGE 36

MEDAILLE D'OR 2 : LENGTH 6¹¹/₁₆ INCHES, RING GAUGE 43

LICENCIADOS

*O*n the market since 1990, the makers of Licenciados chose to take the Disneyesque carriage and scrolls design found on Havana's Diplomaticos brand as their emblem. Blends of Dominican fillers are dressed in light Connecticut shade wrappers for the main range, while Connecticut broadleaf is used for a smaller maduro series, known as Supreme. The Robusto-sized Wavell comes in both wrapper colors. These are classic, mild, Connecticut Dominican Republic cigars, well-made and competitively priced.

SIZES

Name	Length: inches	Ring Gauge
Soberano	8½ inches	52
Presidente	8 inches	50
Churchill	7 inches	50
Panetela	7 inches	38
Excelente	6¾ inches	43
Toro	6 inches	50
Licenciados No. 4	5¼ inches	43
Wavell	5 inches	50
SUPREME RANGE		
500	8 inches	50
300	6¾ inches	43
400	6 inches	50
200	5¼ inches	43

C Dominican Republic
F Mild
Q Superior quality

PANETELA : LENGTH 7 INCHES, RING GAUGE 38

MACANUDO

This brand, founded in Jamaica in 1868, is now made by General Cigar in both Jamaica and the Dominican Republic, under the supervision of Benjamin Menendez. The blend is the same for both countries of origin: Connecticut Shade wrapper, binder from the San Andres area of Mexico, and a mixture of Jamaican, Mexican, and Dominican tobacco for the filler.

These are undoubtedly handsome, consistently very well-made cigars, which provide one of the very best smooth, mild smokes on the market. The word *macanudo* means fine, dandy, or a good thing in colloquial Spanish and, for once in a cigar name, is pretty near the truth.

There is a wide variety of sizes, some of which (mostly larger ring gauges) come in a choice of wrapper color: café (made with Connecticut Shade wrapper), the even milder jade (a greenish, double claro wrapper), and the fuller and nutty-sweet maduro (in which case, the deep brown wrapper comes from Mexico). The Hampton Court and Portofino sizes come in elegant white aluminum tubes. The Claybourne and Prince Philip sizes are made in the Dominican Republic, the others (normally) in Jamaica. Macanudos don't come cheap; the Connecticut wrapper sees to that. They normally come wrapped in cellophane. If there's one criticism, it's that they are somewhat short on aroma, but they are an excellent daytime smoke, or suitable after a light meal. The fuller-bodied Macanudo Vintage cigars are sold at much higher prices and designed for the connoisseur. They are all made in Jamaica, with Dominican filler.

SIZES

NAME	LENGTH: INCHES	RING GAUGE
Duke of Wellington	8½ inches	38
Prince Philip	7½ inches	49
Vintage No. I	7½ inches	49
Sovereign	7 inches	45
Somerset	7 inches	34
Portofino	7 inches	34
Earl of Lonsdale	6¾ inches	38
Vintage No. II	6⁹⁄₁₆ inches	43
Baron de Rothschild	6½ inches	42
Amatista	6¼ inches	42
Claybourne	6 inches	31
Hampton Court	5¾ inches	43
Vintage No. III	5⁹⁄₁₆ inches	43
Hyde Park	5½ inches	49
Duke of Devon	5½ inches	42
Lord Claridge	5½ inches	38
Quill	5¼ inches	28
Petit Corona	5 inches	38
Vintage No. IV	4½ inches	47
Ascot	4³⁄₁₆ inches	32
Caviar	4 inches	36

VINTAGE No. I : LENGTH 7½ INCHES, RING GAUGE 49

DUKE OF DEVON : LENGTH 5½ INCHES, RING GAUGE 42

CLAYBOURNE : LENGTH 6 INCHES, RING GAUGE 31

C Jamaica
F Mild
Q Superior
quality

HYDE PARK : LENGTH 5½ INCHES, RING GAUGE 49

PORTOFINO : LENGTH 7 INCHES, RING GAUGE 34

PRINCE PHILIP : LENGTH 7½ INCHES, RING GAUGE 49

C Dominican
Republic
F Mild
Q Superior
quality

MATACAN

A minor brand from Mexico, made by the Consolidated Cigar Corporation, also responsible for the Te-Amo brand, in the San Andres Valley. They come in light brown and maduro wrappers. They are well made, less tightly rolled than Te-Amo (though they have similar coarse wrappers), draw well, and have a spicy, slightly sweet, if nonetheless rather bland, medium to full flavor. All things considered, they are somewhat superior to Te-Amo, even though they are cheaper. Try the No. 7.

SIZES

Name	Length: inches	Ring Gauge
No. 8	8 inches	52
No. 1	7½ inches	50
No. 10	6⅞ inches	54
No. 3	6⅝ inches	46
No. 4	6⅝ inches	42
No. 6	6⅝ inches	35
No. 2	6 inches	50
No. 5	6 inches	42
No. 9	5 inches	32
No. 7	4¾ inches	50

C Mexico
F Medium to full-bodied
Q Good-quality leaf and construction

MOCHA SUPREME

*T*hese are handmade cigars from Honduras, using Havana seed wrappers. They are well-constructed and, for a boxed cigar, well-priced. Generally they are medium to full-bodied in flavor, but noticeably milder than many Hondurans. There is a woody, nutty hint to their taste.

ALLEGRO : LENGTH 6½ INCHES, RING GAUGE 36

SIZES

Name	Length: inches	Ring Gauge
Rembrandt	8½ inches	52
Patroon	7½ inches	50
Lord	6½ inches	42
Allegro	6½ inches	36
Renaissance	6 inches	50
Sovereign	5½ inches	42
Baron Rothschild	4½ inches	52
Petite	4½ inches	42

LORD : LENGTH 6½ INCHES, RING GAUGE 42

PATROON : LENGTH 7½ INCHES, RING GAUGE 50

BARON ROTHSCHILD : LENGTH 4½ INCHES, RING GAUGE 52

C Honduras
F Medium to
full-bodied
Q Good-quality
leaf and
construction

*M*ontecristo is the most popular Havana by far. Around half of the cigars exported from Cuba in any one year bear its simple brown and white band.

Ironically, perhaps, it started life in 1935 as a brand limited to just five sizes which its founders, Alonzo Menendez and Pepe Garcia, aimed to keep in restricted distribution. They had just bought the H. Upmann brand from the British firm J. Frankau, and their main task was to extend its volume. Montecristo, first known as H. Upmann Montecristo Selection and sold through Dunhill in New York, was a prestigious sideline to test Menendez's leaf skills and Garcia's knowledge of production.

The change of name simply to Montecristo was inspired by another British firm, John Hunter, which was appointed as the British agent. The rival company Frankau handled Upmann and wanted Montecristo to stand on its own. The outstanding red and yellow box design with its triangular crossed swords is attributed to the Hunter company.

World War II interrupted the flow of Havanas to Britain, so the brand's development was concentrated in the United States, mainly through Dunhill's stores. Film director Alfred Hitchcock was an early devotee and regularly sent supplies back to friends deprived by wartime restrictions in England.

After the war the Tubos size was added, but otherwise the line remained the same.

Shortly after Castro came to power, the Menendez and Garcia families moved to the Canary Islands. Some continuity was provided by a legendary figure who remained on the home island. He was Jose Manuel Gonzalez, known as "Masinguila." Considered in Havana to this day as the finest cigar maker ever and one of the hardest taskmasters for the rollers he supervised, "Masinguila" is generally credited with much of the consistency in quality and unique blending that is characteristic of the brand.

In the early 1970s, the Montecristo A and the Laguito (Cohiba) Nos. 1, 2, and 3 sizes were added as the Especial, Especial No. 2, and Joyita. Coincidentally, the brand took off. It became the firm showbiz favorite with the likes of singer Tom Jones and British movie mogul Lew (now Lord) Grade.

Some say success brought its own problems. Certainly to match the quality of the huge volume of Montecristos that go to Spain, for example, is a prodigious task, and many consider that higher standards are maintained only in smaller markets like Britain. However, this did not stop an outbreak of near civil unrest in Spain when the brand was withdrawn following a trademark dispute between Tabacalera (the Spanish monopoly) and Cubatabaco.

The signs are that the trademark issue has been resolved, at least in Spain if not in France. However, this has no bearing on the introduction of a line of Dominican Montecristos in the United States.

Montecristos, with their characteristic Colorado-claro, slightly oily wrappers and delicate aroma offer a medium to full flavor spiked with a unique, tangy taste. The No. 2 is the flagship for the Piramide size, while many devotees consider the No. 1 (a Cervantes) hard to beat.

MONTECRISTO

SIZES

NAME	LENGTH: INCHES	RING GAUGE
A	9¼ inches	47
Especial	7½ inches	38
No. 1	6½ inches	42
No. 2	6⅛ inches	52
Tubos	6 inches	42
Especial No. 2	6 inches	38
No. 3	5½ inches	42
Petit Tubos	5 inches	42
No. 4	5 inches	42
Joyitas	4½ inches	26
No. 5	4 inches	40

ESPECIAL NO. 2 : LENGTH 6 INCHES, RING GAUGE 38

NO. 2 : LENGTH 6⅛ INCHES, RING GAUGE 52

TUBOS : LENGTH 6 INCHES, RING GAUGE 42

NO. 5 : LENGTH 4 INCHES, RING GAUGE 40

C Cuba
F Medium to full-bodied
Q Superior quality

MONTECRUZ

*M*ontecruz was the brand name given to the cigars made by the Menendez family (former owners of the Montecristo brand) when they started a manufacturing operation in the Canary Islands after leaving Cuba. They were then made with Cameroon wrappers, with Dominican and Brazilian fillers. The cigars, with labels very similar to the Montecristo brand are now made (since the mid-1970s) at La Romana in the Dominican Republic, with mid- to dark-brown Cameroon wrappers, by the Consolidated Cigar Corporation. These very well-made, medium to full-flavored cigars (with a distinctive taste and bouquet) come in a very wide choice of sizes. They are described as "sun grown." The "boîte nature" selection is richer, and matured for longer. Montecruz cigars are also produced in a milder range (with different labels and lighter Connecticut wrappers) for Dunhill. The Dunhill cigars come in some of the same sizes as the Montecruz.

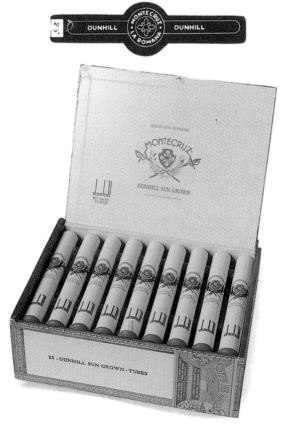

SIZES

NAME	LENGTH: INCHES	RING GAUGE
Indivuales	8 inches	46
No. 200	7¼ inches	46
No. 205	7 inches	42
No. 255	7 inches	36
No. 280	7 inches	28
Colossus	6½ inches	50
No. 210	6½ inches	42
No. 250	6½ inches	38
No. 201	6¼ inches	46
Tubulares	6⅛ inches	36
Tubos	6 inches	42
No. 276	6 inches	32
No. 281	6 inches	28
Seniors	5¾ inches	35
No. 220	5½ inches	42
No. 265	5½ inches	38
Juniors	5¼ inches	33
Cedar-aged	5 inches	42
No. 230	5 inches	42
No. 282	5 inches	28
No. 270	4¾ inches	36
Robusto	4½ inches	49
Chicos	4 inches	28

NO. 200 : LENGTH 7¼ INCHES, RING GAUGE 46

NO. 210 : LENGTH 6½ INCHES, RING GAUGE 42

NO. 220 : LENGTH 5½ INCHES, RING GAUGE 42

C Dominican Republic
F Medium to full-bodied
Q Superior quality

NO. 255 : LENGTH 7 INCHES, RING GAUGE 36

TUBE DUNHILL SUN GROWN

COLOSSUS : LENGTH 6½ INCHES, RING GAUGE 50

MONTESINO

A medium-bodied brand made in Dominican Republic by Arturo Fuente with Havana Fuente seed wrappers, which are mid-brown to dark. These cigars are well made and reasonably priced for the quality.

SIZES

NAME	LENGTH: INCHES	RING GAUGE
Napoleon Grande	7 inches	46
No. 1	6⅞ inches	43
Gran Corona	6¾ inches	48
Fumas	6¼ inches	44
No. 3	6¼ inches	36
No. 2	6¼ inches	44
Diplomatico	5½ inches	42

C Dominican Republic
F Mild to medium
Q Good-quality leaf and construction

NO. 1 : LENGTH 6⅞ INCHES, RING GAUGE 43

*T*he Nat Sherman store at 500 Fifth Avenue is a polished mahogany temple to tobacco, cigars, and smokers' requisites. Its business, which stretches far beyond its doors, was founded in New York's heyday of the 1930s and 40s with stylish cigarettes and strong connections in Havana.

Joel Sherman, its present custodian, anticipated the cigar boom back in 1990 and 1991, introducing four cigar selections, all made in the Dominican Republic but each with a different blend. An additional selection has been introduced since that time.

There is the Exchange Selection, named after New York's 1940s telephone exchanges, including the inevitable Butterfield 8 (a Lonsdale). Four different countries supply the blend of leaves for these cigars including the lightest of Connecticut wrappers. The flavor is mild.

Dressed in Cameroon wrappers, the Landmark Selection (Metropole, Algonquin, etc.) offers another four-country confection

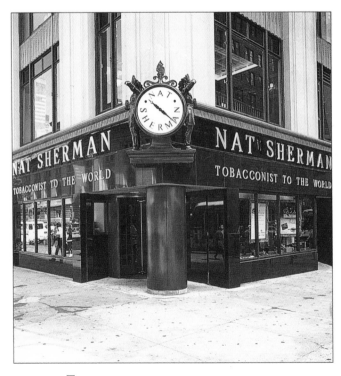

THE FINE EXTERIOR OF THE NAT SHERMAN SHOP IN NEW YORK.

with a bit more flavor and a chocolaty top taste.

Cigar-chomping editors of New York's former newspapers are commemorated by the four hefty, sweet-tasting Mexican maduro sizes in the City Desk Selection. Their mild to medium flavor belies their looks.

On the other hand, the Gotham Selection wrapped in a mid-tone Connecticut leaf delivers a surprisingly spicy, yet well balanced, taste. The latest line, the Metropolitan Selection, is named after some of the more famous gentlemen's clubs in New York. Available in five sizes the blend has a uniquely rich and balanced flavor.

Each series is identified by a different background color to the emblem of a clock on the band. go for gray; go for Gotham.

C Dominican Republic
F Varies according to selection
Q Superior quality

CHELSEA : LENGTH 6½ INCHES, RING GAUGE 38

SIZES

NAME	LENGTH: INCHES	RING GAUGE
GOTHAM SELECTION		
500	7 inches	50
1400	6¼ inches	44
711	6 inches	50
65	6 inches	36
CITY DESK SELECTION		
Tribune	7½ inches	50
Dispatch	6½ inches	46
Telegraph	6 inches	50
Gazette	6 inches	42
LANDMARK SELECTION		
Dakota	7½ inches	49
Algonquin	6¾ inches	43
Metropole	6 inches	34
Hampshire	5½ inches	42
Vanderbilt	5 inches	47
EXCHANGE SELECTION		
Oxford 5	7 inches	49
Butterfield 8	6½ inches	42
Trafalgar 4	6 inches	47
Murray 7	6 inches	38
Academy 2	5 inches	31
MANHATTAN SELECTION		
Gramercy	6¾ inches	43
Chelsea	6½ inches	38
Tribeca	6 inches	31
Sutton	5½ inches	49
Beekman	5¼ inches	28

GOTHAM 500 : LENGTH 7 INCHES, RING GAUGE 50

CITY DESK TELEGRAPH : LENGTH 6 INCHES, RING GAUGE 50

LANDMARK VANDERBILT : LENGTH 5 INCHES, RING GAUGE 47

EXCHANGE MURRAY 7 : LENGTH 6 INCHES, RING GAUGE 38

OSCAR

*T*hese Dominican Republic cigars, named after the company's founder, are well-filled and elegantly presented in claro U.S. Connecticut wrappers. The fillers and binders form a mild to medium blend made from locally produced tobaccos. They have been on the market for nearly a decade and have benefitted from the general improvement in the quality of Dominican cigars. The line covers most needs, including a couple of useful smaller sizes alongside some giants.

SIZES

NAME	LENGTH: INCHES	RING GAUGE
Don Oscar	9 inches	46
Supreme	8 inches	48
#700	7 inches	54
#200	7 inches	44
#100	7 inches	38
#300	6¼ inches	44
#400	6 inches	38
#500	5½ inches	50
Prince	5 inches	30
#600	4½ inches	50
No. 800	4 inches	42
Oscarito	4 inches	20

C Dominican Republic
F Mild to medium
Q Good-quality leaf and construction

HECHO A MANO

PADRON

$\mathcal{F}$ounded by Jose O. Padron in Miami, Florida, Padron Cigars has been producing long-filler premium cigars since 1964. Operating two companies in Central America, Tabacos Cubanica S.A. in Nicaragua, and Tabacos Centro-americanos S.A. in Honduras, Padron Cigars is one among a handful of companies that control every aspect of the manufacturing process.

C Nicaragua/
Honduras

F Mild to
medium

Q Good-quality
leaf and
construction

SIZES

Name	Length: inches	Ring Gauge
Magnum	9 inches	50
Grand Reserve	8 inches	41
Executive	7½ inches	50
Churchill	6⅞ inches	46
Ambassador	6⅞ inches	42
Panetela	6⅞ inches	36
Palmas	6⁵⁄₁₆ inches	42
3000	5½ inches	52
Londres	5½ inches	42
Chicos	5½ inches	36
2000	5 inches	50
Delicias	4⅞ inches	46

There is an emphasis on quality over quantity, and this is reflected in the two lines of cigars that are produced. The Padron—currently available in twelve sizes comes in both natural and maduro wrappers—is very well made, and offers a mild to medium smoke. The Padron 1964 Anniversary Series line has fewer sizes and the cigars are of limited production. All tobacco, from Nicaragua, is aged for at least four years, and wrapped in natural leaf. A medium smoke, this cigar gives very smooth, earthy flavors.

C Nicaragua/
Honduras
F Medium
Q Superior
quality

**1 9 6 4 A N N I V E R S A R Y
S E R I E S S I Z E S**

NAME	LENGTH: INCHES	RING GAUGE
Diplomatico	7 inches	50
Pyramid	6⅞ inches	42/52
Monarca	6½ inches	46
Superior	6½ inches	42
Corona	6 inches	42
Exclusivo	5½ inches	50

PARTAGAS

*P*artagas is one of the oldest of the Havana brands, started in 1845 by Don Jaime Partagas. The old factory still exists, in downtown Havana near the Capitol building (an architectural copy of the United States Congress). The name is still well known, not least because Partagas cigars are produced in large quantities: there are no fewer than 40 types available—many of them machine-made and cellophane-wrapped. There is also a Dominican version of the brand, made with Cameroon wrappers grown from Havana seed, and overseen by Benjamin Menendez and Ramon Cifuentes of the famous Cuban cigar families. The brand is manufactured by General Cigar. The differences between the labels are that Cuban versions carry the word Habana at the bottom of the label, whereas Dominican versions have the year 1845.

The brand was particularly famous between the two World Wars and has the distinction of being mentioned in cigar-lover Evelyn Waugh's novel, *Brideshead Revisited*.

The quality of Cuban Partagas can vary. The bigger sizes like the Lusitania, particularly in Cabinet 50s (a firm favorite with

SIZES

NAME	LENGTH: INCHES	RING GAUGE
Lusitanias	7⅞ inches	49
Churchill De Luxe	7 inches	47
Palmes Grandes	7 inches	33
Partagas de Partagas		
No. 1	6¾ inches	43
Seleccion Privada		
No. 1	6¾ inches	43
8–9–8	6¾ inches	43
Lonsdale	6½ inches	42
Corona Grande	6 inches	42
Culebras (twisted)	5¹¹⁄₁₆ inches	39
Corona	5½ inches	42
Charlotte	5½ inches	35
Petit Corona	5 inches	42
Series D No. 4	4⅞ inches	50
Très Petit Corona	4½ inches	40
Shorts	4⁵⁄₁₆ inches	42

ABC's Pierre Salinger) are very good indeed, but some of the smaller sizes, often when they are machine-made as opposed to hand-finished or handmade, can give draw problems. In general, the brand has a rich, earthy, and full flavor, which is particularly noticeable on the heavier ring gauge sizes like the Series D No. 4 (Robusto). There are two sizes in an 8–9–8 packing; one is a Corona Grande (6 inches x 42) and the other a Dalia (6⅞ inches x 43). The Dalia is seen by Ernesto Lopez, the factory's Director, as his flagship size. They have an altogether smoother finish, but retain the full flavor. There is a Connoisseur series of three cigars, available in some markets, which includes the No. 1, a cigar of the same dimensions as the Cohiba Lanceros but without the pigtail. In general, Partagas is a good choice after a heavy meal.

Handmade Dominican Partagas, although very well-constructed, occasionally have wrappers of variable quality, particularly the larger sizes. The best are very good. They are also relatively expensive. They normally come in colorado wrappers, but there is also a maduro—a 6¼-inch cigar with a 47 ring gauge. The fillers are a mixture of Jamaican, Dominican, and Mexican tobacco. There are 14 sizes, mostly numbered, of Dominican Partagas in all: smooth, medium to full-bodied, and slightly sweet. A selection of sizes is listed.

ERNESTO LOPEZ, DIRECTOR OF THE PARTAGAS FACTORY IN DOWNTOWN HAVANA.

SERIES D NO. 4 : LENGTH 4⅞ INCHES, RING GAUGE 50

CORONA : LENGTH 5½ INCHES, RING GAUGE 42

SHORTS : LENGTH 4⁵⁄₁₆ INCHES, RING GAUGE 42

C Cuba
F Very full-
bodied
Q Superior
quality

DOMINICAN SIZES

Name	Length: inches	Ring Gauge
No. 10	7½ inches	49
Tubos	7 inches	34
8–9–8	6⅞ inches	44
Limited Reserve Royale	6¾ inches	43
No. 1	6¾ inches	43
Humitube	6¾ inches	43
Limited Reserve Regale	6¼ inches	47
Maduro	6¼ inches	48
Almirantes	6¼ inches	47
No. 6	6 inches	34
Sabroso	5⅞ inches	44
No. 2	5¾ inches	43
Naturales	5½ inches	50
No. 3	5¼ inches	43
No. 5	5¼ inches	28
No. 4	5 inches	38
Purito	4⅞ inches	32

C Dominican Republic
F Medium to full-bodied
Q Superior quality

LIMITED RESERVE ROYALE : LENGTH 6¾ INCHES, RING GAUGE 43

PAUL GARMIRIAN

Paul Garmirian's P.G. cigars are among the best on the market certainly when it comes to non-Havanas. Garmirian himself, based outside Washington, DC, has a Ph.D. in international politics and is a real-estate broker. He is also a great connoisseur of handmade cigars, and author of *The Gourmet Guide to Cigars*. He decided to put his 30-year passion for fine cigars to work in 1991 with the launch of his own brand.

His cigars, available only in limited quantities, are made in the Dominican Republic with dark, slightly oily, reddish mid-brown colorado wrappers. They are very well made, have a subtle but noticeable bouquet, burn well and slowly, and are medium flavored. The cigars have a rich aroma, taste pleasantly sweet (the flavor gets richer as you smoke), and are very mellow and well blended. These are very superior cigars, as good as many Havanas, and better than quite a few. The Lonsdale will give you a pretty good impression of the line. Seven more sizes have been added since the first edition of this book, the most recent addition being the Especial.

CORONA : LENGTH 5½ INCHES, RING GAUGE 42

C Dominican Republic
F Medium to full-bodied
Q Superior quality

SIZES

Name	Length: inches	Ring Gauge
Celebration	9 inches	50
Double Corona	7⅝ inches	50
No. 1	7½ inches	38
Churchill	7 inches	48
Belicoso	6½ inches	52
Corona Grande	6½ inches	46
Lonsdale	6½ inches	42
Connoisseur	6 inches	50
Especial	5¾ inches	38
Belicoso Fino	5½ inches	52
Epicure	5½ inches	50
Corona	5½ inches	42
Robusto	5 inches	50
Petit Corona	5 inches	43
No. 2	4¾ inches	48
Petit Bouquet	4½ inches	38
No. 5	4 inches	40
Bombones	3½ inches	43

CHURCHILL : LENGTH 7 INCHES, RING GAUGE 48

NO. 2 : LENGTH 4¾ INCHES, RING GAUGE 48

BELICOSO : LENGTH 6½ INCHES, RING GAUGE 52

CELEBRATION : LENGTH 9 INCHES, RING GAUGE 50

PETRUS

*T*his brand has achieved international acclaim since its debut in 1990, and has been praised by many, Arnold Schwarzenegger among them. Manufactured in Honduras by La Flor de Copan factory, Honduran filler and binder come wrapped in Connecticut-seed leaf grown in Ecuador. The cigar gives a mild smoke, with nutty flavors, and a dry finish. Currently available in 13 sizes, they offer a good choice of cigar at very reasonable prices. 1997 will see the introduction of a limited edition cigar, Etiquette Rouge, using a blend of Dominican, Honduran, and Nicaraguan tobaccos.

ROTHSCHILD : LENGTH 4¾ INCHES, RING GAUGE 50

SIZES

Name	Length: inches	Ring Gauge
Lord Byron	8 inches	38
Double Corona	7¾ inches	50
Churchill	7 inches	50
No. 2	6¼ inches	44
No. 3	6 inches	50
Palma Fina	6 inches	38
No. 4	5⅝ inches	38
Corona Sublime	5½ inches	46
Antonius	5 inches	torpedo
Gregorius	5 inches	42
Rothschild	4¾ inches	50
Chantaco	4¾ inches	35
Duchess	4½ inches	30

... *Tabaco* *Petrus* *Sublime* ...

C Honduras
F Mild
Q Good-quality leaf and construction

PLEIADES

A very elegant range of Dominican cigars with Connecticut Shade wrappers. They are mild, well made, draw well, and are very pleasant cigars with a good aroma. The brand originates from France. Once made in the Caribbean, the cigars are shipped back to Strasbourg, where they are placed in boxes with an original built-in humidifying system, before being distributed in Europe and back across the ocean to the United States.

URANUS : LENGTH 6⅞ INCHES, RING GAUGE 34

SIZES

Name	Length: inches	Ring Gauge
Aldebran	8½ inches	50
Saturne	8 inches	46
Neptune	7½ inches	42
Sirius	6⅞ inches	46
Uranus	6⅞ inches	34
Orion	5¾ inches	42
Antares	5½ inches	40
Venus	5⅛ inches	28
Pluton	5 inches	50
Perseus	5 inches	34
Mars	5 inches	28

C Dominican Republic
F Mild
Q Good-quality leaf and construction

ORION : LENGTH 5¾ INCHES, RING GAUGE 42

SIRIUS : LENGTH 6⅞ INCHES, RING GAUGE 46

ALDEBRAN : LENGTH 8½ INCHES, RING GAUGE 50

POR LARRANAGA

*A*n old brand (the oldest still being produced), dating from 1834, but no longer among the best known. Production is limited, and the cigars aren't widely distributed, but these very full-bodied cigars are sought after by many connoisseurs of traditional Havana flavor. The selection is fairly limited, with about half a dozen machine-made sizes (the brand was the first to introduce machines), some the same (size, not quality) as handmade versions. "There's peace in Larranaga," claimed Rudyard Kipling in his 1890 ditty which includes the notorious line "A woman is only a woman, but a good cigar is a smoke."

These cigars, with their dark, reddish, oily wrappers, are a good choice for lovers of mid- to full-flavored cigars. With their golden bands, they have a distinguished appearance. They tend to be rich and aromatic, with a powerful (rather sweet) flavor, and an aroma less pronounced than some other brands of the same type (Partagas, for instance). The Lonsdale and Corona sizes are as good as most rivals, and the latter is a good after-dinner cigar.

There are also excellent Dominican cigars using the same brand name. They are extremely well made with Connecticut Shade wrappers, fillers blended from Dominican and Brazilian leaves, and Dominican binders. They are full of flavor, especially the Fabuloso (7 inches, ring gauge 50), which is essentially a Churchill.

CUBAN SIZES

Name	Length: inches	Ring Gauge
Lonsdale	6½ inches	42
Corona	5½ inches	42
Petit Corona	5 inches	42
Small Corona	4½ inches	40

FABULOSOS : LENGTH 7 INCHES, RING GAUGE 50

ROBUSTO : LENGTH 5 INCHES, RING GAUGE 50

CORONA : LENGTH 5½ INCHES, RING GAUGE 42

C Dominican
Republic
F Mild to
medium
Q Superior
quality

C Cuba
F Medium to
full-bodied
Q Superior
quality

PRIMO DEL REY

A brand made by the Consolidated Cigar Corporation in the Dominican Republic. The main line consisting of 1–5 sizes dressed in a simple brown and white Montecristo-like band, offers a choice of Candela (double claro), Claro (natural), and Colorado (mid-brown wrappers). Just four sizes make up the Club Selection, which is identified by a red, gold, and white band featuring a coat of arms. They are all very well-made.

SIZES

Name	Length: inches	Ring Gauge
Barons	8½ inches	52
Aguilas	8 inches	52
Soberanos	7½ inches	50
Regal	7 inches	50
Aristocrats	6¾ inches	48
Presidentes	6¹³⁄₁₆ inches	44
Seleccion No. 1	6¹³⁄₁₆ inches	42
Seleccion No. 3	6¹³⁄₁₆ inches	36
Chavon	6½ inches	41
Churchill	6¼ inches	48
Nobles	6¼ inches	44
Seleccion No. 2	6¼ inches	42
Cazadores	6¹⁄₁₆ inches	42
Reales	6⅛ inches	36
Almirantes	6 inches	50
Panetela Extra	5¹⁵⁄₁₆ inches	34
Seleccion No. 4	5½ inches	42
Panetela	5⅜ inches	34
No. 100	4½ inches	50
Cortos	4 inches	28

REGAL : LENGTH 7 INCHES, RING GAUGE 50

SOBERANOS : LENGTH 7½ INCHES, RING GAUGE 50

NO. 100 : LENGTH 4½ INCHES, RING GAUGE 50

ALMIRANTES : LENGTH 6 INCHES, RING GAUGE 50

G Dominican Republic
F Mild to medium
Q Superior quality

PUNCH

A very well-known and widely distributed Havana brand (once very popular in Britain), with lower prices than many others, and as a result, familiar to beginners and occasional smokers. Cigar snobs thus tend to avoid it, mostly without good reason. There is a very wide selection of sizes, most from the La Corona factory, with many machine-made equivalents—as well as types such as Exquisitos and Palmas Reales, which are only machine-made.

The brand, the second oldest still in production, was founded in 1840 by Manuel Lopez with the British market in mind where an eponymous light-hearted magazine (similar to the New Yorker) was much in vogue. A contented Mr. Punch, cigar in hand, remains a feature of each box.

There is also a Honduran Punch brand which comes in three series; standard, Delux, and Gran Cru. These are exceptionally well-made cigars, particularly in the Delux and Gran Cru form. The standard line offers a straightforward, Honduran, fullish flavor, but there is a rare delicacy to the taste in the other two series, even

CUBAN SIZES

Name	Length: inches	Ring Gauge
Double Corona	7⅝ inches	49
Churchill	7 inches	47
Panetelas Grandes	7 inches	33
Punch Punch	5⅝ inches	46
Corona	5½ inches	42
Royal Coronations	5½ inches	42
Petit Corona	5 inches	42
Coronations	5 inches	42
Margarita	4¾ inches	26
Petit Coronations	4½ inches	40
Coronets	4½ inches	34
Punchinellos	4½ inches	34
Très Petit Coronas	4¼ inches	42
Petit Punch	4 inches	40

when maduro wrapped, which suggests substantial aging. The skilled hands and expert knowledge of Villazon's Frank Llaneza lie behind these cigars, which is always a good sign.

With such a large Havana line, it isn't possible for every cigar to be of the highest quality, but the larger sizes, with their fragrant bouquet, distinctive spicy aroma, and reasonably, but not very, full-bodied, slightly sweet flavor, are well-constructed and dependable—the Double Corona, for instance. One complication is that the same-sized cigars are sometimes known by different names in different countries. The famous Punch Punch (Corona Gorda), for example, can be found as a Royal Selection No. 11 or a Seleccion de Luxe No. 1, and even the Petit Corona del Punch is sometimes the Seleccion de Luxe No. 2 or Presidente. Find a trusty cigar merchant to guide you through this choice of first class mild to medium cigars.

There are tubed cigars in both the Cuban and Honduran lines, with names like Royal Coronation.

HONDURAN SIZES

Name	Length: inches	Ring Gauge
Presidente	8½ inches	42
Château Lafitte	7¼ inches	52
Grand Diademas	7⅛ inches	52
Diademas	7⅛ inches	52
Elegante	7⅛ inches	36
Casa Grande	7 inches	46
Monarcas	6¾ inches	48
Double Corona	6⅝ inches	48
Château Corona	6½ inches	44
No. 1	6½ inches	42
Bristol	6¼ inches	50
Britannia Delux	6¼ inches	50
Punch	6⅛ inches	43
Superiores Delux	5⅝ inches	46
Château Margaux	5½ inches	46
No. 75	5½ inches	43
Superior	5 inches	50
Rothschild	4½ inches	48

C Honduras
F Mild to medium
Q Superior quality

DOUBLE CORONA : LENGTH 7⅝ INCHES, RING GAUGE 49

PETIT CORONA : LENGTH 5 INCHES, RING GAUGE 42

PRESIDENTE : LENGTH 8½ INCHES, RING GAUGE 42

C Cuba
F Mild to medium
Q Superior quality

SUPERIORES DELUX : LENGTH 5⅝ INCHES, RING GAUGE 46

BRITANNIA DELUX : LENGTH 6¼ INCHES, RING GAUGE 50

MONARCAS : LENGTH 6¾ INCHES, RING GAUGE 48

QUINTERO

A Cuban brand notable for the fact that it was founded in the southern coastal city of Cienfuegos, and not Havana. Augustin Quintero and his four brothers, who worked in the nearby Remedios tobacco regime, started a small "chinchal" (cigar workshop) in the mid-1920s. By 1940, their reputation allowed them to open in Havana and introduce the brand bearing their family name using Vuelta Abajo tobaccos. Today several of the sizes are both handmade or machine-made, so check for the "Totalamente a mano" stamp on the box. The Churchill is a Lonsdale (Cervantes), but a good one if you like a light smoke. Overall the brand is mild.

PANETELA : LENGTH 5 INCHES, RING GAUGE 37

SIZES

NAME	LENGTH: INCHES	RING GAUGE
Churchill	6½ inches	42
Corona	5½ inches	42
Nacionales	5½ inches	40
Panetelas	5 inches	37
Tubulares	5 inches	37
Londres Extra	5 inches	40
Puritos	4¼ inches	29

C Cuba
F Mild
Q Good-quality leaf and construction

These are among the best of medium-priced Havanas, long well-known and appreciated by serious smokers. The box of this brand, originally created for the English market, carries the unusual legend: "These cigars have been manufactured from a secret blend of pure Vuelta Abajo tobaccos selected by the Marquez Rafael Gonzalez, Grandee of Spain. For more than 20 years this brand has existed. In order that the Connoisseur may fully appreciate the perfect fragrance they should be smoked either within one month of the date of shipment from Havana or should be carefully matured for about one year." The box used to carry a portrait of the great smoker Lord Lonsdale on the reverse side of the lid. The brand is made in the Romeo Y Julieta factory.

These first-class cigars have a delicate, but rich and subtle flavor, and complex aroma (they are much lighter, but have a hint of Montecristo to them). The label is very similar to Montecristo in both color and design. They are very well made and have good burning qualities. The Corona Extra is particularly reputed, as is the Lonsdale. The Cigarrito is a very good example of a size which is often unsatisfactory. The selection of sizes is commendably small. These are, in general, very classy cigars, among the mildest of Havanas.

SIZES

NAME	LENGTH: INCHES	RING GAUGE
Slenderella	7 inches	28
Lonsdale	6½ inches	42
Corona Extra	5⅝ inches	46
Petit Corona	5 inches	42
Petit Lonsdale	5 inches	42
Panetela Extra	5 inches	37
Panetela	4⅝ inches	34
Très Petit Lonsdale	4½ inches	40
Cigarrito	4½ inches	26
Demi Tasse	4 inches	30

TRES PETIT LONSDALE : LENGTH 4½ INCHES, RING GAUGE 40

PETIT CORONA : LENGTH 5 INCHES, RING GAUGE 42

LONSDALE : LENGTH 6½ INCHES, RING GAUGE 42

C Cuba
F Mild
Q The very best quality available

*D*ating from 1837, Ramon Allones, although not one of the best known of Havana names, is a favorite with many connoisseurs, among the best of the full-bodied cigars available. They are near the top of the list of medium-priced Cuban cigars— i.e., below Cohiba and Montecristo, but up there with Upmann, Partagas, and Romeo Y Julieta. Most Ramon Allones are handmade, but there are a handful of machine-made sizes (Belvederes, Mille Fleurs, Delgados, and Toppers among them).

Ramon Allones are rolled in the Partagas factory (known for its full-bodied cigars) and have been since the factory was bought by the famous Cifuentes firm in the 1920s. The brand originated the 8–9–8 form of packaging.

The arms on the box are those of the Spanish royal house. Ramon Allones himself, emigrated from Galicia, in Spain, to Cuba, and was the first man to put colorful printed labels on his cigar boxes.

There is a good selection of Ramon Allones, all of them relatively full-bodied, and well made, with a strong aroma (similar to Partagas, but certainly less than Bolivar, also made in the same factory), good, dark wrappers, and excellent burning qualities. The smaller sizes tend to be lighter in color and somewhat milder. Rich in ligero leaf, these are not cigars for beginners. The 8–9–8 Corona is a good after-lunch choice, just as Gigantes (Prominente), 8–9–8 Churchill, or the Specially Selected (robusto) are all excellent choices after dinner. The very slim Ramonitas aren't recommended. These cigars age beautifully.

There are very good Dominican-produced Ramon Allones, with a similar band (but larger, and square, not round). They are very well made, mild to medium-bodied, and rather expensive. Most of the available sizes, unlike the Cuban brand, are named after letters of the alphabet. The Dominican brand, produced by General Cigar, have medium to dark Cameroon wrappers, Mexican binders, and fillers blended from Dominican, Jamaican, and Mexican tobacco. The Crystals are packed in individual glass tubes.

CUBAN SIZES

NAME	LENGTH: INCHES	RING GAUGE
Gigantes	7½ inches	49
8–9–8	6¹¹⁄₁₆ inches	43
Corona	5⅝ inches	42
Petit Corona	5 inches	42
Panetela	5 inches	35
Specially Selected	4¹³⁄₁₆ inches	50
Ramonitas	4¹³⁄₁₆ inches	26
Small Club Coronas	4⁵⁄₁₆ inches	42

DOMINICAN SIZES

NAME	LENGTH: INCHES	RING GAUGE
Redondos	7 inches	49
A	7 inches	45
Trumps	6¼ inches	43
Crystals	6¼ inches	43
B	6½ inches	42
D	5 inches	42

SMALL CLUB CORONAS : LENGTH 4⁵⁄₁₆ INCHES, RING GAUGE 42

GIGANTES : LENGTH 7½ INCHES, RING GAUGE 49

SPECIALLY SELECTED : LENGTH 4¹³⁄₁₆ INCHES, RING GAUGE 50

C Cuba
F Very full-bodied
Q The very best quality available

C Dominican Republic
F Mild to medium
Q Good-quality leaf and construction

One of the very best-known Havana brands, particularly popular in Britain, Romeo Y Julieta cigars come in a huge choice of over 40 shapes and sizes. Many of them come in aluminum tubes, and there are also a large number of machine-made sizes. Despite the vast range, which inevitably means that not all sizes can be trusted, there are some very good cigars produced under this brand, many of them among the best available in their size.

The brand's early success was directly due to the efforts of Rodriguez Fernandez. "Pepin," as he was known, was originally manager of the Cabanas factory in Havana, but unhappy at its imminent takeover by American Tobacco, he resigned in 1903 to branch out on his own. Using his savings, he bought a little-known factory which, since 1875, had made cigars called Romeo Y Julieta solely for the Cuban domestic market. But he had bigger ideas, and encouraging his employees by distributing 30 percent of profits to heads of department, he traveled the world promoting the brand. Within two years, with his 1,400 workers, he had to move to a larger factory.

For monarchs, heads of state, and others, he specialized in providing personalized cigar bands (at one stage the factory was producing 20,000 different bands). Pepin remained devoted, almost obsessed by his brand, naming his racehorse Julieta, and trying to buy the House of Capulet in Verona, where Shakespeare's play was set. He couldn't quite do that, but was allowed to have a stand under the famous balcony, so that until 1939, every visitor was offered a free cigar in honor of the ill-starred lovers who gave the brand its name. He died in 1954.

The famous Romeo Y Julieta Churchills also come in tubes. They are very well-made cigars, with an excellent aroma, but the tubed versions can sometimes be rather fresh and, as a result, are

MADE IN HABANA, CUBA

not as well matured as the boxed versions. The Churchill sizes, with their distinctive gold bands (the others, apart from the Cedros series, are all red) are, nonetheless, classic medium to full-bodied cigars. The Corona size, often with colorado maduro wrappers, is very well-constructed but inconsistent in flavor. The Cedros de Luxe No. 1 (Lonsdale), is a dark, smooth, medium-bodied cigar, though sometimes not enough for lovers of this size. The Exhibicion No. 4 (Hermoso 4), with its oily wrapper, provides a rich smoke after a heavy meal and is a favorite with many connoisseurs. The Cedros de Luxe No. 2 is a very good corona, with plenty of personality. The Petit Julietas are among the best made and fullest-flavored in their size.

There is no meaningful difference between the various Churchill sizes, but some claim that the Prince of Wales is milder

CUBAN SIZES

NAME	LENGTH: INCHES	RING GAUGE
Churchill	7 inches	47
Prince of Wales	7 inches	47
Shakespeare	6⅞ inches	28
Cedros De Luxe No. 1	6½ inches	42
Corona Grande	6 inches	42
Belicosos	5½ inches	52
Exhibicion No. 3	5½ inches	43
Cedros De Luxe No. 2	5½ inches	42
Corona	5½ inches	42
Exhibicion No. 4	5 inches	48
Cedros De Luxe No. 3	5 inches	42
Petit Corona	5 inches	42
Très Petit Corona	4½ inches	40
Petit Julietas	4 inches	30

than the tubed version. Be sure not to confuse the tubed No. 1, No. 2, and No. 3 *De Luxe* with the similarly numbered tubes without the words "De Luxe"—which are machine-made, and much inferior. In Britain all tubed sizes are handmade, so you can smoke them without hesitation. The Cazadores (6⅛ inches, ring gauge 44), although handmade, is one of the cheapest cigars in the range for the good reason that it is made from less well-selected leaves. They are thus cigars of a different quality.

Dominican Republic cigars called Romeo Y Julietas are also produced in a vintage line wrapped in Connecticut shade and standard selections using darker Cameroon wrappers. Both types are very good and well made, the former offering a particularly delicate smoke. As with the Cuban Romeo Y Julietas, only a selection of sizes is given below.

SIZES

NAME	LENGTH: INCHES	RING GAUGE
Monarcas	8 inches	52
Churchills	7 inches	50
Presidentes	7 inches	43
Delgados	7 inches	32
Cetros	6½ inches	44
Romeos	6 inches	46
Palmas	6 inches	43
Brevas	5⅝ inches	38
Coronas	5½ inches	44
Panatelas	5¼ inches	35
Rothschilds	5 inches	50
Chiquitas	4¼ inches	32

C Dominican Republic
F Mild to medium
Q Superior quality

C Honduras
F Medium to full-bodied
Q Superior quality

VINTAGE SIZES

NAME	LENGTH: INCHES	RING GAUGE
Vintage V	7½ inches	50
Vintage VI	7 inches	60
Vintage IV	7 inches	48
Vintage II	6 inches	46
Vintage I	6 inches	43
Vintage III	4½ inches	50

PRESIDENT : LENGTH 7 INCHES, RING GAUGE 43

MONARCAS : LENGTH 8 INCHES, RING GAUGE 52

CHURCHILL : LENGTH 7 INCHES, RING GAUGE 50

ROMEO Y JULIE

CHURCHILL
Made in Havana, Cuba

ROMEO Y JULIETA
HAVANA, CUBA

CHURCHILL : LENGTH 7 INCHES, RING GAUGE 47

BELICOSOS : LENGTH 5½ INCHES, RING GAUGE 52

EXHIBICION NO. 4 : LENGTH 5 INCHES, RING GAUGE 48

C Cuba
F Mild to medium
Q The very best quality available

ROYAL JAMAICA

*F*ormerly made in Jamaica, production moved to the Dominican Republic following a hurricane in 1988 which destroyed both factories and tobacco crops. They remain among the best of mild cigars. Most Royal Jamaicas have Cameroon wrappers, but the fuller-bodied Maduro range uses wrappers from Brazil.

SIZES

NAME	LENGTH: INCHES	RING GAUGE
Ten Downing Street	10 inches	51
Goliath	9 inches	64
Individuals	8½ inches	52
Churchill	8 inches	51
Giant Corona	7½ inches	49
Double Corona	7 inches	45
Doubloon	7 inches	30
Navarro	6¾ inches	34
Corona Grande	6½ inches	42
No. 2 Tube	6½ inches	34
Rapier	6½ inches	28
Park Lane	6 inches	47
Tube No. 1	6 inches	45
Director 1	6 inches	45
New York Plaza	6 inches	40
Royal Corona	6 inches	30
Corona	5½ inches	40
Buccaneer	5½ inches	30
Gaucho	5¼ inches	33
Petit Corona	5 inches	40
Robusto	4½ inches	49
Pirate	4½ inches	30

MADURO SIZES

NAME	LENGTH: INCHES	RING GAUGE
Churchill	8 inches	51
Corona Grande	6½ inches	42
Corona	5½ inches	40
Buccaneer	5½ inches	30

DOUBLE CORONA : LENGTH 7 INCHES, RING GAUGE 45

PIRATE : LENGTH 4½ INCHES, RING GAUGE 30

PARK LANE : LENGTH 6 INCHES, RING GAUGE 47

C Dominican
Republic
F Mild
Q Superior
quality

SAINT LUIS REY

*T*his Havana brand was created some 50 years ago by British importers Michael de Keyser and Nathan Silverstone. The name originated after the success of the popular American film *The Bridge of San Luis Rey* (based on Thornton Wilder's play, and starring Akim Tamiroff and Alla Nazimova). By lucky chance, there was also a Cuban town called San Luis Obispo.

The characteristic cigars of the brand are heavyweight medium to strong cigars. They are made at the Romeo Y Julieta factory and are in many ways similar to Romeos. The brand has had many fans, among them Frank Sinatra and actor James Coburn. This is a very high-quality brand with a very limited production of only 60,000 cigars a year.

The cigars, which come in a predominantly white box and have a red label, are not to be confused with *San* Luis Rey, a brand made in Cuba for the German market. There is also a range of San Luis Reys machine-made in Germany for the mass market by Villiger using Havana leaf. San Luis Reys have a black label with a similar emblem.

These cigars are among the best Havanas available. The wrappers are dark to very dark, smooth and oily, and the flavor, although full-bodied, is very refined. The aroma of the best of these cigars is superb. The Regios (robusto) is a very fine smoke, as is the milder, and less full Churchill. Saint Luis Reys tend to be cheaper than most other Havanas (certainly others of comparable quality). The selection is small.

SIZES

NAME	LENGTH: INCHES	RING GAUGE
Churchill	7 inches	47
Lonsdale	6½ inches	42
Serie A	5⅝ inches	46
Corona	5⅝ inches	42
Regios	5 inches	48
Petit Corona	5 inches	42

CHURCHILL : LENGTH 7 INCHES, RING GAUGE 47

REGIOS : LENGTH 5 INCHES, RING GAUGE 48

CORONA : LENGTH 5⅝ INCHES, RING GAUGE 42

C Cuba
F Very full-bodied
Q Superior quality

SANCHO PANZA

NON PLUS : LENGTH 5¹⁄₁₆ INCHES, RING GAUGE 42

*N*ot a well-known brand, but good, reliable Havanas, if a little too light and short on flavor for the real connoisseur. But for some, they offer a subtle, delicate, even elegant smoke, particularly the Molino (Lonsdale), although this cigar sometimes has a slightly salty taste which appeals to some smokers, not to others. Their construction sometimes leaves something to be desired: they don't burn as easily as they should. But the Corona Gigante is very well made. Even the torpedo-shaped Belicosos are mild (perhaps the mildest) for their type. The same applies to the Montecristo A-sized Sanchos. The line is small. These are good beginners' cigars, or for daytime smoking. The brand appears intermittently in Britain, but is very popular in Spain. There are plans to distribute it more widely.

SIZES

Name	Length: inches	Ring Gauge
Sanchos	9¼ inches	47
Corona Gigante	7 inches	47
Molino	6½ inches	42
Panetela Largo	6½ inches	28
Corona	5⅜ inches	42
Belicosos	5½ inches	52
Non Plus	5¹⁄₁₆ inches	42
Bachilleres	4⅝ inches	40

🅒 Cuba
🅕 Mild
🅠 Superior
quality

SANTA CLARA

*A*mong the best of Mexican cigars. Made in San Andres with wrappers from the same area. The brand was founded in 1830, is medium flavored, and well made. There is a choice, in most sizes, of pale brown and dark wrappers, with most recent additions including the Premier Tube, and Robusto sizes.

SIZES

NAME	LENGTH: INCHES	RING GAUGE
No. I	7½ inches	52
Premier Tubes	6¾ inches	38
No. III	6⅝ inches	43
No. II	6½ inches	48
No. VI	6 inches	51
No. V	6 inches	44
No. VII	5½ inches	25
No. IV	5 inches	44
Robusto	4½ inches	50
Quino	4¼ inches	30

C Mexico
F Medium
Q Good-quality leaf and construction

SANTA DAMIANA

*S*anta Damiana was once a famous Cuban plantation and brand name. Now it is the name given to a relatively new brand of high-quality cigars, handmade in La Romana on the southeastern coast of the Dominican Republic.

The La Romana factory, near the luxurious Casa de Campo resort, is one of the most advanced handmade cigar factories in the world, applying modern quality-control techniques to the age-old skill of cigar rolling. Different blends and size names are used for the line sold in the United States as opposed to those available in Europe. The American sizes, named Seleccion No. 100, No. 300, and so on, contain a lighter blend of filler unlike the European line which, using traditional names, is designed to appeal to a preference for something fuller-flavored. Both are very well-made, consistent cigars.

SIZES

NAME	LENGTH: INCHES	RING GAUGE
Seleccion No. 800	7 inches	50
Seleccion No. 100 Churchill	6¾ inches	48
Seleccion No. 700	6½ inches	42
Seleccion No. 300	5½ inches	46
Corona	5½ inches	42
Seleccion No. 500	5 inches	50
Petit Corona	5 inches	42
Tubulares No. 400	5 inches	42
Panetela	4½ inches	36

C Dominican Republic
F Mild to medium
Q Superior quality

SOSA

his is a three-country-blend cigar brand founded in Little Havana by Juan B. Sosa in the early 1960s, which then moved to the Dominican Republic in the early 1970s, and is currently starting production at its new plant at the Arturo Fuente factory. Ecuadoran wrappers in darkish, natural, and maduro tones combine with Honduran binders and Dominican fillers to offer pleasant and distinctive, medium to full flavor. There is a definite attempt here to go for the Cuban style of taste in a well-priced cigar.

SIZES

Name	Length: inches	Ring Gauge
Magnum	7½ inches	52
Piramides #2	7 inches	48
Churchill	7 inches	48
Lonsdale	6½ inches	43
Governor	6 inches	50
Brevas	5½ inches	43
Wavell	4¼ inches	50

C Dominican Republic
F Medium to full
Q Could be better

SUERDIECK

$\mathcal{O}$ne of the best-known Brazilian cigars, with a medium flavor. The line consists mostly of small ring gauge sizes, a number of which are very similar. These are by no means connoisseurs' cigars—they are not particularly well made, and the mid-brown Brazilian wrappers (the cigars also use Brazilian fillers and binders) leave quite a lot to be desired. But some people like the flavor.

BRASILIA : LENGTH 5¼ INCHES, RING GAUGE 30

SIZES

Name	Length: inches	Ring Gauge
Fiesta	6 inches	30
Valencia	6 inches	30
Caballero	6 inches	30
Brasilia	5¼ inches	30
Mandarim Pai	5 inches	38

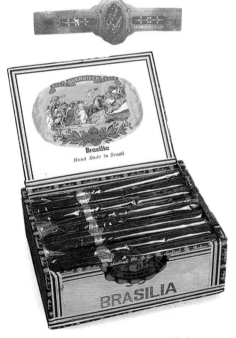

C Brazil
F Mild to
   medium
Q Could be
   better

TEMPLE HALL

*T*his brand, founded in 1876, has been re-introduced by General Cigar. The Temple Hall estates are in Jamaica, and the cigars are a somewhat fuller-bodied version of Macanudo. Like Macanudo, the wrappers are Connecticut Shade and the filler blend a mixture of Jamaican, Dominican, and Mexican tobaccos. The binder is Mexican, from the San Andres area.

These are very well-made, subtle cigars, at or near the top of their line. Temple Hall make a special selection for Dunhill (slightly milder, with a different blend). The 450 is the only cigar which comes in a Mexican wrapper. The brand consists of seven sizes.

SIZES

NAME	LENGTH: INCHES	RING GAUGE
700	7 inches	49
685	6⅞ inches	34
675	6¾ inches	45
625	6¼ inches	42
550	5½ inches	50
500	5 inches	31
450	4½ inches	49

450 : LENGTH 4½ INCHES, RING GAUGE 49

550 : LENGTH 5½ INCHES, RING GAUGE 50

700 : LENGTH 7 INCHES, RING GAUGE 49

C Jamaica
F Mild to
medium
Q Superior
quality

TRESADO

This is a relatively new Dominican brand, made and imported by the Consolidated Cigar Corporation. The cigars are well made and have a medium flavor.

SIZES

Name	Length: inches	Ring Gauge
No. 100	8 inches	52
No. 200	7 inches	48
No. 400	6⅜ inches	44
No. 300	6 inches	46
No. 500	5½ inches	42

C Dominican Republic
F Mild to medium
Q Good-quality leaf and construction

NO. 200 : LENGTH 7 INCHES, RING GAUGE 48

This cigar is still not to be found in any store, but a few—a select few—people have had a chance to smoke it recently. They were the 164 guests at Marvin Shanken's Paris "Dinner of the Century" in October 1994. The one and only Trinidad size, a Laguito No. 1 like the Cohiba Lancero, was served as the first cigar. With a darker wrapper than you would find on any Cohiba and a rich, earthy flavor, there were those present who felt it might have been better suited to the end of the meal.

Mystery now shrouds the origin of this cigar. Non-smoking President Fidel Castro had been credited with its creation as an exclusive gift for heads of state to replace Cohiba after it went public. However, in his interview with Cigar Aficionado (Summer 1994), Castro virtually denied any knowledge of its existence. He was happy to continue offering Cohibas to cigar enthusiasts of his acquaintance.

So, who's idea was it to ask the El Laguito factory to make Trinidad? As yet, outside official Cuban government circles, no one knows.

C Cuba
F Medium to full-bodied
Q The very best quality available

TRINIDAD : LENGTH 7½ INCHES, RING GAUGE 38

ZINO

$\mathcal{C}$reated by Zino Davidoff for the American market when his main brand was still made in Cuba, Zinos are well-tailored Honduran cigars which come in three brands. There is Mouton Cadet, appropriately clad in claret-colored bands and launched during a memorable mid-80s coast to coast tour by Zino himself accompanied by his partner, Dr. Ernst Schneider, and La Baronne Phillipine de Rothschild. These are medium-bodied cigars bearing interesting reddish-brown wrappers. There is the Connoisseur series of heavy-gauge cigars created for the opening of Davidoff's Madison Avenue store, and the standard line, with gold bands, including the 7-inch, 50 gauge Veritas, which gives rise to one of advertising's few classical Latin puns—In Zino Veritas.

SIZES

Name	Length: inches	Ring Gauge
Connoisseur 100	7¾ inches	50
Connoisseur 200	7½ inches	46
Veritas	7 inches	50
Zino Tubos No. 1	6¾ inches	34
Elegance	6¾ inches	34
Junior	6½ inches	30
Tradition	6¼ inches	44
Connoisseur 300	5¾ inches	46
Diamond	5½ inches	40
Princesse	4½ inches	20

MOUTON-CADET SERIES

Name	Length: inches	Ring Gauge
No. 1	6½ inches	44
No. 2	6 inches	35
No. 3	5¼ inches	36
No. 4	5⅛ inches	30
No. 5	5 inches	44
No. 6	5 inches	50

VERITAS : LENGTH 7 INCHES, RING GAUGE 50

CONNOISSEUR 100 : LENGTH 7¾ INCHES, RING GAUGE 50

MOUTON CADET No. 6 : LENGTH 5 INCHES, RING GAUGE 50

C Honduras
F Mild to medium
Q Superior quality

THE STRENGTH OF CIGARS

Cuba is unique to the extent that all Havanas or Habanos are blended from tobaccos grown on the island. They tend to offer medium to full flavors but the enormous variety of leaves available can produce surprisingly mild smokes in certain brands.

Cigars from other places like the Dominican Republic and Honduras are usually made from tobaccos taken from several countries. Hard and fast rules on flavors are therefore impossible to lay down. As a rough guide: Connecticut shade wrapped cigars with Dominican fillers tend towards mildness; maduro wrappers bring a sweetness to the taste, and in general Honduran and Nicaraguan fillers add spiciness.

Below is a selection of cigars by strength of flavor:

COUNTY OF ORIGIN

C Cuba	**D** Dominican	**J** Jamaica
CI Canary Islands	Republic	**M** Mexico
	H Honduras	**N** Nicaragua

MILD

Ashton **D**	Macanudo **J**	Royal Jamaica **D**
Casa Blanca **D**	Pleiades **D**	H. Upmann **C**
Cuesta-Rey **D**	Rafael Gonzalez **C**	

MILD TO MEDIUM

Arturo Fuente **D**	Griffin's **D**	Rey del Mundo **C**
Avo **D**	La Invicta **H**	Romeo Y Julieta **C**
Bauza **D**	Joya de	Santa Damiana **D**
Canaria D'Oro **D**	Nicaragua **N**	Te-Amo **M**
Davidoff **D**	Primo del Rey **D**	Temple Hall **J**
Don Diego **D**	Punch **C**	

MEDIUM TO FULL

Aliados **H**	Dunhill **D**	Montecristo **C**
Cohiba **C**	Excalibur **H**	Montecruz **D**
V Centennial **H**	Henry Clay **D**	Por Larrangaga **C**
Don Ramos **H**	Mocha **H**	Paul Garmirian **D**

FULL

Bolivar **C**	Ramon Allones **C**
Partagas **C**	Saint Luis Rey **C**

3

BUYING AND
STORING
CIGARS

Buying Cigars

When you buy a box of handmade cigars (certainly Havanas) you should ask to open the box to check the contents. No decent cigar merchant should refuse. If he does, he either doesn't know his business, or there is probably something wrong with the cigars. The first judgment to make is purely visual: they have to look good. Make sure that the cigars are all of the same color. They should be properly matched: darkest on the left, lightest on the right. If there is any significant variation in color, it would be sensible to reject the cigars, as as they are likely to be inconsistent in flavor, and the box might possibly have escaped final quality control in the factory. If the cigars differ significantly in color and the box is already open, it is more likely to mean that some of the cigars have come from another box (or somebody: customs, the cigar merchant, has been messing around with them)—another good reason for rejecting them. The spiral of the wrapper leaf should be in the same direction on all the cigars. Don't be afraid to smell the cigars to see if you find the bouquet agreeable—it is part of what you are paying for. If they smell good, they should taste good, too. Smell the cut ends, or take one cigar out, and smell the gap where it lay: that way you will experience the bouquet at its fullest.

And feel one or two of the cigars. They should give slightly when you press gently between finger and thumb, but spring back to shape. They should feel smooth. If they make a noise, they are too old or dry. If they don't regain their shape, they are not well

THE DAVIDOFF SHOP, JERMYN STREET, LONDON.

PREVIOUS PAGE: GEORGETOWN TOBACCO, WASHINGTON D.C. OWNER DAVID BERKEBILE.

made. If the cigar shows no resilience when you press or is mushy, it has been badly stored and will smoke badly. A fresh cigar (less than three months old) will spring back to shape even if your finger and thumb make the two sides almost touch.

If possible, buy cigars in large quantities (boxes of 10 or 25, say) rather than cartons of five which are often less good and less consistent than larger quantities. Nor is it as easy to inspect a cellophaned carton as it is simply to open a cigar box. Some large cigar stores sell cigars in their own boxes or with their "own label." This is normally a marketing ploy: if you have an empty box or two at home, buy them loose; otherwise, you are simply paying for the fancy packaging. The same applies to cigars in polished boxes: if you have the option, buy them in regular cedar, unless you are very fond of boxes or want to present the cigars as a gift. Unless you have sophisticated storage facilities, buy only what you can smoke in the near future (a month or two, say).

Cigars in aluminum tubes lined with cedar (invented by H. Upmann), though very convenient to carry, can sometimes be rather dry as the tubes are not completely airtight. They occasionally lose their bouquet and tend not to be as well matured as cigars in boxes. This applies particularly to small sizes, whatever the manufacturer may claim on the tube. You can, on the other hand, find perfectly well-conditioned cigars in tubes. In the case of the famous Romeo Y Julieta Churchill, the tube states: "The rich aromatic flavor of this fine Havana cigar will be protected by the aluminum container until opened." But many would disagree.

Cigars wrapped in the cellophane can be just as good as those left loose in the box (except, that is, if they are machine-made). They keep well, but mature less. Sometimes cellophane turns brown by absorbing the oils from the cigar it contains. This shouldn't make a difference to the quality of the cigar, particularly if it is then properly humidified. Handmade Havanas rarely come in cellophane, although some sizes of Cohiba do, when sold in small packs.

Some cigars, the Havana H. Upmann Cristales (a corona size), for instance, come in hermetically sealed jars. These are meant to be "fresh" cigars, theoretically unmatured, and tasting like the cigar would shortly after it was actually made.

London (with shops like the 200-year-old Fox & Lewis, Davidoff, and Dunhill) is acknowledged to be the best place in Europe to buy handmade cigars, certainly Havanas. The London branch of Davidoff sells some 400,000 handmade cigars a year in 220 different sizes and brands. But British import and tobacco taxes

THE DAVIDOFF SHOP, NEW YORK.

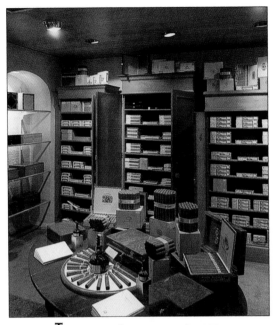

THE HISTORIC DUNHILL SHOP, LONDON.

are high, and the cigars don't come cheap. Paris and Geneva (the headquarters of Davidoff) are also good places to buy. You are unlikely to find non-Cuban cigars using Cuban brand names in most of the leading European cigar shops, so there should be little confusion. Although Spain imports more cigars than anywhere else in Europe (the Spaniards smoke around 30 million Havanas a year, compared to 5 million in Britain), the quality of Havanas there, with many machine-mades on the market to boot, is often dubious, though prices are cheaper than in most of the rest of Europe. Smoking cigars is a particular custom at bullfights. There is a good selection of non-Cuban handmades to be found in London and, of course, in the major cigar stores in the United States.

Beware of apparent bargains—in sales, for instance. These are sometimes machine-made cigars bearing famous Havana labels. As always, check the box carefully. The same applies at airports, where duty-free prices can look very attractive. Storage conditions are often poor, but fast turnover can mean the cigars are smokable. Inspection is not permitted, so there's a risk. You should certainly steer clear of small tobacco stores, news stands, and the like: the cigars will almost certainly be old and badly stored.

Cigars, like any natural product, need to be carefully kept. They should be protected from extremes of temperature and kept in a humidified environment—ideally at 60°–70°F with 65–70 percent humidity. This may be difficult to achieve, particularly in air-conditioned or centrally heated homes. But at the very least, you should keep your cigars in an airtight cupboard or box, away from any heat source, in preferably the coolest place in the house. Keep the cigars in their cedar boxes—the cedar helps to preserve them. You could put a damp sponge in the cupboard. Put the cigar boxes in plastic bags if you like, to stop evaporation, spraying a little water into the bag before you put the box in. If you put a damp sponge or a glass of water in the bag, not too close to the cigars, it will help humidify them (as long as the bag isn't completely sealed—so that there is some air flow—and the box of cigars is partially open).

Some experts suggest that you store cigars in an airtight bag in the vegetable crisper compartment of your refrigerator, but in that case you should take a cigar out of the fridge at least half an hour before you want to smoke it, so that it can get back to room temperature. This is a method of storage which has many detractors, and one you have to be particularly careful with. If you put cigars in the refrigerator, the airtight bag (with excess air expelled before you close or seal it) is essential. You can also get small humidifiers from leading cigar merchants. These come in different shapes and sizes (ranging from pill box types to small strips of plastic), and you put them in the cigar box (having removed a cigar or two). The moistened sponge or chalk in these devices will help keep the cigars humidified (but be careful to check once a month that the sponge hasn't dried out). Metal tubes, which work in a similar way, are also available.

Many importers and merchants use Zip Lock or other sealable heavy plastic bags to send cigars to major clients, and they are very useful, particularly if you are traveling with cigars. Keep them in the box, and put a slightly damp sponge in the bag or spray the inside of the bag with a little water.

If cigars are stored in a warm climate, bugs can sometimes appear—the tobacco beetle, in particular. Heat allows the larvae to hatch. You should never store cigars anywhere near direct sunlight, or exposed to sea breezes. If you store cigars at a low temperature, you have to raise the humidity to compensate.

Humidors come normally made of wood such as walnut, mahogany, and rosewood (though there are also plexiglass models on the market), usually at fancy prices, and in many sizes. They are only really worth buying if you smoke cigars regularly. You should make sure that the lid, which should be heavy, closes tightly and that there is a hygrometer to monitor the humidity level. The humidor should be well made and unvarnished inside. Keep an eye on it, and remember, the humidor only looks after humidity, not the temperature, so you still have to find a suitable location for it. It's useful if the humidor comes with trays at various levels, so that you can store different sizes separately and rotate cigars within the box. Prices can range from $200 to over $2,000—but at the top end you are paying for the humidors as furniture as much as for its functional use. For example, Viscount Linley, cabinet-maker and nephew of Britain's Queen Elizabeth, now offers beautifully crafted humidors through Dunhill starting at $2,000. The plexiglass models retail for under $200 and are serviceable enough. Choose your humidor carefully: many are ineffective or need careful monitoring.

Small humidors made of wood or leather are also available for travelers. Some first such as Davidoff even market briefcases with special cigar and accessory compartments, or built-in minihumidors. There are a number of pocket cigar cases on the market. The best are made of leather, and the most convenient design is the expandable, rigid "telescope" type which can take large or small cigars. Some pocket cases come with mini-moisturizing units. For the cigar smoker who has everything, there are any number of items on the market such as brass, silver, and gold-plated cigar tubes, fancy lighters, and silver match holders.

HUMIDORS. THE SELECTION IS HUGE.

REVIVING DRIED OUT CIGARS

If cigars are very dry, they will be difficult to revive satisfactorily. But, essentially, if moisture can escape from a cigar, it can also be replaced. One of the simplest methods, which usually works, is to put the open box of cigars in a large plastic bag, which is partially, but not completely, closed (it is essential to have a little air flow). You should also put a glass of water or a moist sponge in the bag. Rotate the cigars every few days, remembering also to bring cigars from the bottom of the box to the top, and within three weeks or so the cigars should return to smokable condition. It is very much a matter of trial and error, and means that you have to keep a careful eye on things. They will, however, having been dry in the first place, have lost much of their bouquet and won't compare to a well-kept cigar. In any event, cigars lose moisture slowly and need to regain it equally slowly. You need patience: attempting drastic measures will only ruin the cigars for good.

Another simple way of reviving a box of cigars, after traveling for instance, is to turn it upside-down, and put it under a gently running faucet. Be careful: the bottom of the box should be moistened by the water, but no more. You could use a sponge as an alternative method of dampening the bottom of the box. Shake off excess water and put the box in an airtight bag. The cigars should be in good shape after a couple of days.

Some major cigar stores, particularly if you are a regular customer, will revive a box of cigars for you in their humidified room (it takes around a month) as a favor. The charming and knowledgeable Edward Sahakian of the Davidoff shop in London will even provide this service for people who aren't regular customers—at no cost. "The pleasure of doing it is sufficient for both him and myself," he says.

Top cigar stores will also store cigars for regular clients.

PLACING THE CIGARS IN A PARTIALLY CLOSED POLYTHENE BAG
IS ONE WAY OF REPLACING LOST MOISTURE.

The only serious collectors' market in cigars is in prerevolutionary Havanas. They demand premium prices, about 5 or 6 times higher than the current retail price. The best place to find them is in London, because of the old tradition of laying down large cigar reserves at the main cigar shops. These cigars usually come onto the market when someone realizes that he will never get through the reserve, or when he dies (sometimes there is no obvious beneficiary). They are particularly attractive to American smokers, who have been able to buy and import them with a clear conscience since the trade embargo was imposed on Cuba in 1962. Unopened boxes are the most sought-after, as are sizes and brands which have now disappeared.

You can tell a prerevolutionary box because, the underside will read: "Made in Havana, Cuba," as opposed to the use of Spanish after the revolution.

Whether such old cigars are actually worth buying is a different question. As with old wine vintages, it is a matter of luck. If they have been properly stored and date no earlier than the 1950s, they might well still provide very satisfactory and interesting smokes. But, however well stored, they could just as easily be mere shadows of their former selves, musty with little bouquet. Dark cigars (colorado, colorado maduro, or maduro) are the best bets. Cigars really shouldn't be kept, even in the best storage conditions, for more than 10 to 15 years: the longer you leave cigars, the more of their bouquet and aroma they will lose.

THE MARK ON ANY PREREVOLUTIONARY BOX OF CIGARS.

INDEX

DANJU GIG

DANJU GIG

☆ CAROLYN WESTON ☆

RANDOM HOUSE ★ NEW YORK

FOR JSL

DANJU GIG

1

There is always some guy with a bright idea. Like let George do it. Or instead of George—*me,* Marty Brom thought as he stared glumly at the silvery expanse of aircraft wing outside his porthole window. The pressurized pane gave back a ghostly reflection of himself—Palm Springs tan, Sebring haircut, jet-set threads, the works. Go-go stud goes eastward into Eden. He belched softly, tasting lox and the faint flavor of last night's gin. Beyond the wing tip, clouds parted, furnishing an ephemeral glimpse of the earth far below. Scorched earth it was, wrinkled and scored like Colorado, or maybe Arizona. Only this was the Sahara. Sucker, Marty thought. He'd stepped right into the sandbag on this one.

Abby Golden, his great and good super-wheeler-dealer partner had argued him into it. "Look, if Burton and Taylor can go to Africa, why not Shad Smith? And why not Golden and Brom right with him?" Then he'd gone on to explain the whole cocka-mamey idea—how Shad Smith, their super-client, was crazy to do this African picture, but he wouldn't do it unless locations were just right. "So he gets this idea to make a flying trip, see. Just a couple guys to look the scene over before we start hag-gling about costs and all that."

"So have a nice trip," Marty had said. "I'll keep a candle burn-ing in your girl friend's window."

"So funny he is. A regular comedian. Listen, it'll be a ball, sweetheart. I mean, why not? All expenses paid. Practically a world tour! What's wrong, you lost your spirit of adventure or something?"

"I get all the adventure I want on the Strip every night. Look, he's your baby. Your big blue ball of fire, Abby. So he wants to go to Africa, *you* go with him."

"With *my* heart? With *my* blood pressure? What kinda partner wants to send me ten thousand miles from the only doctor can keep me alive? I ask you, what kinda partner is this? A monster!

A murderer wants his best friend, his partner, to commit suicide!"

Looking back, Marty realized he knew from the beginning he was sandbagged. I mean a client like Shad Smith, you don't go letting him out of your sight even for the john, much less on a safari to Africa . . . So to make a long story short, here he was. Nursemaid yet to a million-dollar package with ants in his pants. And headed across the Sahara. What if we crash? Me and the one and only Shad Smith.

Beside him in the double seat, the one and only stirred restlessly, stretching his long Glen-plaid legs a little longer. Handmade shoes the size of boats stuck up at a deadman angle. Making a mental note for his own wardrobe, Marty inspected his client's thin silky light-wool socks. Spun out of selected spider webs probably, twenty bucks minimum the pair. Sighing, Marty let his eyes slide up the long expensive star-status length of his seatmate, discovering one humorous eye peeping at him out of the brown sleeping face. Trust Shad to catch him with his PR face down.

Shad Smith and Success were synonymous. After three top-ten Nielsen seasons in a TV series, a public appearance tour in forty states to capacity crowds, an hour TV special, two weeks at Tahoe, and a Standing-Room-Only holdover at Melodyland, Shad was big-time; after twenty years in show biz—with a slight interruption for the hostilities in Korea—incorporated, packaged, a million-dollar proposition.

Of himself, Shad always said, "Lucky, man, it's all luck." For like an idea which cannot be resisted when its time has come, Shad had arrived at the right place in the right role at just exactly the right time—and he knew it. "I mean, look at the trends," he sometimes commented. "In the fifties, I'd be dead before I was born. Who needed me when all they wanted was coffee-colored Adonises, Belafonte style? But in the sixties, the scene got blacker, remember? The big ideal wasn't Adonis any more, it was a true-blue black-boy thespian name of Sidney Poitier. Then what came next? The breakthrough, man. Shad Smith. Me, yeah. An old brown boy with an old brown boy's phiz. Just the spade next door, that's me."

Success. Shad Smith. Synonymous. But who'd have believed it, he thought, five years ago? Who'd have believed it in those dear dead days of weekend gigs at off-season toilets called So-and-So Lodge and This-and-That Beach? Shad Smith at the piano. Songs, dances, patter they sometimes laughed at. The sober ones, that is—that occasional cat not too drunk to hear the words. The rest had just waited for the blue gags, the scat ditties they expected him to sing. Niggers knew dirtier ones than anybody. Shad Smith was nothing to them, nothing at all. He was show biz' own Invisible Man . . .

But in Shad's mind was more than self-congratulation as he pretended to doze beside Marty Brom. For he, too, had been sandbagged. By an old friend, one of those old soldiers who never die. This one evidently hadn't even faded away.

In his mind's eye, Shad saw again their meeting in New York— a meeting which led him somewhat more unwillingly to another less happy one in Lisbon. They had just left that shining white ancient city where—somewhere beyond the wide boulevards, the plazas dominated by heroic statues—a black man sat waiting, hoping against hope.

"The name he's using is Fernando Corraia," the colonel had said in New York. "But don't try to find him, Shad, he'll find you."

"Like show biz." Shad had laughed, still amused by the cloak-and-dagger bit. Was this old soldier putting him on? "Don't call him, he'll call me."

"Don't worry, he'll contact you all right. But only when he's ready. And only when it's safe."

Carried back to the fifties and an army-issue cubbyhole at headquarters in Seoul, Shad had almost snapped the old boy a salute. But instead he had grinned, waiting for the gag. But there hadn't been any, the colonel was serious. "Look," Shad had said as mildly as possible, "I'd like to help you, no jazz, but—"

"You're the only one who can, Shad."

Only one—was that what had grabbed him? Anyway, he'd fallen for it. Instead of Nigeria, he'd agreed to go to a place

5

called Danju and see, like Joe Patriot, what he could see.

What the hell, he had thought at the time, it didn't hurt to say yes, did it? Any good cat would do the same. But now he wasn't so sure. Not sure at all. Not since Lisbon and the frightened black man who went by the name of Fernando Corraia.

"I won't tell you his real name," the colonel had said, "but if you're curious enough you can find out for yourself in any newspaper morgue—"

That word morgue had clanged in his mind, echoing spookily. Morgues mean death, man.

"All I'm telling you," the colonel went on, "is not to use it. Not for any reason, Shad. He's as shy as a mouse in a houseful of cats—and twice as scared. You understand?"

Shad had been standing at the sitting room window, looking out at the UN building shining like a temple against the gray eastern sky. Flags in front of it flapped at street level like naval semaphores. From this distance he couldn't identify any of them, not even the good old red-white-and-blue. "What's their flag look like?"

"What's that? Whose flag?"

"Danju's."

"Oh." The colonel looked surprised and put out for a second. Shad could almost hear him thinking it: God, *civilians*.

"Nemmine, Cunnel, suh—go on."

"All right, I'll make it brief." He grinned a tight-lipped gung-ho military acknowledgment of the alteration in their respective positions. "I realize your time's valuable—"

"Don't put me on, Colonel." Shad laughed. "Come on, what's the word on this? What's his name. Hernando."

"*Fer*nando. Corraia." He cleared his throat. "I should've brought a map so I could show you where it's located. Danju, that is. But anyhow, it's West Africa. It was a colony until—let me see—1959, I think it was. Then they got independence. Fernando Corraia was instrumental in that, and like most of the nationalist leaders in these little republics, took over as premier once they were on their own."

"Nice work if you can get it."

"Sometimes. Sometimes not." Again the colonel smiled thinly. "Witness, for instance, Lumumba and company."

"I see what you mean." Morgue meant dead.

Hitching forward in his chair, the colonel stared at Shad, appearing oddly sorrowful and unexpectedly old. "We've got a real hellish stew brewing there, Shad. In Africa, that is. The Russians and Nasser. The French and Belgians still meddling around in the Congo." Then abruptly, as if forcing himself, he leaned back in his chair, crossing one thin baggy tweed leg over the other. His shoes, Shad noticed, were in need of half-soling. God's own devoted citizen soldier—no time in *his* cruel and demanding world for comforts or amenities of any sort. "Anyhow, I'll give you briefly what we know, Shad. Corraia can fill you in on whatever I miss—if he can, that is."

"What do you mean *can?* Alive to do so?"

"I should have said able. If he's able to meet you some place safe enough to talk freely."

"Look," Shad protested, "if somebody's gunning for this cat—"

"No, no, that's the least of our worries right now. He's an old hand at the assassination game."

Shad laughed somewhat more feebly than usual. "Now there is one sport I mean to miss, Colonel. I mean—*entirely.*"

Disapprovingly, the colonel waited.

Finally, feeling years younger, a callow corporal in the presence of official deity, Shad said, "Sorry, sir. Go on."

For ten years, the colonel continued, Corraia had led his tiny republic from its first beginnings into something like prosperity and stability. There were grants of aid from the United States, of course, help in the areas of agricultural and trade development. The infant republic seemed well on its way to a stable statehood, politically firm in its loyalty to the West . . .

"Then we started getting wind of something," the old man said moodily. "Nothing any of our people could get their teeth into. Nothing in the way of hard fact. Just whispers here and there, a seepage of trouble. Some new Eastern European trade representatives suddenly on hand. Some loose money floating around that hadn't been there before . . ."

Then suddenly, without warning, revolt caught like a grass fire in Danju, led by a man Corraia had trusted implicitly.

"His name is Okefe. You'll be meeting him, Shad. General Albert Okefe. He's now, to all intents and purposes, military dictator of Danju."

"Already I don't like this stud. Do I have to deal with him?"

"As an honored visitor, of course."

Shad jingled change in his pocket. A habit when he was nervous or confused, his fingers found his lucky penny—an Indian head with a hole in the middle that he'd carried for as long as he could remember. "I'll tell you something, Colonel, this don't smell so sweet I'm beginning to like it yet. This Danju gig. I mean look, I got my responsibilities now. A couple million bucks going on this new picture. A lot of people depending on it getting off the ground . . ."

As his now-famous voice trailed off, the colonel kept looking at him. A natural mimic, Shad stared back, mirroring his expression. Then suddenly the old man started to laugh.

"What's the gag?"

But the colonel didn't answer, only laughed and laughed like a paid claque with tomorrow's hamburgers depending on their volume.

"Okay," Shad snapped, really annoyed. "All right, I get it. Whichever way I wiggle, you'll bag me, right? Keerist, you always did!"

Wiping his eyes with a spotless handkerchief frayed at one corner, the old man nodded. "I know you, Shad. Men don't change that much. You always tried to weasel out of the easy ones, then you'd turn right around and volunteer for the dirtiest duty you could find for yourself." Again he laughed, shaking his head. "Perverse, that's you, Shad. The most perverse damn soldier I ever did run across."

Recognizing that he was beaten—I mean, a guy pegs you *that* good, you might as well give up—Shad said, "Okay, okay, I surrender, Boss. Gimme the shaft, I'm braced for it."

"You don't need me to give you anything, Shad. Because the rest you can guess, can't you?"

"The Russians Are Coming?"

"Wrong tense, we think. They're already there. But where in Danju or why, we don't know. Any official eyes and ears we had—our consular staff—was pulled out after Okefe took over." Again the colonel shifted forward in his chair, eager now, impatient as he always was when the job was set. "Danju is a police state now, Shad—as carefully combed by secret police as any Iron Curtain country. We've lost all but two undercover people there—most of them by 'accidents.' The chance of our finding out what's going on isn't near as good as an iceberg's in hell. That is unless"—he paused—"some sharp-eyed tourist spots something. Someone whose word we can absolutely depend on."

"But what if I don't see anything?"

"Then we'll know there's nothing to see."

Shad blew out his breath. Caught, buddy boy. "You're going to stake *that* much on me? The whole bit?"

"The whole bit, Shad."

A soft thump sounded in his head then. Imaginary, sure, but all the same he felt its thud clear through to his toes. The sand-bag, man. Walked right into it. Shad Smith, Boy Spy. "Keerist," he said. "Kee—rist!" Then he shook the colonel's hand and saw him to the door of his hotel suite, feeling trapped and yet proud —perhaps foolishly so—that he was the one they had chosen to trust.

It was only later he remembered that it probably hadn't been choice at all, since there was nobody but him, let's face it, to choose from.

But by that time, he was in Lisbon, having left New York and his wife behind; having left what remained of what the colonel called his "perversity" behind, too. Perversity, he thought, meaning self-preservation. But too late now. He was committed.

2

The plane lurched and momentarily the dead land below drew closer. Then they rose again—with the swiftness, Marty thought, of an express elevator in the Empire State Building. An old gag occurred to him thinking this: would you please go back and get my stomach? Again he belched. Lox and gin. Five martinis he'd waited through in the bar of that palace called Hotel Something-or-Other, Lisbon, Portugal . . .

"You are enjoying our country?" the barman had asked courteously with the second drink. "Many visitors come to see us now."

"Yeah, it's great," said Marty who had seen nothing so far but the airport terminal and this mammoth birthday cake of a hotel. "By tomorrow I'll probably be addicted, yeah."

"Addicited?"

"I'll like it so much I'll hate to leave." In a pig's eye.

"Yes, I see. Oh, very true, this must happen. You must make motor trip to Estoril. Very beautiful. Very chic. All the best people are at Estoril."

"You don't say." Marty looked at his watch. Where the hell was Shad? He tried to figure the time, but found himself beaten by international zoning. "Hey, what time is it, George?"

The barman looked around. "You speak to me?" His cheery face clouded with Latin pride. "I am Jaime, senhor. Allow me to present myself."

"Yeah, okay. Marty Brom here. You got the time, Hymie?"

It was late and getting later—too damn late, he thought, to be guzzling gibsons. Chewing the cocktail onions reflectively one by one, Marty arranged the toothpicks on the bar before him. One for each half hour, say. Four now. That was two hours he'd been waiting for that crazy stud who was probably out chasing Portuguese tail.

"One more?" the barman suggested.

"Took the words right out of my mouth."

"Pardon?"

"You know what Thurber always said about martinis."

"Senhor?"

"One is fine, two is too many, three is never nearly enough."

"So."

"Yeah, so." Juniper rising gently into his nostrils, Marty nodded tipsily. "S'truth, buddy, you better believe it."

"I am not Boddy, senhor. It is—"

"I know, I know," but he couldn't remember. A real Yiddische name and can't remember. Stoned, friend, really stoned. Marty smiled benignly. Guy made a hundred-percent gibson, though, you had to say that for old Samele or whatever his name was. "You ever see television here?" he asked, feeling a sudden warmth for his attentive companion behind the polished expanse of a foreign pub bar.

"Oh, yes. The teevee. Very nice."

"Ever see the Shad Smith Show?"

"Pardon?"

Marty sighed, and suddenly bored, started looking fuzzily around the bar lounge. It was filled with people in evening dress. "These cats really take their threads serious, don't they, hey?"

"Pardon?"

"Never mind. Hey, what's the time now?"

From somewhere in the hotel came a low throbbing voice— man's, woman's, Marty could not tell. Like chanting it was.

"Fado," the barman explained soulfully. "Is our national music, fado."

Sounds like a Yiddische funeral, Marty thought. Papa is all, oi vey iz mir. Where had Shad gone? Crazy schwartzer. Into the ginny euphoria of four and a half gibsons, a tiny serpent of

11

alarm intruded. Trouble, Marty thought. They all get in trouble. Make a few bucks, see their name in lights, and what happens? Trouble, of course. News hounds calling with tomorrow's headlines. Joe Q. Star has changed his name to Trouble.

"Look," Shad had said, "I got a call from this old buddy of mine, Mart. I'm going to meet him, see, and rap for a while. Meet you back here in a couple hours."

But there hadn't been any call. Hadn't he answered the phones himself? All right, a note, then. But none had been delivered. But something had come, somebody had knocked on the door. Oh, yeah, a bellboy with ice they hadn't ordered. Shad had tipped him some fantastic amount. The next thing I knew, he was out the door.

Feeling cold suddenly, soberer and worried, Marty pushed away the balance of gibson in his glass. And when the barman inquired if something was wrong, he shook his head and threw a bill on the bar. He rushed out into the ornate lobby as big, he was sure, as Buckingham Palace. "Any messages?" he asked at the desk, hopefully.

The clerk in his soup and fish looked to see. All these flunkeys here look like ambassadors, Marty thought. He could see for himself there was nothing in the box under Suite 615.

Where had Shad gone? Feeling awash in gin, nauseated now, Marty rode up in the gilded elevator to the sixth floor. But once inside the sumptuous sitting room which connected their two bedrooms, he could only stand indecisively, wondering how long he should wait before he set up a howl. I mean, call the fuzz? he asked himself. Shad would cut his throat if nothing had happened.

To comfort himself then, Marty began to rage in imagination at Abby Golden. He's your client, for chrissake, your baby you always said. Hell, I never even got a chance to know the guy. Don't know Shad Smith from Adam, you fink.

But it didn't work, he was not comforted. And imagining his next transatlantic call to his partner, Marty Brom could only shudder. Negro Star Found Dead in Lisbon Brothel. There's some nice news for a partner with a cardiac condition. Salazar

Bans Shad Smith from Portugal. Oi vey Maria, what should he—?

The door opened.

"Shad! Where the—?"

"You left your key in the lock." Shad tossed it on the table, scratching the mirror finish. "What you been doing that smells like gin, man?"

"Three hours I been chewing my nails. Three, count 'em! While you been wandering around a foreign burg . . ."

Shad had only laughed, of course, suggested drinks and some dinner downstairs. I mean, what's a guy to do? He wouldn't say where he'd been, no details, no explanations. As he watched the dry baked land passing far below, Marty tried to guess for the hundredth time just what his client might have been up to. Shouldn't he ask? Didn't he have a *right* to know? Glancing over at the long sleeping form of his seatmate and client, he thought, Star, schmar, I don't have to put up with that!

But it seemed he did, 'twas a PR man's fate. Feeling put upon and consumed by curiosity, Marty signaled the steward and in a stage whisper ordered himself a nice cold gibson. "Dry as dust," he added redundantly.

"Make it two," Shad muttered without opening his eyes.

I shoulda done like Mama said, Marty thought mournfully. Been a doctor, a lawyer, say. Something square and peaceful-like.

On his closed eyelids, Shad watched again as the black man emerged out of swirling smoke. The room where he had been sent by the bellboy's note had been low, jammed with people, a popular nightclub or restaurant. It smelled of heat and bodies and sharp resinous wine. The music of guitars filtered under the din of a hundred conversations in a sibilant, throaty language he didn't dig.

"Mr. Smith?"

"Hernando, I presume."

"Senhor Corraia, please." With his dull black fingers tense around the back of a spindle chair lacquered a shiny orange, the man glanced around the room slowly. Then at last, seeming satisfied, he sat down.

"Wine?" Shad asked, not quite believing any of this. "It's got glue in it."

"A little if you please."

Dig this spade with a British accent yet. Shad poured a glass from the dark green bottle he had ordered by pointing, then holding up two fingers. The international language, money, had come next. Shad had a strong feeling he had paid at least ten times what the bottle really cost.

"Keep your voice quite natural," Corraia said when they had silently toasted each other and sipped their wine. "A conversational tone."

"How's this?"

"Splendid."

"I wondered how good your English would be." Shad grinned. "Is my face red."

With a curious look, both measuring and haughty, Corraia surveyed him. "Red?" he asked finally. "I presume this is idiomatic. A figure of speech."

Shad drank instead of answering, for the first time in years, feeling his color.

As if he guessed this, the man who called himself Fernando Corraia smiled. In his black face gold teeth glinted briefly. Then serious again, he said in his gentle, cultivated way, "There are new friends in my country. Generous friends. Very fortunate new friends for a poor and backward people." As Shad was about to speak, he held up his hand. "No, let us not name any names, please. Or nationalities. What troubles me is that friendship, of course, is a two-way thing. And I think to myself, Yes, these new friends, so generous, are fine—but what does my country have to offer in return? We are poor, undeveloped, underpopulated. I say to myself, What could it be that we might give a new friend? What gift in return for all their generosity?"

"You got any ideas?" Shad asked.

"Yes, of course." Corraia shrugged, spreading his pale-palmed hands. "But of what use are the ideas of a man so far away? So useless?" Again he glanced around slowly—covering, Shad saw, every face nearby. Then turning back, he leaned forward

14

slightly, and like a man telling a fascinating anecdote, began smilingly to recount what had happened in Danju.

There were whispers, he said as the colonel had, ripples like wind shadows on the surface of a pool. But never, not once, was there a hint of the real foment which worked like acid under the skin of his government. General Okefe was his oldest friend and most trusted ally. They had gone to England together—two picked out of hundreds, thousands, to be educated for the future. Corraia had gone first to the London School of Economics, and then to Cambridge. "Years of study," he said flatly, unemotionally. "Years, you understand, preparing myself for what must come. The same as Albert, General Okefe. Selflessly, you see, out of devotion to the future of our country which must be."

Did Mr. Smith know what it was for a man to sacrifice his youth for an ideal, an ambition? To deny himself everything now so that later he might serve as he had trained himself to do? Shad thought of his answer: Yeah man, I dig you, baby. And his own struggle rolled over him, the endless-seeming years when it appeared he would never be more than second, third, fourth rate. But he knew better than to speak, not to a man like this. To Corraia, ex-premier of a new nation, the story of an American entertainer could only seem silly.

"They took us by surprise," Corraia was saying calmly. "A slaughter. Quite merciless. It was only by a miracle I escaped with my life. Then my friend, my oldest friend, like a brother to me, declared himself dictator of our country. And he set a price on my head. A fortune. For whoever brings back my head to General Okefe—" He stopped, drank some wine, and leaning back, breathed in deeply. "Well, no matter," he said at last. "You must travel. I urge you, Mr. Smith. Fly, if you can. See every inch of Danju if possible."

"But what shall I look for?"

"God only knows. Something, Anything." For an instant Corraia closed his eyes, his hands clasped tight before him as if he suffered, or prayed. "I can only say, look. Listen. Because there is something there you must see, something you must hear

15

of." Then abruptly, he pushed back his chair. "You must forgive me, it is time to go."

"But, listen—"

"No, I dare not linger anywhere. They have already found me twice." Again the gold teeth glinted. "Very, very narrow escapes, both. Very hard on the nerves." Then he was gone, disappearing into the smoke, the crowd . . . And the music had risen, louder and louder—strange, sad, plangent chords struck angrily off guitar strings. And a woman's low voice came through the smoke. And as if on signal, the room fell silent. Fado. The soul music of Portugal.

With his eyes still closed, Shad hummed a phrase he thought he remembered and opened his eyes to see Marty looking at him.

"Hey, what's that? I like it, I like it!"

"Fado, man. Big sad fado song. Real groovy Portagee spiritual."

Then the steward came with their gibsons.

3

Since no international airline landed in Danju, Marty and Shad were booked as far as Ikeja Airport at Lagos in Nigeria. From here, on a Nigeria Airways plane, they would go on to Porto Saba, the coastal capital of Danju. As they drank the last of their gibsons, the land below them began to change, turning green and mottled brown, like a colored relief map. The coast of West Africa was discernible suddenly between fleets of low-hanging rain clouds as they approached their destination. The slave coast. The gold coast. Africa!

Fasten Seat Belts flashed on as they both munched cocktail onions. *No Smoking.* Shad stubbed out his Benson and Hedges long. The steward came by and picked up their glasses and rumpled cocktail napkins. Reflectively, feeling somewhat restored, Marty picked his teeth with the colored toothpick advertising their airline.

They began to descend then, entering their landing pattern; and as his body felt the unease of lowering altitude, the tilt of the plane, Shad was suddenly assailed by disbelief. Corraia was unreal, and their encounter last night; like a vehicle hitting an ice patch, Shad's mind kept slipping, sliding, unable to grasp his situation as anything but a joke, or worse, a trick. Too crazy, he thought. *Too* crazy! Somebody's got to have blown his mind.

As a point of reference, something truly real and really known, Shad began to think about his wife. The last thing before leaving the hotel this morning, he had called Gloria in New York, waking her, of course, it was hours earlier there.

She missed him already, she had grumbled sleepily. Did he know what *time* it was, for God's sake? Even the milkmen weren't up yet. Picturing her tucked up in the luxurious hotel bedroom, Shad had felt an immense relief, a kind of lifting gaiety. "Hey, baby," he had said. "You remember when your daddy said you couldn't marry me? He wasn't going to have any two-bit song-and-dance man for a son-in-law?"

Her yawn had come across the Atlantic so intimate and sweet he had felt tempted to take the next plane back. "God," she had groaned, "are you out of your mind? Shad, are you drinking?"

"Plead sober, judge."

"Then what in the world made you think of that?"

"I don't know. Just thinking in general, I guess."

Well, it was too early, she said, for all that stuff. But here was a kiss to take along with him. Would he please hurry back? She meant really hurry. She didn't like this being a widow at all.

The plane swooped at an alarming rate, as if sliding down an invisible chute over a harbor and then a white city. They saw the airport tower in the swift-approaching distance—green-tinted glass flashing in brilliant sunlight. Then they were down, bouncing once, zooming over the tarmac toward the terminal building. Thank you for traveling with us, the steward announced unctuously, his multilingual accent almost unrecognizable over the loudspeaker. Marty—an impatient and practiced jet-setter—was already gathering their hand luggage together before the plane had even stopped rolling.

In billows, fierce and unbelievable in its sudden ferocity, the steamy heat of Africa poured over them. Immediately, before they were even down the boarding stairs of the plane, their clothing was sticking to their drenched bodies.

"Jesus," Marty said.

"Keerist," Shad answered.

In the blinding sun, they rushed across to the terminal building, taking what was evidently a side entrance.

"That gin's bubbling like antifreeze in me," Marty complained as they headed for the Nigeria Airways counter. Couldn't they change the location of that opus Shad was so in love with to someplace civilized like Palm Springs?

"You kill me, baby," Shad said, and mopped his face again, pleased by the scenery behind the counter they were headed for.

Yas, the gorgeous brown-skinned girl said, the gentlemen's aircraft would be departing on schedule. Nigeria Airways flight so-and-so, departing from that gate over there. But the gentlemen had been through customs? When they confessed they had not, her smile turned sour. They must attend to the customs without fail.

"Relax," Marty said to Shad, "I'll take care of it." But as it happened, a very stern customs official demanded to see Mr. Smith and his passport in person.

Schwartzers, Marty raged inwardly as the man spent minute after minute scrutinizing their papers. Give 'em a uniform and they . . . but then he had the grace to stop this line of thinking. His bread and butter, after all, was this elegant Negro standing patiently beside him.

"Nigeria Airways flight—" A loud electronic buzzing buried the number and the curiously accented voice announcing it over the loudspeaker.

"I think that's our connection," Marty said to the customs official. "They told us in Lisbon it was a close one."

Unblinking, the man surveyed him calmly. "One must complete the formalities," he chided in a sing-song voice, "no matter what the urgency of transport."

"But we'll miss our plane!"

The man shrugged, continuing to study their passports. "Shad Smeeth. Occupation, actor," he read aloud to himself. "Purpose of trip—" he glanced at Shad with a vague sort of suspicion— "beezness?"

"Look," Marty cried furiously, his pale, freckled face growing fiery, "this is Shad Smith, one of the biggest TV and film stars in the United States. He isn't a spy. He isn't a—"

"Last call for Nigeria Airways—"

"You hear that?"

"Thank you, gentlemen, for your courtesy," the customs man said, bowing slightly. "We are honored to acknowledge the presence in person of a United States TV and film star of the first magnitude . . ."

"Jesus," Marty grumbled as they raced for their embarkation point, "all that crazy jig—all that crazy character wanted to do was practice his English on us."

"Pretty fancy too, you got to admit it. Very, very fancy lingo."

"Yeah, so damn fancy we nearly miss this plane!"

Steaming with perspiration, they bolted up the steps and past the smiling stewardess. Marty's color-consciousness paused abruptly. A black Sophia Loren? Wow-wow-wow! Mopping his face, he glanced about at the other passengers, who were almost all Africans. The motors were being fired up one by one. As the door was closed and sealed shut, Marty—who had flown hundreds of thousands of miles—experienced a sudden sinking attack of panic. Africa, he thought, and felt doomed, helpless. No place for a white man, particularly Mama Brom's little blue-eyed blonde-haired Yiddish boy.

The flight was brief and for Shad and Marty—accustomed as they were to transcontinental high altitudes—a frighteningly low-level hedge-hopping one. Over steamy-looking green mats of jungle they watched the plane's shadow skimming like a gigantic winged lizard. Then the coastline swooped up at them again, so near this time they could see the breakers foaming white on deserted yellow-hued beaches. Gulping, Marty spied a herd of animals grazing in what looked like a dry meadowland. *Wild* animals, he thought. Zebras, giraffes, the whole schmag. He yearned wildly for Sunset Boulevard.

Then ahead in the distance they spied another harbor, a white city which looked incandescent under the ferociously burning sun. Temperature in Porto Saba, Danju, the next stop, was ninety-eight degrees, the stewardess announced over the loudspeaker. Some turbulence was expected soon, so passengers would please keep seat belts fastened. Through passengers must also keep their seats, since the landing at Porto Saba would be brief.

Marty and Shad then listened to the same instructions given in French. After this, a language which they decided must be an African dialect issued from the loudspeaker. Swahili? Africa's soup language.

A sailing sloop in the harbor below caught their attention. "Looks like a lot of meters there," Marty commented. "Transoceanic racing stuff."

"You a sailing man, Mart?"

"Yeah, sort of. In between skiing and skin-diving, that is."

"Groovy." Shad laughed. "Real sportif! You ever try flying?"

"Sure, I've got my license. Bet I've logged more hours in the air than the cat that's steering this crate."

Shad's mouth pulled down comically—a Stepin Fetchit expression. "Baby, somehow I wish you hadn't said that!"

With a sinking feeling in the pit of his stomach, Marty wished he hadn't, too.

Both fell silent then, introspective, as the plane began to rush downward, all souls on board imperiled by its headlong earthward plunge.

"The gentlemen depart at Porto Saba?" a prosperous-looking Indian across the aisle from Marty asked. "One's deepest sympathies if so, for this is a city no longer hospitable to foreigners."

Sweating heavily, smelling his own anxiety, Marty hoped that Shad wasn't listening.

"I am in textiles and this very unfriendly government has stolen away my branch there," the Indian went on serenely. "However, I have others—" he spread his hands, a philosophical man ready to take his lumps—"so this is not a financial tragedy. However, it is only the kind thing to do, I feel, to warn others of the fate which befalls me in this poor country we now land upon."

"Well, that's—uh—nice of you to let us know," Marty said as Shad poked him.

"What's he saying?"

"Something about business, I don't know," Marty lied. "Hey, you sure these cats expect us here?"

But the answer was soon obvious as their plane landed and rolled toward the terminal building. A small uniformed band waited in the blaze of afternoon, a guard of honor of some sort, and a group of glittering limousines. Two small children wearing glistening white clothing held a printed sign which said Danju welcomed Shad Smith.

"Gracious heavens," the Indian across the aisle said as he goggled at the array outside their windows. "There is some visiting dignitary, no doubt."

"Two," Marty replied. "Us, that is." As the plane door opened and a brassy blare faintly recognizable as "America the Beautiful" floated in at them, he rose from his seat. "Come on, Champ," he said to Shad, who already looked bored. "All your fans're out there clamoring for you."

"Dignitaries!" the Indian kept crying excitedly as they made their way to the door of the plane. "Do you see that? Those were most assuredly dignitaries to whom I myself was only now speaking!"

Then the sun hit them, the steambath heat, and there they were in Danju.

4

A long time afterward when they compared notes, Marty was to see truth again in that old saw about the eye of the beholder selecting its own view. He, for instance, had been conscious only of blackness at first—wherever he looked, everyone was black. Shad noticed how carefully cautious everyone seemed. Like maybe, he said later, Big Bubber was listening?

Marty laughed at this. "Wrong again, it was *Little* Brother," and laughed again at Shad's expression. "Didn't you know that's what they called that Haile Selassie-sized general? Little Brother of the Knife, yet."

Porto Saba was smaller than Lagos, they discovered driving in, less developed industrially than the Nigerian city. From the airport where they had been ceremoniously received, Marty and Shad rode with a bemedaled officer—General Okefe's aide—careening in the middle of a procession of limousines along a dusty highway in need of repairs. Poor-looking small farms flashed by, a gas works, a power plant, as the general's aide delivered a rapid-fire running commentary on the government's ambitious Five-Year Plan. His handsome black face shone as he talked, his eyes glittered with what looked to Marty like fanaticism. What's this guy, some kinda nut or something? He wondered if Shad were nervous, too.

Clusters of mud huts appeared then, and after them, at the edge of the city, a shack settlement which looked like pictures they had seen of hobo camps. *This* is Africa? both thought. Dirt streets teeming like anthills wandered off from the main road in every direction. Ragged-looking children waved as they passed. In the gutters beggars with maimed limbs and ghastly sores on their faces and bodies held up helpless, hopeless hands, begging futilely as the limousines sailed by. The heat was so intense it numbed them; dust blowing in through the open windows smelled like the effusions from an outhouse.

Then abruptly they bounced onto a concrete boulevard, wide and palm-lined, and the aide sighed, falling silent at last. Peering out at the pleasant aspect of low white colonial buildings, spacious streets, green parks, Marty experienced a relief so powerful it felt like joy. Civilization, he thought. Hallelujah. As usual in a new town, he wondered where a guy might find a little action.

"Hey, this is all right," Shad was saying. "Nice, yeah. Real pretty. Looks kinda like Santa Barbara."

Appearing pleased, the general's aide pointed out the telephone exchange, the radio station, and a taller building which he said was the trade mart. "Soon you will see what was once the Governor's Palace," he went on. "One of the finest structures of its sort in all of West Africa. Of course the colonial government built it with *our* effort—you shall forgive me—with *our* sweat. All these structures were by rights always ours."

More and more frequently as they approached the heart of the city, Marty noticed groups of uniformed men either stationed at intersections or patrolling in open trucks, their automatic rifles sticking up like the thin periscopes of a school of minisubs. There was no other traffic save buses on the streets. "How come all the military around?" he asked the aide finally. "You got troubles or something?"

"Troubles!" The aide looked shocked. "Most assuredly not, Mr. Brown—"

"Brom," Shad said.

"Mr. Browm, yes, sorry. Danju is a peaceful country. A serene land. You will see that, I am sure."

Glancing at Shad, Marty lifted his eyebrows. Jesus Christ, looks like Watts that summer, he thought. Riot-town. Had he better call Abby? Look, bubele, this place gives me the creeps. Like Nazi Germany yet. Then he realized he knew a better comparison, having traveled only last year in the Caribbean.

Haiti, he thought. Yeah, man. Old Papa Doc's little suicide paradise—that's what this peaceful country, this serene land of Danju, reminded him of.

"The general will be astonished at the smallness of your party, Mr. Smith," he heard the aide saying. They had arranged for Mr. Smith and his entourage to occupy the entire third floor of their very beautiful Hotel Splendide, one of the finest of such structures in all of West Africa.

"Well, that's mighty hospitable of the general," Shad said—playing heavy, Marty noticed, on a Southwestern drawl. "We sure do hope we haven't put anybody out."

"Please. No, of course not. We are honored by your visit, Mr. Smith."

Squinting out the window like Gary Cooper casing the main drag of a new tough cowtown, Shad said, "You sure *do* have a lot of law around."

"It might appear so," the aide replied stiffly. "But only for the sake of our people. And," he added, "our visitors."

The train of limousines then made a sharp turn around what appeared to be a small park in the center of a town square. Two armored cars were parked in the shade of a gigantic baobab tree. Uniformed men lounged at each of the four corners of the square, weapons glinting oily and dangerous as serpents in the brilliant clear light. Ahead lay a long white stone wall pierced by heavy gates. A bugle blew somewhere—one thin high note, and the gates swung open, the lead car turned in.

The first thing Marty noticed as they entered the gates were the barrels of machine guns trained on them—one behind each gatepost—manned by black men who looked as though they meant business.

But ahead lay dappled shade, an idyllic short drive through the luxurious tropical gardens which surrounded the imposing colonial-style white stucco edifice inside the walled half-acre they had entered. Peacocks strutted across diamond-shaped lawns. Flocks of white doves fluttered up like confetti as the limousines approached. On what looked like a belltower atop the three-story building, an enormous flag hung limp in the still heat; then lifted by an onshore breeze from the Gulf of Guinea, it suddenly billowed out black and yellow and orange—the national banner of the Republic of Danju.

At the top of ten wide marble steps, shadowed by the archway entrance, stood a group of officers in full dress. Gold braid gleamed, dress swords flashed. All but one were magnificent.

This man, small and brown, was dressed in casual khakis and rope-soled sandals—a dull duckling in this gathering of swans. Not even Louis B. Mayer, thought Marty, could have staged it better . . . "His Excellency himself," the aide whispered, confirming his guess.

"Which one?" Shad asked, and Marty hid a grin, wondering if the general, too, would be bothered by competition.

But as it turned out, General Okefe was strictly—as Shad said later—underplay all the way. A quiet welcome, the hospitality of his country, he offered, then they all trooped into the cooler interior of the Premier's Palace where drinks were waiting in a long state reception room.

No gin, Shad noticed, but plenty of vodka in label-less bottles. Vodka that had a kick like a mule. Where you hail from, mule? Moscow, maybe? No, he said, he was not from the place called Watts. Yes, of course, he said, he deplored the tragic death of Dr. Martin Luther King. Don't anybody want to talk about show biz around here? Alternately gazing into the serious anxious-to-please faces around him and the bottom of his glass, he suffered through the hour of their official greeting, longing for the lightness, the put-on jazz, the gaiety of his own kind.

"None of those long-face cats wanted to talk about anything but *race*," he complained to Marty later when they were finally back in the limousine again, headed sedately for the Hotel Splendide. "I mean, a hundred-percent black country, why all that hype?" Then he punched Marty's arm, grinning suddenly. "How'd it feel, baby, to be the onliest, hunh?"

"What you talking about? Jesus, the *heat!*"

"You mean to tell me it didn't bug you, being a one-man minority group at that wake we just left?"

Marty opened his mouth, then closed it again. And suddenly they were both laughing hard—two stray cats a long long way from home. In the rear-view mirror, their driver watched them, baffled. Such a strange people, these Americans. Could a white man and a black truly find such joy together? From what he had been told, they should be bitterest enemies, silently tolerating each other's presence. He worried because so far there was nothing significant to report to those who had told him to eavesdrop on the visitors.

"I got news for you, baby," Marty was saying. "Like all the wrong threads we pack for this safari."

"No uniforms, you mean."

"I mean black tie, sweetie. These cats go strictly by Esquire, I guess."

Shad laughed. "You're putting me on."

"Not me, sweetheart. There's a big bash scheduled for tonight. Dinner, dancing, the whole bit. His Excellency's flack nearly swallowed his drink, glass and all, when I told him all we had with us was our Sy Devore Nehru coats."

"But that's the *style,* man—didn't you tell him?"

"So next year maybe it'll reach 'em. *Mean*while—"

"Down at the palace."

"Yeah, us two tourists'll be strictly underdressed. Just thought I'd give you the word," and Marty made a merchant's gesture. "You win a few, you lose a few. How was I to know anybody but the English still dressed for dinner in Darkest Africa?"

"Well, don't take it to heart, man, don't take it to heart. We'll pig along and make the best of it."

Was he mad? Marty wondered. Maybe touchy on account of that Darkest Africa crack? Settling back, he looked gloomily out the window at the passing scene. If this is like Santa Barbara, I'll—but here his mind failed him; he couldn't imagine anything crazy enough.

The Hotel Splendide lived up to its name—on the outside, anyway. A rambling three-story balconied structure, it sat back from the boulevard, half-obscured by a garden approach full of luxuriant tropicals, jacarandas blazing with purple blossoms, tall waving palms. On a tennis court they could just spy through

the foliage, two Indians in shorts and turbans were lackadaisi-
cally batting a ball back and forth. Brilliant-hued parrots flashed
like meteors through the trees. As the limousine passed beneath
them, a swarm of tame monkeys leaped and chattered, pelting
the rooftop with a rain of leaves and pods. Then the drive
widened, curving before the entrance of the hotel where the
manager in a swallow-tailed coat waited to welcome them
effusively.

Honored, honored, honored, he cried, bowing in perfect
rhythm. Allow him, please, to escort them to the Hotel
Splendide's choicest accommodations. Were the gentlemen
aware that many famous personages had been sheltered here?
Oh, yes, it was true. The Hotel Splendide, take his word for it,
had entertained all the great of the world.

The huge lobby was deserted except for one desk clerk and
a tiny bellboy in a uniform two sizes too big for him. No sign
of anyone through the teak-framed opening labeled Bar Lounge.
Not a soul to be seen in the immense dining room which over-
looked the garden in front.

"Looks like we're off season," Marty muttered, intimidated by
the tomblike silence they walked through.

"Front!" The desk clerk called loudly, his voice shattering the
stillness when they had registered. The tiny bellboy leaped
as if stung, and struggling manfully, tried to manage their
luggage.

"Boy, you got more ambition than you have muscle," Shad
said finally. "Here, gimme that." He grabbed his flight bag. "You
just carry the key and lead the way."

Ducking the manager, who was fussing at the desk clerk in
the furious-sounding gutturals of some African dialect, they
entered the grilled lift which carried them by slow jerky stages
upward to the third-floor corridor. Also deserted. No whisper
of sound issued from behind any door. A dusty, musty odor of
desuetude pervaded the place.

"Listen, kid, tell me something," Shad said as they stopped
at a door marked 301. "Is there really anybody but us staying
in this place?"

"Take the Fifth Amendment," Marty advised the boy sourly.

★

"That's a question it won't do anybody any good knowing the answer to it."

But blinking, his small black face a blank under the pillbox cap too large for him, the boy considered the question. Suddenly he smiled. "Is many peoples expecting presently," he piped. "Many peoples!" Then he unlocked the door, and strutting like a puppy with its first bone to chew, ushered them into a mammoth sitting room with tall windows and a balcony overlooking the gardens in front.

"Hey," Shad said, pleased, "dig the view, Marty."

But Marty was too busy staring around him, dismayed by peeling paint, threadbare carpets, the moldly splendor of greasy brocade furnishings which hadn't been cleaned since before he was born. "Jesus," he breathed. "Jee-*sus!* You mean to tell me we got to *sleep* in this place?"

Rushing across to a connecting door, he flung it open, revealing another huge room dominated by a canopied bed as big as a barge. Mildewed mirrors hanging on every wall cast his own face back at him. Through an open door beyond the court-sized bed he spied, then smelled, the cracked marble bathroom where rusty water dripped viscously from corroded taps. In an ornate tub sitting high on brass dragon's paws lay a selection of dried-up insects.

"Is not beautiful?" the little bellboy asked proudly behind him. Then he slid under Marty's arm, and clucking over the entomological display in the tub, began to casually collect the carcasses, using his cap for this purpose. "Will be maid soon," he declared manfully, eyeing Marty's expression. "Good maid. Very pretty."

Groaning, Marty turned away, closing his eyes. For this my momma sent me to college? Golden, you fink. Ah, Abby, you momser. Weakly he opened his eyes just in time to see a large bug of some kind scuttling across the bedroom ceiling. There was indeed no business like show business.

5

Through the long sizzling afternoon both Marty and Shad pretended to sleep—Shad lying under the huge canopy, Marty on a smaller more modest sleigh bed next door which he had policed first for crawlers. Out in the garden, the parrots cried shrilly in the breathless heat; as if in answer, the monkeys chattered and screamed. Somewhere in the simmering city a bugle blew, a motor backfired . . . Or was it a shot? Both Shad and Marty started up in their beds, listening. Then lying back in the damp of their own sweat, each stared upward, thinking hard.

Call Abby? Marty tried to decide and could not. I mean, come on, he argued with himself, a few bugs, a few soldiers around, what's the big tsimmis? This was Africa, after all. The Dark Continent. A guy on a safari has to expect a few items he's not used to, don't he?

But his eyes caught the flick of a lizard down the wall, a shadow of something flying in the gloom above his head. Rising without sound, he crossed to the lattice-shuttered windows, and opening them, suffered the glare and heat pouring in. Anything was better than not seeing, he decided. Better heat prostration than bugs any day.

Shad, too, was trying to make up his mind. How to get away alone—and when—was his problem.

Into the imaginary possibilities which came to mind, the face of Fernando Corraia kept intruding. A frightened black man with a price on his head . . . Or was it all some kind of exaggeration? Some self-important melodrama dreamed up by a has-been?

Like a pendulum, his mind kept swinging to and fro, coming to a stop at the colonel every time. Maybe he couldn't quite believe Corraia, Shad thought, but for sure he had to believe the old man, didn't he? Unless they're both kinky. No, can't think that way. Unless they're both a pair of red-scare kooks.

Groaning softly, he turned on his side, staring mesmerized at a slender shaft of sunlight which pierced through the shutters into his cavernous bedroom. Motes like gold dust shimmered along the beam; where they struck the worn carpet, muted color came to life, psychedelic in the surrounding shadows.

The note which had been folded into his breakfast napkin in Lisbon this morning had given him the name of a contact here. *Without fail talk with Joseph Akabane—grocer—Old Town.* Without fail. He had memorized the name, but the street eluded him for the moment. Old Town, he thought. Was that inside the city?

Then the street name drifted up from another level of recollection. *Shepherd's Lane.* Trust an actor, when he had to, to remember the line.

Shepherd's Lane. But how would he find it? Rubbing sweat from his face, Shad rose and sat on the edge of his bed, oppressed by the stifling, gloomy room, a strong sense that he was playing the fool here.

Beside his bed on a nightstand spotted with cigarette burns stood an antique-looking telephone. Prewar European design, Shad decided. He had seen the same kind in old foreign movies with subtitles. Lifting the receiver, he listened to a pulsing silence. No answer from the switchboard. Maybe there wasn't any—answer or switchboard. Jiggling the receiver bar, he waited again, but nothing happened. "Keerist," he whispered. "Keerist!" Danju schmanju. No picture of mine—and that's a promise, dad—is ever going to get made *here.*

About five the sun was suddenly blotted out by the boiling clouds of an approaching rainstorm. Wind smelling of the sea rattled in the tropical garden. The tall palms bent into wild arcs, fronds turning inside out before the guests. As lightning began to play like fireworks over the white city, the monkeys and parrots in the garden disappeared.

"Hoo—ee!" Shad cried, "*look* at that sky!"

Alarmed, Marty joined him, gaping at the weather. "Wha hoppened? What's going on? Hey, for chrissake, it looks like the end of the world!"

"Grab your love beads, baby—maybe it is."

From the sitting-room balcony, they watched in silence as thunder boomed and torrential tropic rain began to fall.

"Feel that cool, man." Shad breathed deeply. "If I was a nudist, I'd be out there running through that bare-assed as a baby."

"Don't tempt me." They grinned at each other. "And a couple of chicks in the buff, too, maybe?"

"You got a filthy mind, man."

"Listen, Nature Boy—" but Marty stopped, gaping as the rain stopped abruptly and a gigantic rainbow shone over Porto Saba. "Will you look at that? Hey, the sun's shining again! What kinda cockamamey weather is this?"

As the garden began to steam and the monkeys reappeared, they sat mopping streams of steambath perspiration off their faces, drinking Beefeater's neat from Shad's private stock. Streamers of trailing cloud flamed orange and pink and yellow to the west as the storm hit the jungle and traveled onward. Reluctantly Shad said they had better start dude-ing up, since the general's aide would be along pretty soon. "And we don't want to keep those boys waiting, do we? Not with that firing squad they got sitting there by that gate."

A costume designer's dream in his brilliant, formal evening uniform, General Okefe's aide appeared promptly at seven— early, he said, in order to assist them. But assistance, it seemed, meant a kind of briefing. The general was very particular, he explained; it was quite necessary to know the procedure.

"Okay, what's the drill?" Marty said crankily. "We curtsy, maybe?"

Shad hooted. "How's this for starters?" And segueing into a campy performance, he swished two mincing steps forward, gracefully delivering a low, sweeping curtsy.

"Very amusing," said the aide. "But—you shall forgive me, gentlemen—I am quite serious?" Surveying them—Shad tall and lean, Marty shorter and chunkier—each in his new silk Nehru coat, he sighed. "This Hindu style is quite correct in your country for evening wear? I may inform His Excellency of this?"

"Better believe it," Shad answered. "I mean, when Sammy Davis shows for Oscars in one? This is in, man. *In*sville! You tell the general that's the real true word." Taking a turn before a large mildew-speckled gold-framed mirror, he mugged for a second. Then watching the aide in the glass, Shad said casually, "Some guy was telling me you got a neighborhood here called Old Town. How about it? Maybe something we could use for a location?"

Now what kind of a put-on was this, Marty wondered. Since Lisbon they hadn't been separated for a minute. Shad hadn't talked to anybody alone. This was the first *he'd* heard about—

"Old Town." The aide seemed to hesitate, choosing his words carefully. "This is hardly worth your attention, Mr. Smith. Not a town at all, as it might seem. Simply a settlement outside the city."

"Oh, I get it. We must've passed through it coming in, then— right?"

"Yes, that is correct." Disapprovingly, the aide shrugged. "A terrible area as you saw. One of the first projects on His Excellency's agenda." Then he changed the subject.

Because of the curfew, he said, the evening had been planned somewhat earlier than was customary. But not being Europeans perhaps Mr. Smith and Mr. Browm would not be too upset in their usual dining habits? The general wished them to understand that the curfew, while severely kept, was only for the purposes of protection. For the citizens, that was. Their protection.

And there goes any action, Marty thought. Feeling frustrated, he complained about the water supply. "No hot," he grumbled, "and hardly any cold comes out of those taps." No girls, no kicks, no nothing.

"Item two," Shad added, "what's with the phone service around here? We can live with the curfew, but we got to have phones. I tried to call out awhile ago, but—"

"Perhaps some difficulty," the aide interrupted smoothly. "If you will tell me where it is you were calling."

"New York. The hotel where my wife's staying—why?"

Instead of answering, the aide apologized profusely, deploring these faulty services which the general, of course, would make right again soon. "I will speak to His Excellency this evening," he went on. "Perhaps you will be able to call from the palace, Mr. Smith."

"Well now, that's right friendly," Shad drawled. In the mirror again, he glanced at Marty. "These folks run a real tight town here, don't they, friend? Yessir. Real tight."

"I am afraid—you shall forgive me—I do not understand the meaning—"

"Say, talking about service," Marty interrupted, "how about using your influence for me, too, Captain?"

"My rank is Major, Mr. Browm. Of course. There is something you require?"

"A bug bomb." Ready to elaborate, Marty found himself suddenly rendered speechless by the major's horrified expression. He'd never seen a Negro go pale before. "Look, I only meant something to kill bugs," he explained. "Hey—you want a drink of water or something?"

"Bugs." The major shook his head as if to clear it. "Bugs?" Then his color returned. "Ah, insects," he said, and smiled stiffly. "I will notify the management on your behalf, Mr. Browm. Of course we are most desirous of your every comfort."

"What'd I *say?*" Marty whispered to Shad when they were finally on their way out, preceded by the brilliantly uniformed aide. "What was all that tsimmis about me asking for a bug bomb?"

"Dirty word, man. In Danju, bomb is in the four-letter class."

"The—? Oh," said Marty weakly. "Oh, yeah, I get it," and more unhappy than ever, he stepped into the elevator, his heart as well as his stomach sinking as they slowly descended to the deserted lobby.

6

Browm, a voice in his dream said, and he wakened abruptly, aware of blackness and oppressive silence. Reaching out, Marty fumbled for the lamp, found it—but nothing happened. Curfew? he wondered. Meaning lights out, too. Everything in Danju quits at eleven, including—*Gott sei dank*—their so-called parties.

Rolling a sticky tongue around his champagne-dried mouth, Marty thought about the stiff, sedately boring evening which had caused his heavy thirst for bubbly. And he grinned as he remembered Shad's face, unbelieving at first, then finally resigned. What a bunch of squares! He grinned in the dark. Don't anybody tell *me* they got kicks born in the blood.

But ice, they'd had ice, buckets of it. Tortured by thirst, Marty pictured himself tipping up one of the champagne buckets, drinking his fill. No such thing to be had at the Splendide, of course. Should he try that stuff from the bathroom tap?

In his mind's eye, the bathtub rose up, littered with the carcasses of many, many insects. His flesh shrinking while his thirst grew, Marty suffered and prayed for dawn.

Then he remembered the pocket flashlight shaped like a pen which Abby had given him for a going-away present. Big deal, he'd thought then, that cheap momser. But now he was thankful —not too late, he hoped. And where had he put the thing? Where, O Lord.

Tentatively, he sat up in bed, swinging his feet over the side, not touching the floor. Sucking in his breath with urbanite horror, skin crawling, he touched one toe to the dusty carpet. Nothing moved underfoot; after a moment, bravely, he set both feet down. And as he did—eureka!—he remembered where it was. One pen-shaped pocket flashlight right there in his breast pocket where that cheap momser had put it. Here's a present for you, bubele, nothing much, just a little something to remember me by. Well, I'm remembering you, Abby, baby. Cheap conniving schmuck.

Blindly, fumbling, he bumped first into the end of the sleigh bed, and then, after a wild push forward into the thick blackness, into a chair. The very chair where his coat might be hanging? Feeling suffocated, a sense of tiny furtive movement all around him, Marty choked a cry of frustration. Where *was* the effing thing? He scrabbled madly, cursing himself for closing the shutters.

Then his fingers closed on a metal tube. Two metal tubes—one his pen, the other the flashlight. A click in the dark. No miracle light. That cheap bastard, didn't he even put batteries in it? Another try and a blessed little beam shot forth bravely, altering his blindman's view of the world. Boldly, Marty went into the bathroom. The water tasted even worse than he remembered.

Later he was to wonder what had made him stop at Shad's door connecting into the bathroom. Suspicion maybe? Not in *this* town. But anyway, like a good PR momma, he quietly turned the knob and peeped into the moonlight-flooded room. Shad was nowhere to be seen.

Transportation had been his biggest problem—that and dodging the military patrols. But by ducking down alleys and side streets, heading always eastward away from the harbor, Shad had managed so far to avoid an encounter.

Eerily silent except when a patrol cruised slowly by, the streets seemed glazed by the brilliant moonlight. City of the dead, he kept thinking. Great title for a horror pic. Using the light sparingly, keeping to the dark side of each avenue, Shad kept glancing at his watch. Keerist, he'd be all night at the rate he was going, And if Marty just happened to go looking . . . Well, he'd worry about that when it happened.

The tropical sky looked frosted with stars, galaxies, dazzling planets. Like the sky, he decided, of some sci-fic opus. Dr. Urg on Venuscraft X–16, do you read me? Yowsuh, boss. Lost in Waste. Nielsen says go . . . Man, he thought, eyeing the blazing moon, wouldn't Gloria think this was—what? His excitement took a bump and abruptly collapsed. Crazy was what his wife would think. Irresponsible, etc. Chicks just don't dig the adventure bit. He decided to wait awhile before he told her when they got back. And then he decided maybe he never would.

In the mouth of an alley, he spied a bicycle evidently abandoned. And on a second take, in the patch of moonlight nearby, he saw a human foot, bare and still. The bike was an old one with a piece of iron pipe fitted where the handlebars should be. And the foot? Lord God, not a corpse, please.

His scalp prickling, Shad crept closer; close enough finally to hear breathing. A smell of stale alcohol drifted to his nostrils. Twitching his toes, the sleeper gave a gentle snore . . . and a moment later, was the victim of a theft. Pedaling madly, Shad sailed down the deserted street, his Nehru coattails flying behind him.

Shepherd's Lane in Old Town. Joseph Akabane, a grocer. It seemed to Shad he was hours pedaling to the outskirts of the city, and hours longer riding slowly up and down the littered streets as narrow and fetid as Casbah byways. Looking for a name, a sign, any hint of his contact, he dodged scrawny cats that darted spitting away from him, piles of refuse iridescent with maggots. Keerist, the smell! In the black and silver night it was palpable, a presence. The ancient stench of poverty and disease.

Occasionally as he pedaled slowly by one of the tin-roofed shacks, a dog would bark. But no door opened to see who passed, no face appeared at any unglazed window. Yet he sensed eyes watching him, furtive movement behind his back. Where Porto Saba was a city of the dead, this, the Old Town, was a graveyard full of ghosts.

The streets were not marked, nor were most of the anonymous-looking stores, each pasted with weathered posters advertising tobacco and rice and something called millet. Here and there, through a chink in a board, a shuttered window, he could spy lantern light. Did he dare knock on a door and inquire the way? No, Shad decided, best wait for a time. But Shepherd's Lane. Which one could it be?

Then he spotted a sign that was almost unreadable. *J. Aka e Prop.* Inside, a lantern cast wavering light which he could see through floursacking curtains at the roughly cut window. Resting the bike against the thin wall of the shack store, Shad paused for an instant, again attacked by disbelief. Me *here?* And on *what* business? A legion of hard-bitten black faces under battle helmets surged through his mind as the quiet voice of General Okefe said again: "It is ugly, of course. Revolution. Ugly and bloody and merciless, Mr. Smith. But there is no other way, you see. Not for people like us. For us, the only answer, you see, is to destroy. To kill. To kill and kill."

Shivering in the steamy darkness, dizzy suddenly with the stench of Old Town, he smelled again the fumes of champagne and candlewax, heard again the high laughter of gowned women at the sumptuously laden dinner table as the general's quiet voice said *No other way . . . kill . . . kill . . .*

He knocked softly and heard movement inside. The warped door opened a crack, and an eye peeped at him A child's eye, at once wary and innocent. "Hey, boy," Shad whispered. "I'm looking for Joseph Akabane. A friend of his told me to come see him. You dig me, kid? A real good friend."

The door closed. Pressing his ear against it, Shad heard whispering, a clink of metal against glass. Then there was silence and a long wait which tolled like clockwork in the beating of his blood. Kill, the general had said, his mild, brown face untouched by passion or sorrow or remorse. Light from crystal chandeliers had rained down over a meal which would have fed all of Old Town. Around it, the closed, cautious, ambitious faces of men on the make. Black men. But their women had been fine. Were women better at things like conspiracy, revolution? As he waited with his heart thudding like a bird in his breast, Shad thought, maybe yes. But a woman's hand never holds the knife that slices the throat of a good old soul brother.

He was just about to knock again when the door opened. The ragged boy beckoned him in, pausing long enough before he closed the door to look up and down what must be Shepherd's Lane.

His watch read after midnight, going on one. In less than five hours it would be dawn here. Jesus, Marty thought, and then what? They were due at the airport an hour after daylight to board the general's own private plane. Sorry, General, I've mislaid my boy. Trust that swinging spade to find himself some action, even here in the Black Hole of Calcutta.

Since discovering his client's disappearance, Marty had prowled the hotel like a ghost with one eye—climbing stairs (the elevators were off), checking the lobby below, even trying the rooftop reached by a staircase which had creaked and swayed alarmingly under him.

The lobby had been the worst, though—an immense blackness with a single lantern shining on the desk clerk's long counter. In the amber light a soldier had slept, one hand curled laxly around the stock of a rifle.

Like a spelunker lost in some mammoth cavern where dragons lived, Marty had crept through the public rooms of the Splendide, knowing as he did his search must be futile. But if Shad wasn't here, where could he be? Picturing a car waiting, some Danju official's gorgeous brown wife out for a midnight boffing, Marty shuddered for the consequences. Negro Star Dies Mysteriously in West Africa. Shad Smith Banned from Republic of Danju. Oh, mama, mama, what do I *do* with this guy? Every time we hit some burg, he's the original Lone Ranger.

But a niggling suspicion began gnawing at Marty after he had given up his search and returned to Suite 301. First Lisbon— that good old buddy Shad had to visit for a while. Now a midnight ride in this battened-down town. It just don't make sense, he kept thinking. No sense whatever. I mean, in the bright lights maybe, a chick to ball, a few kicks to be had . . . But in Porto Saba? Just don't make sense . . .

The one-room shack was small and dirt-floored, a kind of store and living quarters combined, Shad saw. A few shelves fastened to the walls held meager supplies. At the back, in a shadowy corner was a pallet bed, a nest of rags. Near the hissing oil lamp standing on a packing crate, a stoney-faced woman perched on a rocker with no back. She did not move or speak, only stared at Shad. In the soft unsteady light of the lamp her black eyes glittered, empty, opaque.

"Ma'am, my name—well, you don't care about that," Shad began. "A man you know—a big man—told me to come here and talk with Joseph Akabane." He hesitated. "He your husband maybe?"

"Ta papa," the boy whined. "Ta papa," and fell silent again as the woman looked at him.

"Sonny, if you know where your daddy's at," Shad urged, "you go get him. Will you do that? Get your daddy so I can talk to him?"

But it wasn't any good, nothing he said, for the boy didn't understand English evidently, and the woman only sat there rigid, unspeaking, her ageless face like a carved black bone, impervious to the winds of all his persuasions. In a fever of frustration, Shad tried money at last, but she didn't seem to notice the bills he placed on the packing case before her. Looking around the abjectly poor shack, Shad tried desperately to think what he should do now. Leave a note for Akabane? Try talking to the neighbors?

"Listen," he tried one more time, "I'm here to help, for God's sake. You understand? But I can't help you—or your husband either—unless you tell me how I can find him."

There was a soft susurrus—a sigh?—he couldn't tell. Then, with a slow movement of one hand—a sleepwalker's gesture— the woman signaled to the boy. Some warfare seemed to occur between them, a silent revolt in the boy which the woman's slow dull stare defeated. Hanging his head, the boy scuffed at last through the shadows beyond the lamplight, and crouching in the corner, scrabbled in the nest of rags there. Bringing back a battered tin which had once held pipe tobacco—Rigley's Rough

Cut—he stood silently before the woman. Reluctantly, he set the tobacco tin on the packing case before her. As if this were a ritual which both understood, he pried open the vacuum lid.

Inside lay something withered, dead. And as his stomach caved in, Shad recognized what it was. A human hand. A man's strong fingers, a wedding band. And he understood. His stomach turned over. That was all that was left of Joseph Akabane.

7

The general's plane was an old two-motored Douglas model of a sort which had been used in the forties by airlines in the states. Marty could remember flying on one from Chicago to New York with his grandfather. He was five years old then. Which makes this crate—his mind boggled at the age of the aircraft. Couldn't still be flying, could it? A plane that old? He wished suddenly he'd brought a parachute.

From the low altitude, they could see the city complete below them, the harbor and the wide estuary of a river flowing into it. Referring to a map he had begged off their hotshot, gung-ho pilot, Marty traced the river beyond the coastal plain, through the green mat of jungle they circled over, to its tributary sources far inland. "From the looks of this map it must be wild country back in there," he said, pointing eastward. Through a heat haze shimmering in the distance, they peered inland, but saw only jungle. "According to this—" Marty poked at the stiff cartographer's paper lying spread out on his knees, "there's some mountains and a high plateau." He squinted at the terrain mapped without designating any sign of civilization. "Nothing there for us. The palm of my hand looks more interesting."

Shad kept staring at the river, which made a snake's path across the coastal plain below them, into the jungle *Opp,* the boy had said, *reeber.* Upriver. Remembering the small shadow in the darkness, the frightened glistening of the boy's eyes, he unconsciously shook his head. Where upriver? What?

After leaving the shack store which had once belonged to Joseph Akabane, he had slowly pedaled down the dark street, Shepherd's Lane, his mind fixed, stunned, on that withered, severed brown hand wearing a cheap plated wedding band. Executed? Murdered? His skin prickled over the possibilities of how the woman had got hold of her husband's dead hand.

But a scuttling under his bicycle wheels had shocked him awake. Rats? Cats? Hoping for the latter, he peered into the shadows. Then, in a patch of moonlight, he stopped long enough to light a cigarette, using the gold lighter Gloria had given him for his last birthday. Solid gold, heavy and sleek. It had cost enough, he thought, to feed the Akabanes for a year or more.

Feeling guilty somehow, soiled and spoiled by this revelation, he threw the cigarette away. And from out of the dark a hand reached out, snagging the long, still-burning butt. Transfixed, Shad neither breathed nor moved—until he saw it was the boy again. Akabane's son inhaled deeply, blowing out a long plume of smoke on the hot still night air. "You're pretty young to be hitting the nicotine—"

The boy hissed and made a gesture to silence him. Moving closer, he whispered, "Opp reeber. Go opp reeber." Then trailing smoke, he was gone as suddenly as he had appeared, moving swiftly and silently through the dead shadows of Shepherd's Lane . . .

Go upriver. To where? To what? Watching the land below as it slid by under them, Shad realized then that his question might be—to whom? Somewhere up that wide brown oily-looking waterway was another contact perhaps, help of some sort.

Pointing to the river on the map, he asked Marty what was there, upriver. "Any towns or anything you can see? Any place we ought to have a look at?"

"I told you—nothing." Marty glanced out the porthole window. "Nothing we're going to see on this trip, either. That flyboy keeps figure-eighting like he's on a track or something. Hell, if we wanted to look at Porto Saba and the beach, we could've done it in a car."

"Could be we're seeing all His Excellency wants us to," Shad commented incautiously.

"What're you talking about, 'all he wants'—?"

"Nothing," Shad said hastily. "What the hell, there's nothing but jungle to see, is there?" Then an idea struck him. Hey, how about that, he marveled at himself. The quick-thinking milkman. Like maybe he had a gift for this cloak-and-dagger con? Grinning at Marty, he said, "Five bucks says you can't fly this crate. How about it, buddy old buddy?"

Never a man to turn down a chance to make a fast few, Marty bit on the bait. "The hell I can't!"

"You mean it?"

"Sure. Look," Marty said with the superiority of one whose reflexes have been tested by many sports, "I told you I could fly, didn't I? I'm licensed for everything but jets already." Then suspiciously he peered at Shad. "What you cooking up, Champ?"

"Me? Nothing—just wondering." Again Shad grinned. "Fella can't never tell when he'll need him a flyboy for a friend, now can he?"

This cat is up to something, Marty thought sourly. But what could it be? Running through the usual list of clients' failings—broads, booze, boys, banana peels—he couldn't decide. Had to be something, though. Got to be when a guy comes waltzing home two, three in the morning out of a dead town that's been pitch black for three hours or more . . .

"So what's it this time?" he had yelled furiously last night when Shad had slid in the door. "Another good old buddy? Jesus, you scared me blue! You got friends even in Darkest Africa you got to go play with till three in the A.M.?"

But, oh, the relief seeing that grinning brown face in the trembling light from his pocket flash!

"Man, if you don't sound just like somebody's old lady." Shad had laughed in the dimming beam. He had held up his hands to shield his eyes. "Turn off the spot, Marty. Show's over. Curtain down." And just like that, not another word but good-night, sweetheart, he'd gone waltzing off to bed . . .

Shad yawned. Marty echoed him. "You and your midnight prowling," he grumbled. "I just hope it was good. You got another old buddy lined up for tonight?"

"Nobody but the general. Dinner for three with him and you, baby."

"Another jolly evening." Marty yawned again. "You got a drink handy in your first-aid kit?"

From under his seat, Shad pulled a battered leather traveling bar. In it were two bottles—Scotch and gin—two aluminum mugs, and a large supply of fast-acting purgatives. Years on the road had made him chronically constipated. "Beefeater's, J and B, Ex-Lax?" he offered. "We also have a nice selection of Calso water and Carter's Little Pills."

"Hey, chocolate Ex-Lax, for chrissake. I haven't seen that since I was a kid."

"Think of it as luck, man. If you had my gut you would. How about a little touch of Beefeater's for an eye-opener?"

"Don't mind if I do, guv."

They both sniffed the heady aroma, then knocking back mouthfuls, sighed in unison, longing for ice, tonic, maybe even a lime. Decadent Americans. What a guy has to put up with, Marty thought, broadening himself with travel.

At the Splendide, the general's aide and the hotel manager waited in the lobby with an array of staff behind them. There were maids in starchy uniforms, waiters, an elevator boy, and a tall man in a black uniform with a heavy chain of a sommelier hanging like a golden yoke over his shoulders.

"What happened?" Shad asked, clowning surprise. "The strike over? Business as usual now?"

Unamused, the aide explained that the staff had been away "on holiday." Mr. Smith must remember also that he had arrived a day before he was expected.

"What're you talking about?" Marty bristled. "We said the fifteenth—that was yesterday. I got my watch here to prove it."

He displayed his chronometer, which not only told the time but also the day and month of the year.

"Well, yes," the aide admitted. It seemed that through some error in transmission, their representative in New York had informed the general incorrectly that they would be arriving the day after—which was today, was it not?

"Well, for chrissake, why didn't they say so yesterday," Marty carped when he had the chance. But his irritation was brief, powerless, smoothed away by the busy maids, the two waiters who served them a sumptuous lunch on the sitting-room balcony, a bottle of wine which the sommelier brought, compliments, he said, of the general.

"Show biz." Shad grinned, lifting his glass. "We must've bugged them plenty raising their curtain before the stage was dressed." He sipped the wine. "*If* we did. Ah, this is great, man. You think those chicks in there are Equity?"

"Whatever they are they're—" soulfully—"dolls. You think whoever directed this show would mind if we borrowed a couple of his cuties for the day?" But the maids, though charming, were all mutes, it seemed, able only to giggle when Marty approached them one by one. "You know what I think?" he said finally, exhausted with his efforts. "I think it's some kinda local torture. You know—look but don't touch? No spikka to the ladies?" Glowering through the French doors at the lissome maidens in their rustling skirts who were dusting and vacuuming so prettily, he sighed. "Gimme some more of that fruit of the vine. I see a long dry season's ahead of me."

That afternoon during their siesta, Shad dreamed of his wife, and not pleasantly, for this time she rejected him. No two-bit song-and-dance man for her. She laughed and walked away with her father, clinging like a child to his surgeon's skilled hand. Then later in the dream he saw her sitting in the front row out at Melodyland, crying as he sang about love. But when he went to find her, she had disappeared. The house grew dark, and there was nowhere left to look. He knew in his dream he would never see her again.

Although it was stifling in the huge bed with its drooping

canopy, Shad was shivering when he wakened. His mouth tasted musty and winey still. Along his nerves the sadness and heartbreak of the dream still lingered, seeming now like a warning. Dizzily wakeful, blinking in the dazzle from outside, Shad felt the dire portent of his subconscious, some danger he had not yet faced. And lying on his back with his hands under his head, watching the shadows of palm fronds flickering across the incandescent windows, he listened to the parrots screeching, the insane chatter of the monkeys. No matter how he tried, he could not make himself believe in this blazing, tranquil, tropic afternoon the hazard which his dream seemed to try to tell him.

Up the river. In his mind, the colonel nodded. That's it, Shad. You've got to find it.

But what was it? A person, a thing? Whatever it was, Akabane must have known. Or if he hadn't known, someone thought he did.

A mummy's disembodied hand. In a tobacco tin. The pathetic dime-store wedding ring seemed printed on the air above Shad's head, the exact curve of the fingers, the dull nails, amber colored, split, and roughened from a life of hard work.

No, he thought. Akabane wouldn't have known any secrets. His purpose must have been to point the way. And the dead hand had. He must follow where it directed. Upriver. Somewhere up that brown oily river through the jungles of Danju . . .

"It's great you letting us use your plane, General," he said that evening over the dinner which was served in a small dining room. "But maybe we'll need to have a closer look, too. For scenic stuff. Maybe along that river we saw?"

"The Mobene, yes. There is a riverboat occasionally. If you wish I can arrange for one anytime, Mr. Smith."

"Well, we don't want to cause a lot of bother—"

"No bother, Mr. Smith," the general said calmly. "We are delighted, of course, to cooperate in any way we can."

A searchlight began flickering through the foliage in the garden outside.

"About that river," Marty was saying, "am I wrong in thinking that means crocodiles in this part of the world?"

"No, you are not, Mr. Brom. They are plentiful in our Mobene River . . . Merely a patrol," he interrupted himself in answer to their unspoken question as the searchlight flared in at them. "There is always a good deal of unrest after a change of government, you understand. One finds it necessary to be somewhat more watchful, especially at night—"

A sharp crack of rifle fire froze them in their seats. Swiftly the general pushed back his chair, rising.

Knowing before he asked, Marty said, "Was that a shot?"

"Please do not be alarmed." Small and plain in his ordinary uniform—out of place really in the small elegant room—General Okefe smiled. "But perhaps we should have a little less illumination?"

Must be a generator on the grounds here, Shad decided. Lights out for everybody but the Boss. Except now. Their host crossed quickly to the electric switch. Above them the crystal chandelier dimmed like stage lights. In silence, listening to one another's breathing, they waited. As if on some silent signal, Marty bent over the small dining table, blowing out the candles in their silver holders.

Through the windows came a curious, high keening cry, distant but unmistakable. An animal? A human? His scalp prickling, Shad moved closer to the wide screened panels which were locked shut on the garden. The scent of some night-blooming flower drifted in on the humid air. He could imagine he smelled the sharp pungence of cordite from that single shot they had heard.

A blade of light sliced their protective darkness as the dining-room door was flung open. The major whose name neither Shad nor Marty could pronounce yet called something in a guttural tongue to the general.

"Please be kind enough to turn on the lights," Okefe said.

Reaching out in the dark, the major flicked the switch. A crystal blossom, the chandelier bloomed against the ceiling, turning from a yellow glow into a full white brilliance.

"Gentlemen?" the general said, and returned to the table.

From the doorway, the major watched him, his face grayish.

Remembering his upsetting bug-bomb request yesterday, Marty felt a shivering chill down his spine. Scared then and scared now. What in *hell* was going on out there in that imitation jungle inside the wall?

"Let me pour you more wine," the general was saying hospitably. "That will be all, Major. Please close the door. Mr. Smith—more wine?" He insisted cordially as the door drew slowly shut. "This is a particularly fine year, I believe. A gift to my predecessor from his friends abroad. Pity he cannot be here to enjoy it with us." The general shrugged. "Fortunes of politics . . ."

A frightened black man hiding in Lisbon. And they were drinking with his would-be murderer. Fortunes of politics, hell, Shad thought. This was war. He must remember that. It was war, and as anybody who'd been to one knew, a guy could get killed getting mixed up in a war.

An hour after daylight the next morning, they took off again in the general's plane. But to Marty Shad seemed restless this time, uneasy some way. After patting a lumpy pocket stuffed with Kleenex, he said he was going up front to chew the rag with the pilot. "Maybe he'll have some bright ideas about locations, hunh? Anyhoo, I'll try him, see what he has to say."

Locations, Marty thought gloomily after he'd gone. Meaning we really have to come back to this endsville part of the world? Eccch, I can't hack it. I mean, I really can't! Let Golden do it the next time around, bring his lifesaver doc with him. "Sweetheart," he heard himself saying, "I got my own cardiac to worry about since that free world trip you sent me on to Danju."

His stomach lurched gently as they banked and turned for the tenth time. Mr. Figure-eight at the controls again. For chrissake, couldn't he fly any other pattern? Closing his eyes against the white glare of the morning sun, Marty dozed and dreamed of Beverly Hills. Lust over lunch at the Polo Lounge, say. A frosty gibson by some sassy chick's pool. Oh, mama, mama, am I ever hurting . . .

His eyes snapped open. That wacked-out spade is up to something. Clients, he thought bitterly. Better I should handle polo ponies, and that's the truth. Polo ponies? He smiled feebly to himself. Workhorses is what you want, baby. At least you can lock 'em up when they're not slaving.

Sitting in the co-pilot's seat, Shad gabbled and wisecracked, softening up the pilot—a gung-ho type who'd seen far too many flying movies of an elderly vintage. But he was a big film fan who'd read all the releases the wire services had ever picked up. Knew all about the marriages and tragic ends of Misses Mansfield and Monroe, for instance, the confessionals of long ago given out by Miss Day and Mr. Curtis—feature stuff in the ladies' mags. So troubled, poor artistes, he murmured pityingly. But was not that the way of the world? One rises to fame only to fall ill of its poisons.

"Yeah, it's a little disease called Newman's Law," Shad said finally, tiring of the dialogue. "Your PR guys keep saying you're the greatest, and pretty soon you begin to believe it." Then he steered the subject to imports and exports. Did the Republic of Danju do much business with the States?

"Not at present, I believe," the pilot replied cautiously. "But of course quite soon we expect to be trading again. The general himself assures us we will."

"Then you people must be pretty short of goodies by now. Luxuries, I mean. You know—like canned goods and stuff like that. Sweets," he added. "Chocolate. The big calorie scene."

"Oh, but we will soon again have these items," the pilot said defensively. "Our people do not suffer for these luxuries." But he swallowed visibly as Shad pulled the wad of Kleenex from his pocket, unwrapping it to reveal a foil candy wrapper.

"Chocolate," Shad said, making the words as sweet as the thing it stood for. "Got an awful sweet tooth myself." And he turned the bright foil back, breathing out with relief as he saw that the bar was only sticky, not melted as he'd feared. "Have some?"

"Oh, many thank yous, but no." The pilot couldn't take his eyes off the candy.

"Come on," Shad urged, "I got lots of these. Here," he said generously, "you take this bar, why don't you? I got plenty back in the cabin with me." Leaving the pilot munching happily, he slid out of the seat beside him into the cockpit. "See you later? I got to check with my boy back there. We're going to find us a place to make a picture today."

"Thank you very kindly for the sweet." The plane veered slightly as the pilot turned and smiled, his mouth full of the sticky chocolate.

"How we doing up there, Champ?" Marty asked sarcastically when Shad returned to his seat. "Figure-eighting right by the manual, are we?"

"Don't you worry about a thing, buddy. Just don't you worry, we going to have us a ball yet." Looking satisfied, Shad leaned back and closed his eyes.

A little over an hour later, after a pleasant snooze, Shad sat up and looked at his watch. "What's doing, anything?"

"We're still on that same old track up in the sky, podner. Listen, why waste time like this, Shad? Let's either get the job done or cut out, hunh?"

"Now, don't go getting feverish," Shad soothed. "We're going to do the job all right, believe me . . . How about a little refreshment for your nerves? Very good for the nerves. Old Doc Smith recommends it."

They had a Beefeater's neat, and another right away. Then looking covered-up clever, Shad suggested that Marty try flying this crate.

"Are you kidding? That flyboy would probably get boiled in

oil if he let anybody else take the controls." But even as he protested, Marty got that old feeling. A losing proposition. And anyway, hadn't he walked right into this one yesterday? Yeah man, he had. "Okay, so for five bucks' profit, I'll try," he said finally. "But if the pilot says—"

"He won't." Shad beamed. "I got a feeling that boy *needs* you, Marty—needs you real bad."

How could Shad have known? Marty pondered the mystery for some time after he'd explained to the sweating sick-looking pilot that he could fly, and without a word, the guy had nearly pulled the controls out of the panel, handing them over to him. He had bolted out and in the door of the head. Not a sign of the guy since then. Tourist trots, Marty decided. Must be really bad around here when the locals got them too.

Pleased with himself, he tested the controls and revved the old motors. She was a good enough old bus, he decided—if you liked old buses. And it was fun to be flying again—

"Hey," Shad yelled behind him, and sliding the radio earphones to one side, slipped into the co-pilot's seat beside Marty. "You're too much, baby. You know that? You drive this thing like you was *bawn* to do the job!"

He had the map with him, Marty noticed. And he seemed to understand all about the pilot's sudden attack.

"Turn east," he said, all business all of a sudden, the map spread out on his knees. "Let's go criss-cross clear to all of the borders if we can. This thing got enough gas to do it you think?"

"Gas we got, but how about permission? We can't just high-jack this crate without reporting to the tower."

"Such a law-abiding citizen. Man, it does my old shriveled heart a world of good to see you shape up like this." Shad stopped his hand as Marty reached for the earphones. "Come on, Marty, cool it. You know what'll happen. They'll tell you to get your ass like quick back to that field."

"So—"

"East," Shad said. "I mean it, Marty. I want to cover every inch of this Danju Republic."

Now I'm sure of it, Marty thought as he banked and turned

eastward. But what could it be that Shad was up to? Or after? "Okay, Chief," he said drily, "we're headed east—now it's a search pattern you want?" And his voice hardened. "For what, buddy? What kind of a cockamamey gag are you running?"

"No gag. I just want to look at the country."

"Yeah, sure." Marty spied a wadded foil candy paper on the floor, then. And suddenly, with a chill, he knew the nature of the pilot's unexpected complaint. "Ex-Lax," he breathed. "Chocolate Ex-Lax. For chrissake, are you crazy or something giving the pilot of a plane a dose like that?"

"What's the big flap, man? You said you could fly this thing. Look, relax, Marty, I'll tell you all about it some day."

"Some day, yeah. Like while we're both squatting in some lousy cell in the Porto Saba Alcatraz? Listen, Shad, you can't clown around with aircraft like this. They cost money, see? They're valuable. Guys don't like other guys just running off with their planes."

But it wasn't any good. Shad just sat there looking like the cat that had got one on the wing, tracing on the map as they criss-crossed the country, bird-dogging for what, Marty couldn't guess.

Beyond the green mat jungle lay miles of dry savannah dotted with herds of wild game they couldn't identify. They recognized elephants—you'd have to be blind not to—and right after the elephants, a band of giraffes. Excited in spite of themselves, they zoomed down for a closer look. No stock shot ever gave you what the real thing was like.

The land began to rise after a time, then, and distantly they could see a great rocky projection which the map told them was an escarpment called Abessa. Like a great wall it towered over the savannah, seeming from their view to spring up from the gently rolling land like the thrust of a cataclysm which had only just occurred. Beyond it, they found themselves over an arid land like a moon landscape—all rocks and gullies and formidable wind-sculpted stone formations.

"Looks like Arizona, only worse," Marty commented. "Like to do your picture in that hellhole down there, Champ?"

But Shad wasn't listening. His eyes were glued either on the map or the landscape below. "Half of those canyons aren't even marked here," he said. "Less than half. Even the big ones. I bet nobody's ever even crossed that country down there."

"Maybe not on the hoof." Marty's sharp eyes had caught sight of something which had to be manmade farther ahead to the east. "But sho nuff they been crossing by air." And he pointed. "Look there. See that?"

Squinting in the glare, Shad peered out the window, seeing at first only the rugged biscuit-hued wasteland. Then he spied it: a long smooth track which looked like the work of a giant bulldozer.

"Airstrip," Marty said. "You want to go down and have a look?"

"No, keep circling." Shad swallowed an acid gorge which kept rising in his throat. His eyes burned and watered from the glare. The gin he had drunk rose nauseatingly into his nostrils.

Then his breath caught, he felt throttled by shock as they banked and turned—and below them he saw an enormous excavation containing a spidery structure which, even from this height, looked to be as tall as a tall building.

"What the—?" Marty breathed. "Hey, that's—." He turned in the seat and stared at Shad, his face gone blank with disbelief. "That's a gantry," he whispered as their plane began to wobble. "For a rocket, Shad. Couldn't be anything else. For chrissake, that's a *rocket* silo down there!"

The earth seemed to tilt, then it straightened again. Shad kept swallowing and swallowing, his mouth bitter and dry as he heard again the voice of Fernando Corraia: What does my country have to offer in return? What gift in return for all their generosity? Their. They. They're there, the colonel said. Already there, but where or why in Danju, we don't know. But now Shad did.

"There's a plane," Marty muttered. "Jesus, it can't mean anything, can it, Shad? For chrissake, they haven't even tried to camouflage—"

"Maybe not yet, but they will later."

"What the hell're you talking about, later. Why later? Listen," he cried wildly as the wings wobbled and the plane bucked, "are you trying to tell me—? I mean, are you *crazy* or something? So, it's a rocket base, that don't mean it has to be—" Then he stopped yelling and began to fly again, his freckles standing out like measles on his face. "Oh, Christ," he kept murmuring. "Oh my Christ. And look at that plane. Will you *look* at that plane down there? He'll be up and on our tail in—"

"Let's get out of here."

"Baby, you took the words—" Marty's voice shook so badly he could hardly talk—"right out of my mouth!"

9

He felt like Snoopy in the comic strip Peanuts, Marty told it later. "You know—I'm gonna get you Red Baron, you foul fiend? Only the tables were turned. You better *believe* they were! We lit out of there like a pair of striped-ass apes." And he'd laugh here, pause for appreciation of his modest self-kidding; it made a great story of a great experience, although his telling of it was pure fiction.

For what he really felt like as they streaked westward, seeming to stand still as the other plane closed in, was a hare hunted by bloodthirsty hounds—one heavenly hound with jets propelling it. Mouth dried and hands freezing, he started telling his flight manual like beads in his mind, trying to remember all the dodges he'd ever read about low-level flying.

"Can we beat him running?" Shad kept saying anxiously. "Keerist, Marty, he's almost on our tail!"

"If he's armed—" Marty swallowed—"start praying, buddy. Start praying anyway! And hold on, here we go."

Bucking like an amusement-park roller-coaster car, the old plane fell like a stone, wings flapping, motors screeching, every rivet and bolt straining at the seams.

"What're you *doing?*" Shad yelled as the sunbaked surface of the plateau rushed up at them. His mouth opened in a silent scream. He gulped it back as Marty wrestled the controls, finally pulling back as their swooping shadow raced across the rocks only yards below them, slipping like a sting ray through some clear tideless incandescent sea.

"Where's he now?" Marty asked hoarsely, rivulets of sweat pouring down his face. "Never mind, there's his shadow—"

"Above us to the right." Shakily, Shad examined the fast-looking slinky jet that fish-tailed so near he could almost count the rivets on the plane's underbelly. "Can he force us down?"

"Not—I hope—unless he wants to crack up, too." Feeling fragile, frail now as an ant underfoot, Marty throttled back. "I'm going to try something."

"Hey, you're slowing down!"

"It's our only advantage. He's got the speed, sure, but he'll stall out if he tries to hang here with us." I hope, thought Marty. Oh, Jesus, how I hope. And then what? He could not think.

The jet pulled ahead of them, zooming up, banking sharply in a tight turn. White hot reflections bounced back from the swept-back wing surfaces. Twin trails of dark smoke followed as it swung at them, head on, streaking.

"Brace yourself," Marty said grimly. "He'll probably give us a buzzing that'll straighten your hair."

"Oh, Jesus, look at him. Look at him *come!*"

They both yelled, ducking involuntarily as the jet shot over them, pulling up the second before they crashed. Buffeted by the wash of its passing, the old plane rocked like a rowboat in a storm. Marty fought the controls, sweating and praying, for there was no margin for error at this altitude. Skimming was for kites, not aircraft.

"He's going to try again." Shad swiveled around in the seat, watching as the jet climbed again behind them, turning to streak back, sharklike, implacable.

"Grab that wheel in front of you, and hold it steady," Marty commanded. "But if I say drop it, you drop it fast—dig me?"

Nodding, Shad grasped the co-pilot's controls before him. In his hands, he could feel the pulse-beat of the plane. "Here he comes!"

"Okay, hold her steady, whatever you do!"

Yelling and sweating, arms aching, they wrestled the old airliner's bucking as the jet buzzed them again and again, its wash bouncing them like a cockleshell. The ground below rose and fell dizzily. Fumes of jet fuel billowed against the clear plastic panes of the cockpit, so close did the other plane pass over them.

On the earth below, the shadows of the two planes collided over and over again, slipping free, soaring apart, only to meet once more suicidally. Strained, sick, desiccated by fear, Shad kept thinking of his wife, praying wordlessly, his lust to live so powerful that it seemed beyond hope, beyond prayer, beyond anything like a wish to stay alive. Consumed with this passion, he grinned once at Marty, and with a kind of surging love, felt Marty's own fever, his own desire to conquer this violence which, if they lost, meant certain death.

"Here he comes," Marty yelled.

"Screw him!" Shad cried—and the pursuing shadow gobbled theirs. Cursing like maniacs they fought with gravity, holding the old plane to its ground-skimming course.

Then ahead lay the escarpment of Abessa, and beyond that, the vast savannah. No place to land, no place to hide; neither the brittle earth nor the blazing sky could shelter them, caught as they were in limbo between them.

"Let go," said Marty as they approached the escarpment.

Shad mopped his face, peering in every direction as they went sliding over the towering cliff—at a level so close they could see the textures of the sunbaked ancient rock—meeting their shadow again below. Trying to shade his eyes against the glare, Shad kept looking back, upward, and to either side of them. "That sneaky bastard. I can't see him any place."

"Probably hiding in the sun to see what we'll do next."

"You mean land or something?"

"Quit kidding. That's a washboard down there." Marty blew out his breath, feeling suddenly calmer, free for a moment's rage at Shad. "Jesus, all the goodies you got in this world, now you got to play James Bond games too?" He squinted at the sky. "Where *is* that mother? What's he waiting for? I'm telling you, Shad, this old bucket of bolts can't be good for much more of this knocking around."

They flew steadily on, both searching the heavens as the altimeter needle wavered in the red hundred-foot levels. Had the jet given up? They hardly dared hope as five minutes went by, then seven, then ten. Finally they looked at each other, cautiously hopeful. Below them, clumps of thornbush rushed by, rough cairns of morain-like rock, waterholes dried and crazily cracked.

"Hey," Shad breathed finally, "you think maybe—?"

"I don't know, buddy, so don't stop praying." Cautiously Marty increased their speed a bit, then growing bolder by the minute, lifted their altitude fractionally. "Take another look, hunh?" He swallowed noisily. Maybe they were saved after all? He was afraid to even think it. "He's probably back there somewhere, ready to pounce the minute we lift up . . ."

But there was nothing in the sky behind them, only a vulture wheeling around and around over some dying creature in the bush below. Shad leaned forward in the seat, his drenched shirt unsticking from the leather with a tearing sound. Nothing ahead and above them either—only the empty, white-hot African sky curved like a burning-glass over this wild and empty land.

A hundred feet at a time, Marty increased their altitude, their flying speed. Listening to the steady beat of the old motors, they sat silently, still watchful, not yet free enough to feel optimistic. Fifteen minutes passed, then twenty-five. With a sudden lift of heart, Marty leaned forward and fondly patted the instrument panel. "You're the best, baby—an old bag, but the best." Then flushing, his fear adrenalins transformed into fury, he turned on Shad. "Okay, sport, let's have it, hunh? The big story of Shad

Smith, Snoop? You crazy bastard. I mean, you knocked-out kook! What the hell got you going on this—this *caper?*"

So Shad told him from beginning to end, leaving no detail untold or unexplained.

"Oh, Jesus," Marty kept murmuring. "Sweet suffering Christ!" And by the time Shad was finished, he was speechless with shock. I mean, what do you say? He felt caught in a whirlwind. Nothing he knew made any sense any more. "You mean," he asked weakly at last, "it was *official?* Some intelligence cats really *knew* that base existed?"

"They knew something was going on, but there wasn't anybody to find out what it was."

"So you were elected. A big star, worth a million bucks, they ask you to do their—" then Marty stopped. "They who? What am I talking about? They're my guys, too." He beamed at Shad. "Hey, you know something, Champ? You're some stuff, baby. You are really some stuff! You're that truth they keep talking about that's stranger than fiction."

"Likewise, I'm sure." Surprise blanked Shad's face. He snapped his fingers. "Hey, we forgot! That pilot's still—" and he scrambled for the toilet.

The pilot lay curled on the floor, groaning piteously, certain if he did not die of his ailment, he must surely die anyway when this aircraft crashed. Americans obviously had no fear for their lives, flying in such a reckless manner. He was sure they were doomed by that white man's piloting. A man most assuredly bent on the grave . . .

Suffocated by the stench, Shad propped the door open, trying to reassure his miserable victim. No, it wasn't poison he had given him. Wouldn't he be more comfortable lying in the cabin? A drink might help, a little gin maybe? But the flier only groaned and would not budge; nothing Shad said could make him move.

"Poor guy," he said guiltily after reporting to Marty what he had found. "But, no kidding, Marty, it was the only thing I could think of to do."

"Serves him right for not listening to his ever-loving mama."

"What you talking about, man?"

"Taking candy from a stranger."

In an excess of high spirits, they both guffawed. Even the tiredest gag now would have broken them up. But there was still the problem of what came next. Did they dare land in Danju? Not, they decided, if there was the remotest chance that a radio signal could have been beamed from the interior.

"So, does it stand to reason," Marty challenged, "they wouldn't have some kind of communication?"

"And if they do, it means—" Shad sliced a finger across his throat. "We haven't got a chance if they get hold of us. Anyway, I've got to get the word to the colonel, and fast."

"Grab that map again." Marty inspected the gauges. "I don't know for sure, but I'll make an educated guess. We got about an hour's more flying time left in old Dolly here. That is," he added, "if these gauges are right. On a crate this old they could be way off."

Ahead lay the rainforest and beyond that the coastal plain. Using the river as a marker, they decided to fly due west for another half hour, then north across the Danju border.

"If we could get to Nigeria, to Lagos," Marty said, "we could be in New York like real fast—"

Gloria, Shad thought.

"—but we haven't got the gas, so let's forget that quick."

They decided finally to cross the border, and at the first paved road or airstrip they saw, to land there. "Stands to reason there'll be a phone or something we can get hold of to yell for help," Shad said. "Then whatever way we can, we'll shoot on home."

From high above the jungle they could see the coastal plain finally, the Mobene River flowing into it, the harbor, and Porto Saba. In the sky over the city, a speck glinted, catching the sun. A plane, Marty said, probably circling the city. Their welcoming committee from General Okefe?

Turning north then, they crossed the river that flowed parallel to the Danju border fifty miles away. But unlike the map on Shad's knees, there was no line of demarcation to show them when they were no longer over Danju. Marty made a guess from his instrument readings, and when he thought they had crossed, dropped altitude again, looking for a place they might land.

"What's the map say?" he kept asking. "For God's sake, can't you tell me what the map shows?"

"Doesn't go this far," Shad finally admitted, sheepishly folding it up. "I figured you'd feel better if I faked it for a while."

By this time, Marty saw, their fuel was getting low. Should he head for the coast, try a landing on the beach? Then Shad gave a whoop.

"Look there." He pointed ahead. "Isn't that a town over there?"

"More like a city, I'd say." Marty relaxed. "And—unless I'm mistaken—isn't that a beautiful little airport tower over there on the right?"

Without attempting radio contact with the airport tower, Marty let down over the city, and watchful for air traffic, mindful of the onshore wind, slid into a landing pattern. Signal lights flashed at them frantically. As they drew closer to the long tarmac strips laid down between parklike stretches of trees, they saw a crash truck careening across the field.

Shad crossed his fingers as he had as a boy, squinting ferociously in the glare as the ground rose up. The wings wobbled briefly. Marty kept muttering to himself, pulling knobs and levers, his face looking pale and measled again. Then the wheels struck and they bounced high in the air. Shad sighed gustily as they hit again, staying down to roll this time.

"Old Mama Earth," Marty breathed.

"Yeah, man, and I'm a mama's boy from now on."

As the plane rolled to a stop, several vehicles converged on them—the crash truck, what looked to be an ambulance, and two passenger cars, both long, shiny, and jet black.

"Dig the welcoming committee," Marty said as he unstuck himself from the pilot's seat. "You think we'll have problems about not having our passports with us?"

But Shad was staring out the window at one of the long black cars that carried miniature flags on the front. A diplomatic car, had to be. And the flags were orange, yellow, and black—the same as the banner he had seen in Porto Saba, flying over General Okefe's palace.

10

Protesting feebly that he was better now, the pilot was loaded into the ambulance, looking to Shad more frightened now than griped. What would happen to him? If he were blamed by Okefe for losing control of his plane, could he take refuge in this country? Shad turned to the black man who had ridden in the second limousine. Captain Hougene, he had said his name was, muttering something vague about police. But as Shad was about to speak, he was stopped as the man from the car bearing the flags stepped forward to present himself, not unexpectedly, as the Danju Ambassador's First Secretary. "Mister Hugo Boumette at your service!" he cried, clicking his heels, looking anxious and concerned. "You must reassure me immediately. All of us—" he gestured toward Captain Hougene and two men with him who looked like professional assassins—"you are quite well? You are not in need of medical attention?"

"If the gentlemen will accompany me to the terminal building," Captain Hougene said, without waiting to hear their reassurances, "perhaps we will take a statement?"

"But—for what purpose?" the Danju First Secretary asked blandly. "Please, must we further complicate this unfortunate incident?"

"We'll make a statement, all right," Marty said, glancing at Shad. "How about it, Champ?"

Shad nodded. Maybe when they were alone, he thought, he could ask Hougene to help the pilot.

"Statement," Mister Hugo Boumette was saying with theatrical distaste, his black Arabic-looking features haughty and scornful, as if of barbaric practices. In his immaculate white shirt, sincere tie, gray weskit and black coat, he was the essence of diplomatic disdain. "Such an unfortunate necessity. Surely a statement could be waived under these circumstances?"

Stalwart, middle-aged, policeman written all over him, Hougene shrugged. He opened the rear door of his black car. "Gentlemen?"

They got in. Hougene slid into the front seat beside the driver, turning so that he faced them. His aides were left to walk to the terminal building. Both looked sweaty and very unhappy as the car slid away through the sizzling heat, followed by the Danju limousine.

"Now," said Hougene emphatically, "off the record, as they say, you will tell me, please, what has occurred?"

"Why off the record?" Marty asked. "Can't we wait till we make our statement?"

"A pilot falls ill. Fortunately the passenger is able to fly his plane." Hougene smiled slightly. "A great misfortune is avoided by a miracle. General Okefe himself called our president, asking that we do not detain his illustrious visitors. Such a curious word in this instance—detain." He examined his shiny fingernails then, as if waiting for either Shad or Marty to speak. And when neither did, he went on: "There was, one understands, a general alarm throughout all of West Africa. Needless to say there is great rejoicing in all states that the illustrious visitors to Danju are thankfully safe from harm." He looked up then—a penetrating glance at Marty, then Shad. "The alarm went out hours ago, gentlemen. Hours. As soon as contact with the plane was lost. One may wonder then—since the passenger was able to fly here—why he did not fly directly back to Porto Saba?"

As Shad opened his mouth, Marty nudged him. What's a PR man for if he doesn't have the answers? "Well, Captain," he hastily extemporized, "it sounds pretty crazy, I guess. But the fact was, I got turned around. You can up there, you know. Just like trying to navigate in an open sea sometimes."

"I see. You lacked—what is the word? Ah yes—bearings? Is that it?"

★

"That's it, Captain."

"Then where did you fly while you were—lost? Inland, perhaps, across the Abessa Escarpment?"

"No, just around," Marty lied smoothly. "A figure-eight pattern. Over the jungle mostly. We just kept flying till we spotted this field."

They had pulled up by this time, stopping before the modernistic terminal building. As Hougene and the driver got out of the front seat, Shad whispered, "Why didn't you *tell* him?"

"Without witnesses? Listen, for all we know, he's trying to pump us for that other one. The Danju cat." He grinned out at Hougene when the door was opened. "Plenty hot here, isn't it? You think there's any chance of us getting a little drink maybe?"

"Of course, I will see to it. If you will follow me, gentlemen?"

The terminal was jammed with African travelers, some stately in their flowing robes, others sweltering in Western clothing. A family of Indians took emotional farewell of each other, weeping, kissing, bowing with the palms of their hands pressed together. Immaculately dressed children dodged wildly through the crowd, their faces shining with excitement.

"This way," said Hougene, leading them away from the babel-like din down a long corridor to a silent office. "Naturally, Mister Hugo Boumette must be present during our interview, since you are guests of his government." Again he smiled slightly, his tough black cop's face full of an ironic intelligence. "Perhaps you will wish to have spoken freely as we rode in the privacy of my car?" Then he shrugged. "Well, no matter—"

And Boumette bustled in, sweating slightly now, his fresh collar perceptibly wilted. "Such a pity all this," he was saying mournfully. "So trying for Mr. Browm and Mr. Smith after their unfortunate flight. So unfair, also, to the charming Mrs. Smith after all her hours of worry."

Shad gaped at Marty. Looking sourly at them, then around the small stuffy office, Captain Hougene pulled up a pair of straight-backed chairs, gesturing for them to sit.

"Mrs. Smith," Marty said when he had regained his voice. "You did say *Mrs.* Smith."

"Yes, Mr. Browm, that is what I said."

"But—" Shad stopped then began again. "But, my wife's in New York."

"Oh, no." Boumette beamed. "It was to be a surprise, you see."

"You mean she's here?" Marty asked weakly. "I mean there? In Danju?"

Shad sat down suddenly and stared at the floor while Hugo Boumette explained to them that while they were still in Lisbon, the Danju representative to the UN had personally carried General Okefe's invitation to Mrs. Smith at her hotel in New York. "So pleased was the general over Mrs. Smith's graceful acceptance that he has planned a great ball in her honor this very evening. And for the gentlemen, a ceremonial hunt tomorrow." Then Boumette's face fell. He wrung his hands. "Poor lady," he cried. "No sooner did she arrive than your plane was reported missing! General Okefe himself took the terrible news to her, and stayed by Mrs. Smith's side through all these long hours!"

"Does she know we're safe?" Shad asked dully.

"But naturally, Mr. Smith. As soon as your plane was sighted, His Excellency, the ambassador, personally contacted the general."

Marty looked dizzily around the room. A blackface nightmare. Witnesses, he thought, sickened as he recalled his own cleverness. Too late now to try to tell anybody. Didn't dare now.

Looking bored in the silence, Captain Hougene sighed deeply. "Well, gentlemen?" he said finally. "Shall we make our statement?"

You win a few, you lose a few. But at Russian roulette, you only lose once. Thinking later about that stuffy little office, the lying statement they gave Hougene, Marty decided they had to be the worst moments of his life. So near yet so far from freedom, from safety.

Shad made his statement like a hypnotist's victim, his famous voice lifeless, his expressive face blank. and when Hougene thanked them ironically for their patience, he rose like a sleepwalker and without answering, headed for the door.

Following him, Marty whispered, "Take it easy, Champ. We'll be all right—"

Behind him, Hugo Boumette was saying brightly that His

Excellency, the Danju ambassador, would be delighted if they would consent to take tea with him. By that time the plane would be checked out, refueled, and ready again. A distinguished pilot had already been engaged to fly them back to Porto Saba...

Porto Saba. Their prison now? And you shall henceforth be taken to a place of detention where on a fixed day of this calendar month you shall be—

But the moment of our deaths is mercifully unclear to us.

11

"Oh, baby," Gloria cried, clinging to him. "Shad, baby, what I've *been* through today! What *happened* to you? I've nearly gone crazy. Shad, they wouldn't say *any*thing except they'd lost contact with the plane—"

"So regrettable," General Okefe's aide was saying to Marty, "that as well as the aircraft, Mr. Browm, you were not also able to manipulate the radio."

"Well—" Marty swallowed nervously, watching Shad who still looked numb. "I guess I never thought about it." He tried a laugh. "Believe me, it took everything I had to fly that thing!"

They both looked at the plane which a lackadaisical flight crew clambered over, securing it. Their "distinguished" pilot had already gone, whirled away in a waiting army vehicle.

"By the way," Marty said as casually as he was able, "what happened with our other flyboy? He's okay by now, I guess. We asked the ambassador, but—"

"Your pilot is resting, as they say, comfortably. Here in Porto

Saba." Hot as coals, in his calmly smiling face, the major's eyes fixed on Marty's for an instant. "We have his full report, incidentally. A most interesting story. His Excellency found it fascinating."

"—And I was so lonesome in New York," Gloria was saying. "Shaddie, you're not mad, are you, I went along with this gag? It seemed so kicky having that delegate call on me—"

"Yeah, they told me all about it. A big surprise."

"Well, you needn't sound so downbeat—"

"Hey, Champ," Marty stepped into the breach—a good PR man to the end, he thought. "You still reeling, hunh? Listen, Gloria, the way we heard you were here! Like socko, baby, right outta the blue. I mean, how could we guess? Isn't that right, Shad?" Beaming, he included the major, then. "Looks like we almost bollixed up the general's act, right?"

"His act, Mr. Browm?"

"His surprise, I should have said. Having Gloria here."

"Indeed. Well, I am sure His Excellency is only thankful now that our fears for you today were not, after all, necessary."

"Yeah," said Marty on a falling note. "Yeah, sure."

Gloria beamed at him, taking his arm and Shad's, linking them as a threesome. "You sassy swingers. I want to hear what you were *really* up to, disappearing like that. Thought you were going to get away from momma and have a few kicks, didn't you?"

"Oh, we had 'em," Marty said, more weakly than he had meant. "Believe me, honey, we've had a coupla kicks."

"This is a word I do not understand," the major said very quietly. "Kicks."

"Adventures," Gloria explained before Marty could stop her. "It's sort of hip-type idiom . . . Look, I'm frying in this sun." She glanced at Shad. "You look so funny, baby. Aren't you *ever* going to say anything?"

"Give me a chance." He looked at Marty. "Anyway, you heard the man. I'm reeling." And he kissed her.

"Attaboy," Marty cried. "Make 'em know it!"

His heart feeling squeezed by iron fingers, Shad made himself grin, made himself perform. "Hey," he murmured to his wife, "new threads?" wondering how long he would be able to fool her. "What's this you're wearing—mini-mini?"

"Like it?" She took a Twiggy pose before the three men, radiant in the heat, dismissing for now her flickering sense of something strange in her husband, something artificial.

"Most charming," the major commented mildly, his African modesty affronted by the scarcity of her mod dress.

Again it was Marty who filled in enthusiasm. "Wow," he said soulfully, and meant it, for she was even more gorgeous, he decided, than Diahann Carroll. And that is some gorgeous. Gloria's legs were beautiful—and so much of them to see. Long, brown, groovy as Dietrich's. Better, maybe, he couldn't remember. La Kraut now performed in floor-length beads.

For the first time, in this state of anxiety, Marty experienced a kind of envy, looking at Shad and Gloria. Maybe he better start looking for a wife, too? Then, as he glanced at the waiting major, reality struck him like a blow from the dark. Chances were he'd never have the chance now. *Merde,* he thought, we'll get out of this somehow.

A loud roaring echoed across the airport then, and squinting in the low sunlight which struck in brassy bolts on the tarmac, they watched a line of dump trucks filing out onto the field. "What's going on?" Marty asked the major.

"Pardon? Oh, that." General Okefe's aide smiled subtly. "Repairs, Mr. Browm. Regrettably, we find we must close this excellent airport for a time. His Excellency, General Okefe," he explained to Gloria, "is always mindful of such matters as public safety."

Shad and Marty exchanged a blank look as Gloria said, "But how're we supposed to get out of here if it's closed for repairs?"

"Not to worry, Mrs. Smith." Again the major smiled. "Be assured that His Excellency will arrange everything."

"Well, if you say so." She turned to Shad. "Baby, you're dead, aren't you?" And as he gaped at her, appalled, she went on innocently, "You've got to have a nap before that wing-ding this evening. You'll get rested in a couple of hours, won't you? Won't he, Marty? Shad, this place is really the most." Again she took his arm. "And the major. He's been darling to me. Took me all around what they call the marketplace this morning when I got here. And, Shad, I saw the darlingest things to take home with us. And so cheap! I'm just dying to have one of those white robes the men wear. You know the ones I mean?" They walked slowly in the blazing heat of early evening to the limousine that awaited them.

Once more as the sun dipped in the west, great billowing clouds boiled in off the sea, blotting out the sunset. Wind lashed the palms lining the boulevards. As they passed through the city, its white-robed inhabitants fled the storm, taking shelter in doorways as the limousine passed. By the time they had turned into the garden in front of the Splendide, the first huge drops began to plop-plop down on the roof of the car. A second later they were buried under a torrential downpour which roared like kettledrums all around them.

The desk clerk ran out holding a mammoth umbrella. "I feel like a potentate," Gloria said under its shelter. "Next thing you know I'll be wanting a palanquin."

"A what?"

"Sedan chair. You know. One of those fancy rigs they have in all the biblical movies? Queen of Sheba stuff."

Trying to match her gaiety, Shad laughed as they ran up the steps and waited for the umbrella to return with Marty. How could they find a chance to talk alone, to plan? Talk, he thought, like with every room probably bugged.

"Speaking of rain," Marty puffed as he dashed up to meet them. "Where Ah comes from, podners, this here means floods."

"The poor monkeys," Gloria mourned. "Where do they go, I wonder?"

"Ask his nibs," Marty cracked, jerking a thumb toward the major who was sedately climbing the wide entrance-way steps to shelter. "He probably doubles in the front office there."

"Hey," Gloria protested, giggling. "You got a grudge or something, sweetie?"

"Nothing a few less brass buttons wouldn't help," Shad filled in hastily. "This cat hates uniforms, I find out. Says this place reminds him of—" He grinned as the major arrived beside them. "Nice weather for ducks, Captain."

"It's major," Gloria hissed, looking puzzled.

"Sorry about that. How about a drink, Maje? That is, if I've got any left in old Doc Smith's handy medicinal supply."

Marty held his breath, thinking, Oh no, not again, as he pictured the gin and Calso-water highball which would put the general's aide on the absent list this evening. But the major said no thank you, perhaps later. He would return at nine o'clock precisely to escort them to the Premier's Palace.

"Precisely nine o'clock." Marty imitated him as they entered the lobby and crossed to the elevator. "Pree—cise—uh—lee!"

The elevator gave a great leap upward, throwing them back against the gilded filigreed wall.

Gloria watched the desk clerk's amazed face slide out of sight below them. "These poor people. They won't know what hit them after you two have gone."

Over her head, Marty looked at Shad. The three most precious words in the language? *After we've gone.* Or were they the most doomful? On both their faces were hope, dismay, a lingering disbelief.

The elevator stopped, and as Gloria stepped out, the door to the sitting room swung open. On the other side stood the smiling sommelier, and beyond him, on a table, champagne chilling in a huge silver urn.

"Home was never like this," Shad said, and as Gloria stepped in ahead of them, again looked at Marty, unbelieving.

"Oh, bubbly, bubbly, the Yiddish downfall," Marty cried rubbing his hands together briskly. "Compliments of His Serene Excellence, I presume?"

"Of General Okefe. Right, sah." The sommelier beamed. "Shall pour now, or later, please?"

"*We* shall pour now." Shad tipped him. "Thanks, that's all." As the sommelier bowed himself out, Shad poured three glasses, taking a quick gulp ahead of everyone else. "Ah, that's better. Keeps the mildew out."

"Is that why I like champagne?" Marty took his glass and began to wander around the huge sitting room, idly peering behind chests and under tables. "I always thought it was good for—" he stopped, peeked at something behind a garish oil painting of charging Arab horsemen, then went on—"the imagination. You know—you think you imagine something—" he looked at Shad— "and then, after a glass of bubbly, you realize all of a sudden it's really so?"

"What in the world are you talking about?" Gloria asked. "Marty, are you looking for—?"

"Great connoisseur, this guy," Shad interrupted. "Didn't you know that, baby? Marty's always looking for that off-beat piece that'll send some art dealer right up the wall."

"Well, at the risk of sounding snide—"

"Don't say it," Marty advised her. "I had the same reaction to this palatial slum we fondly call our accommodations." He lifted his glass. "Well, here's to it, kids—long may it wave." And he wondered if the general was listening in.

12

"Champagne, champagne," Shad intoned, resting his glass on his naked chest. "Makes hearts happy. Makes hearts light. Hard hearts. Broken hearts. All kinds, makes 'em—" Abruptly he sat up, spilling a little from his glass. The drops frothed gently on the laundry-thinned sheet. "Speaking of hard hearts—you just going to sit there brushing your hair while your poor old daddy keeps a-suffering in his bed?"

"You go to sleep like you're supposed to." Gloria kept on counting brushstrokes, her face on the moldy mirror that of a sorceress in the gloomy room.

Outside the shutters, the cloudy sky shone like polished brass in the afterglow of the sun now far below the horizon. The heat was tremendous, steamy, overpowering. Against the ceiling, a slow old-fashioned fan stirred the humid air as gently as a chef stirring soup. Parrots screeched in the dusky garden in front of the hotel, but the monkeys this time were silent after the storm.

"That's the last word, hunh?" Shad asked. "Sleep?"

"The very last." Gloria put down the brush and in the mirror studied him. "Maybe then you'll feel like talking."

"What about?"

"Oh, Shad, stop. I know an act by now when I see one. You and Marty have been playing verbal ping-pong over my head for the last hour."

"I don't dig you, baby." He slid down under the damp sheet again. "But I guess it's all right. You'll let me in on what you mean when you're ready." Avoiding her steady gaze on the mirror, he pounded his iron-hard pillow futilely. "What a dump this is." He pretended to yawn then closed his eyes. "Wake me up when they sound the beat."

Watching him in the mirror, Gloria caught her long silky black hair back in a severe knot, fastening it with two hairdresser's clips. What's bothering him? she wondered. Something, for sure. She knew him too well to be fooled by all his fooling. But what could it be? Something happened today—something worse, maybe, than that story they had told?

As she tested her own feelings, suspicions, her face in the glass took on the arrogant blankness of a fashion model's. And behind its beauty, her mind worked like a computer, trying this answer and that. Not for nothing was she the daughter and granddaughter of scientists.

Through slitted eyelids, Shad watched her lovingly, desire and fear warring in him. Could they keep her off it, protect her from knowing? Ah God, he thought, what a lousy hangup. If only he'd told the colonel—but he couldn't have, could he? From hindsight, the answer always looks different.

There was a rustle as she moved, silky and soft. Then he smelled her fragrance as she stopped near the bed. A shadow crossed his eyelids—her hand, he guessed—confirmed an instant later when the champagne glass was delicately pulled from his lax fingers. As it clinked gently on the nightstand near him, Shad was tempted to reach out, pull her to him, tell her everything. In the dripping dusk she would love and understand— what? That he had trapped them all? His inside squirmed. His scalp crawled. Wonderboy Smith has gone and done it, all right. Newman's Law, he thought bitterly, remembering his explanation to the pilot he had tricked. He'd begun to believe his own publicity. The beginning of the end, man.

In the cavernous bathroom a tap was turned, water trickled hollowly into the claw-legged tub. Then the door shut. He heard it latch, and waiting what seemed an endless time, Shad finally heard his wife splashing in her bath.

Grabbing his silk robe off the bottom of the bed, he padded barefoot into the sitting room, but Marty was not there. As he started for Marty's bedroom door, he heard a wicker chair creaking on the balcony. Letting out an unconsciously held breath, he turned toward the wide screened open doors. "Hey," he called softly to the dim shape sprawled in a lounge chair.

Wicker creaked loudly as Marty sat up. "What's this? You two have a fight or something?"

"Glory's taking a bath. Listen, buddy, we've got to talk and fast."

"Here, maybe, but no place else in there."

"You find a bug behind that picture?"

"Yeah, just like the movies, boss. You go look for yourself you don't believe me."

"It's probably a phoney."

"Like hell it is! I saw it—"

"Okay, so you saw it." Shad slid down onto the tiled balcony floor beside Marty. It was wet from the rain and mercifully cool. "Listen, Mart, planting bugs behind pictures went out while you were still playing at your mama's knee—"

"Or—like the joke says—at some other low-down joint?" Marty sniffed at his own antique humor. "So, it's outdated planting bugs behind pictures. Isn't everything else in this place the same vintage?"

"The furniture maybe, but not the smart boys behind all this.

You saw what was back there in those mountains. Did that look outdated to you, buddy?"

"Okay, so let's have the news."

"Jesus Christ, how I wish I had it!" Shad gnawed his thumb. "They must've spotted me in Lisbon. With that—" He stopped, groaning. "What a lousy scene. I ought to be shot."

"Don't hold your breath, baby—they might just oblige you." Marty sucked in his breath. "Listen, what're we gonna do, that's what I want to know."

Shad rubbed his head, his mind a blank. "That bug's got to be phoney. Something they put there for a couple of hip types like us to find—"

"So we find it—then what?"

"I don't know. Honest to Christ, I don't know how we should play this!"

"Play, he says. What you're missing is your scriptwriters, baby. You think it matters how we—quote—play—unquote?" His face spectral in the deepening darkness, Marty cried softly, "What we've got to think about, man, is getting out of here! Like up, up, and away—you dig me?"

"How, for instance?"

"How the hell should I know? You're the big noise around here. *You're* the one they elected Spy of the Year. *You* tell *me* how we get out of this mess, and I'll be only too glad to keep playing Follow the Leader!"

"Okay, okay, calm down. Cool it." Shad gnawed his thumb again. It tasted salty, he noticed vaguely. Man is a creature, he had read somewhere, made of solids and liquids. Salty solids and saline liquids. They even had the formula just how it went, but no genius yet had found the magic to make it live . . . "All I know to do is play it by ear," he said slowly. "They can't murder us in cold blood, for chrissake."

"You hope."

"But they've got to shut us up somehow."

"As if I didn't know. Like three hairy accidents maybe? Big news for a whole day or two." In the long silence that followed, Marty sighed finally, only half-joking as he added, "I sure did want to live at least long enough to see the first Mars shot."

"The first—? Oh, for chrissake, *space*."

"Well, it's important, man!" Marty shook his head. "You show-biz cats. There's nothing happening but you, is there, baby?"

"Right now, no. Just me—and incidentally, sweetheart—*you*."

"Not to mention your wife." Marty hesitated. "That's the big hangup, isn't it?" Then he softened. "Sorry, Champ. Believe me, I dig what a skunking it gave you when that jazzy diplomatic cat came on with that one. All of a sudden it was for keeps— right?"

"I can't take any chances, Marty. Not with—"

"I know, I know." Again Marty sighed. "Like we both know the answer. We got to play it cool and split when we can. But the big sixty-four-dollar one is—"

"Shad?" Gloria's voice drifted out—from nearby, Shad guessed, in the sitting room.

As Marty started up, Shad pushed him back in the chair, calling, "Yeah, baby, we're out here."

"You're supposed to be sleeping." She seemed to float in the dark onto the balcony. "What're you two doing out here— hatching up something *else?*"

Ignoring her emphasis, Marty said they were trying to cool off. "But it's no good. You know, I figure the mean temperature here is about the same as the steamroom at the Beverly Hills Health Club?"

Gloria laughed dutifully, and leaning against the railing, sniffed the verdant tropical air from the garden below. "I know it's terribly hot. But it's beautiful here too, isn't it? So peaceful. Just look at the city. All the lights look so little and fuzzy."

"Enjoy, you're entitle," Marty said. "They go out promptly at eleven."

"You're kidding."

"Wait, you'll see. They got a hundred-percent curfew here even a baby would squawk about."

"Come on, sit down." Shad pulled a chair so he would be sitting between the two of them. "Have a nice bath?"

"I guess you might call it therapeutic. That is, if you can absorb iron by osmosis through the skin."

"Just think—if you can," Marty quipped, "no more tired blood."

But no one laughed. Aware of his wife's scrutiny, Shad touched her lightly. "Drink, baby?"

"No more champagne for me. But if anybody mentioned Scotch right now—"

Shad bounded to his feet in one jump. "How about you, Marty?"

"Gin, thank you kindly, sah."

"I wonder what'd happen if I asked for ice?" Shad snapped his fingers. "I'm fixin' to try just that!"

"What's eating you two?" he heard Gloria asking as he crossed half-blindly to the phone in the sitting room. There was a lamp on the table beside it. He heard Marty make some laughing answer as he switched the lamp on and the bulb glowed like a huge firefly in the velvet darkness.

"Sah?" A switchboard voice answered surprisingly, almost at once.

"I marvel," said Shad. "Look, is there any chance of getting some ice up here?"

"Ice. Certainly, sah." He heard the man breathe once, twice. "You are aware, sah, of the message in your box?"

"Message! No. Who's it—uh, never mind. Send it up with the ice, will you?"

Fernando Corraia, he thought as he hung up. By some wild chance—? He stopped himself from hoping. Fernando Corraia was helpless here. As helpless, he realized, as he himself was. The message was probably a gambit—the opening play in the fatal game between the three of them and General Okefe.

13

Behind the high gates of the Premier's Palace the peacocks had disappeared, the flocks of doves, but in the dark gardens, torches flickered. Patrols? Marty wondered. Had to be. Tonight every tree probably had a marksman behind it. But once inside the brilliantly lighted building, all sense of hazard, reality, was gone. The ball was like a lavish fairy tale told by the Danjuans to lull them.

At one end of the grand ballroom blazing under crystal chandeliers a military band sat on a raised dais playing Strauss waltzes and sedate foxtrots. At the other end of the quarter acre of waxed floor stood a buffet bar featuring a champagne fountain. Waiters with bubbly, laden trays circulated among those who watched the dancing. Fans flickered in jeweled, black hands. On the breasts of the gentlemen, decorations gleamed.

"You know what I feel like? Cinderella!" Gloria cried after she had danced for half an hour and finally nailed Marty, forcing him onto the floor with her. "Doesn't this remind you of something?"

"Yeah," said Marty, counting step-slide-close like at dancing class all those years ago, "an old, old De Mille production."

"And all in blackface. Crazy, ain't it?"

Gloomily surveying the gowned black women and their splendidly uniformed escorts, he sighed, wishing that were his only problem. "Don't rattle those color chains, beautiful. I only meant the music."

"I know you did." She laughed in his face. "Smile pretty and say cheese now, baby. That lens over there is pointing our way."

Blinded by the flash from the Danju newsman's camera, Marty kept moving his feet to the dragging beat—step, slide, close, step, slide, close—his mind fixed on the message they had received.

"I bet you danced better at your bar mitzvah."

"I'll dance better at my own funeral."

"It is kind of draggy." Gloria leaned against him briefly. "Cheer up, baby, maybe they bugaloo at midnight."

A piece torn from an old sheet of music. What could it mean? (Step-slide-close.) What kind of message was a scrap of score printed by G. Schirmer, Music Publishers?

It was old, Shad had said, he knew that much. If Marty didn't believe him, take a sniff. "That's real bottom-of-the-trunk stuff, buddy."

"So, it's bottom-of-the-trunk—what does that mean?"

Shad had rattled ice the bellboy had brought them with the message, making ordinary noises for Gloria's benefit. She was still in the bedroom dressing. "Pour you big or little, baby?" he had called.

"Little—and loaded with ice, please!"

"Roger, over and out! Means something, yeah," he muttered. "But what, for chrissake?"

"Listen, you read music. Maybe it's in the notes?"

With a handful of ice poised dripping over a glass, Shad had studied it, humming a scrap of melody which neither of them could recognize. "Real square old harmony," he said. "Look at that chord progression. Strictly schmaltz Guy Lombardo stuff."

"Now about that drink!"

"Comin' up, baby!"

Glaring at the scrap as if to scare its secret from it, they both sighed unconsciously.

"What bugs me right now." Shad inspected the drink he had poured for Gloria, adding more ice. "How'd it get here? There's got to be a catch. Either that, or the desk clerk—somebody here in the hotel's on our side."

"So, what's the difference? We don't know what the cockamamey thing means anyway."

Before nine o'clock when the major arrived, they tried all the
obvious things they could think of—a transatlantic call was impossible, they were told, since regrettably there seemed to be
trouble with the circuits; then a cablegram which the man at the
desk assured them would be sent out first thing in the morning.
To whom did the gentlemen wish the message addressed? Abby
Golden, they decided, who else was there? And the message
itself—well, just help will do, Marty thought, get us the hell out
of here. But the chances of any contact were so dim, they decided, they might as well play this one straight down the middle.
"Need assistance," he dictated over the phone, glancing at Shad.
"Locations so far undiscovered. Charter ship and crew immediately for coastal cruising."

"Hey, I like that," Shad whispered. "Coastal—"

"—Cruising," the desk man repeated. "Yes, sah. This is the
total message, sah?"

Marty hesitated. "No, add this," he said. "Confirm soonest.
You got that?"

"Confirm soonest. Yes, sah."

"Dreamer," Shad muttered. "But at least it'll give 'em something to think about." Then peeking into the bedroom where
Gloria was still busy, he continued in a conversational tone after
Marty had hung up: "You think there's a chance they might send
that?"

"Not unless somebody makes a mistake."

"Yeah, like never happen here." Shad sliced one finger across
his throat. "Too expensive these days."

"What's expensive?" Gloria called from the bedroom.

But the major arrived then, resplendent in a white military
monkey jacket with gold shoulder boards and black instep-
strapped trousers with gold braided stripes down the seams.

"You're a dream, Maje," Shad said, closing the drawer where
they had concealed the scrap of music score. "Come on out of
that bedroom, baby, we're on!"

The dancing would begin in precisely half an hour, the major
announced. With Mr. Smith's permission, Mrs. Smith would be
His Excellency's first partner of the evening.

"What fun," Gloria cried, her voice muffled. "The belle of the ball, that's me." And breathtaking in a Grecian-draped white chiffon gown, she whirled out of the bedroom, making a Loretta Young entrance. "Don't bother to applaud, boys, you might turn my head."

Five minutes later they were on their way.

"Gloria says she feels like Cinderella," Marty reported after he had circulated the ballroom for another half hour and finally caught up with Shad again. "Tell me, ole buddy, what do *you* feel like?"

"Why talk about it?" He stopped a passing waiter, taking a pair of glasses off his tray. "Here, have some giggle juice, it's just what you need."

"Not me, friend, what I need is air. Like about ten thousand miles of it, say—between me and this place?"

"Then, I am not wrong in my suspicions," a mild, now-familiar voice said behind them. Whirling around, they both gaped at the general, who smiled benignly. "Forgive me for eavesdropping, but I did fear Mr. Brom might not be enjoying himself tonight."

"Who says I'm not?"

"Then you are, Mr. Brom?"

"Sure," Marty lied. "I'm having a ball."

"So glad, Mr. Brom." The general turned to Shad. "No ill effects then, from your trying day?"

"None at all, General." Shad beamed at him. "Everything's comin' up roses with us."

"Splendid. May I say how I enjoyed dancing with your charming wife? She seems delighted to be here in Danju—" and his tepid smile broadened. "We, of course, feel most fortunate in having her."

"I don't doubt that for a minute, General."

"Yes. Well." As if distracted by some troubling idea—a small man in a plain black uniform—he glanced around the ballroom, clasping white-gloved hands behind his back, rocking on his toes several times. "So limited," he murmured. "In our resources, you understand. When one's choices are narrow, one inevitably feels frustrated." Then he smiled again, and as if enjoying the intensity of their attention, added, "Forgive me. I was thinking aloud. Of our opportunities? Opportunities, that is, to extend the hospitality of our poor small state."

"Oh, don't you worry about that," Shad said huskily. "Remember, we came here on business, General."

"Yes, I know. But having accomplished—"

"Nothing yet," Marty filled in desperately, feeling out of his depth. "We just got through sending a cable saying so. To my partner. A very budget-minded guy, incidentally. Abby Golden. Maybe you heard of him? He's the kind of a guy—to give you an idea—flies ten thousand miles to save ten bucks. Wouldn't surprise me a bit if he showed up pretty soon."

"Really," said the general. "How interesting, Mr. Brom. A pity then, he cannot be here in time for our hunt tomorrow. He would find it most fascinating, as you will, I am sure."

"Sounds great," said Shad, ignoring Marty's look. "But what're we hunting with, General? We got the threads but no equipment."

Was that so, the general asked, as if he didn't know. Well, no harm done, since he himself was amply supplied. "In fact, you may select your weapons this evening." He beckoned to his aide who hovered nearby. "Major Belelondres will show you our complete collection of hunting rifles—right now if you wish. Be assured that whatever weapons you choose will be prepared for your use tomorrow."

"Smells a lot like rat out tonight," Marty muttered as they took leave of the general, following his aide through the exotic-looking crowd which parted for them, soberly respectful—as if, Marty thought, they were already sacred relics. "And tell me something—just tell me, please—if you've got any idea of shooting your way out of this—"

"Cool it, man, we'll talk later."

"Yeah, when—from grave to grave?"

14

Whenever any of them thought of that evening again, and the hunt next day, the two events always ran together in a chiaroscuro, surrealist nightmare which not even time or distance could make clear. One minute they were prisoners of a dead city spellbound in blackness, the next—it seemed in memory—they were careening out of Porto Saba under a nacreous sky—dawnlit but not sunny yet—piled into a Land Rover with the major. Ahead rode the general in a bullet-proof car; they were tailed by a jeepful of Danjuan newsmen. Before and behind the three vehicles, fatigue-clad troops rode shotgun on the procession. Dust devils whirled like dervishes across the empty coastal plain which rapidly fell away behind them. The major's voice droned on and on, briefing them for the hunt which only Gloria did not dread . . .

"Why didn't you tell me right away," she was to cry later, infuriated when she finally knew. "Didn't you know I'd help you? Didn't you think I could?" But all she could do by then was guess at the suffering she had caused them, how the idea of her must have paralyzed them both. She was the X-ingredient, she was to realize sadly, the alchemist who made fear seem helplessness . . .

"Our meeting point will be the village of B'akou," the major was explaining over their compulsive yawning as they bounced along in the Land Rover. "Here we will break our fast with the paramount chief." He smiled as if at some secret joke. "One hopes you will find our indigenous food palatable. At any rate— you shall forgive me—do not fail to eat a bit of everything offered you. Not to do so, I assure you, would give offense to the chief."

There would be tribal dancing in their honor, he went on, and a choosing of honorary warriors for the hunt. Each of them would have a gun bearer, of course, trained men on whom they could rely. "Naturally," he added, "it is not expected that Mrs. Smith must shoot."

"Why not?" Gloria asked crossly. "I'm not coming on this clambake just to sit here and knit while you cats have all the fun."

"But, Mrs. Smith—"

"Better listen to the lady," Shad advised gloomily. "When she makes up her mind, that's it, Maje."

Full of lies, love, sleeplessness, he had spent the night trying to decide what he must do. But his mind had kept slipping, unable to keep a grasp on the perilousness of their predicament. A guy with his luck in a fix like this? A man in his position? He had felt himself the center of a complicated gag, a practical joke. With a kind of horror, Shad recalled now, he had found himself smiling again and again in the dead blackness—even as he worried, unable to really believe his worries.

"Hey, Tiger," he called across the rumbling Land Rover to Marty, who looked sleepy and miserable. "You all set to bag you a coat?"

"Mr. Smith," the major chided, "surely you must know there are not tigers here."

"No tigers! Well, how about that?"

"Oh, Shad," Gloria murmured, "cool it, why don't you?"

"Me no get tiger, me not hunt," Marty said. "How about we go fishing instead?"

"Mr. Browm—" the major appeared genuinely shocked— "surely you cannot be serious?"

"These two don't know the meaning of that word." Gloria smiled at him. "Relax, Major. Just point them both in the right direction, they'll shoot at whatever they're told to."

"Izzat so?" Marty argued. "I'll have you know I am a very choicey kind of hunter. Blonde," he began to enumerate. "Preferably about 38-22-28—"

"Stop the car," Gloria said grimly. "I want to ride with the general, please."

"Mrs. Smith, you are serious?"

"No," said Shad. "Just point Mrs. Smith in the right direction—" he grunted as she elbowed him in the ribs. They smiled at each other, for an instant alone, completely unaware of the others.

They passed through groves of palms and great fields of crops which the major said were government owned, farmed on shares by peasant families. "There is millet," he pointed out. "Groundnuts, which you call, I believe, peanuts. There is rice there in the lowland . . ."

Over a mud embankment road so narrow it seemed impossible it could hold them, they passed through a mangrove swamp full of tortured-looking trees draped heavily with moss and ugly creepers. Mosquitoes attacked them in humming hordes, but the respite from the sun seemed almost worth it to them.

Then the procession emerged into a meadow-like flatland dotted here and there with copses of trees. Once a forest logged off by generations of greedy colonials, the major informed them, this land was now free for farming. "Unfortunately our agricultural system is as slow to develop as our industries," Belelondres admitted wryly. "Our people are reluctant to move, reluctant to change. A family is a village, you see, perhaps centuries old. And the land is sacred, the trees around it. One cannot force such poor ignorant peasants to uproot themselves for an intangible like the welfare of the state."

Twice there was rain, sudden and violent, and each time afterward, steam rose as if the earth itself were on fire. In the distance the jungle shimmered in the misty haze—more like a theatrical backdrop, Gloria decided, than anything as real as the dense humid undersea world which they found when they entered it.

"Note our precious woods." The major pointed to trees as they passed by. "There is mahogany here, ebony there. To the west is a large rubber plantation. That road there—" indicating a narrow branch off their own—"leads to a sawmill."

"I'd never have believed anybody could work here," Gloria

said, shuddering unconsciously. She felt buried in greenness, overpowered by it. "It's so thick! Isn't it simply crawling with snakes and things like that?"

"Oh, quite," said the major. "Look there—" and he pointed again at a mottled green and black limb lying in a clearing by the side of the road. "Watch it closely."

"Why it—it's moving!"

An instant later, the limb disappeared, transformed into a long snake which the major said was deadly—a mamba.

"Sure you won't change your mind and take up that knitting you were talking about?" Shad asked his wife. His own vote, he decided at this moment, also leaned strongly toward knitting.

Half an hour later, the jungle thinned again, becoming occasional woods separated by open grassland. They saw smoke ahead, a long stretch of dry-looking meadow, and at the end, a village which the major announced as their destination, B'akou.

As they drew closer, they heard drumming like a pulse-beat over the sound of the motors, and a cloud of saffron-colored smoke rose up, a wavering column in the still hot air. Then they plunged into the village of B'akou, circling a huge bare dusty compound surrounded by round mud houses with thatched roofs and walls painted with weird white and black animistic graffiti.

"Just *listen* to them cats beating the skins!" There must be twenty or thirty drummers, Shad decided, all of them sweating and pounding away, filling the air with that curious pulsing which was more than just sound. To the right of them stood a group of tall coal-black men, some dressed in the white robes which Gloria so admired, others half naked in skirtlike wraparounds of brilliantly striped cotton. One of these, a fat old man with crinkly white hair, also wore a kind of cape of animals' tails fastened together. Over him a woven canopy of matting was held by four youths with heavily painted torsos. The old man—obviously the paramount chief—held a small black-painted stool in one hand, a horsetail fly whisk in the other. Both of these he lifted—as if offering them—as the procession stopped, the troops jumped down forming a guard, and the general emerged from his heavy limousine.

"We must wait," Major Belelondres said, "while His Excellency pays his respects." He beckoned to someone they could not see. "Perhaps you will allow our photographer—?"

"Sure," said Shad. "Why not?"

"Now aren't you glad I forced you two to go to Abercrombie and Fitch?" Gloria said. "You'd look pretty silly getting safari pictures taken in sandals and meditation shirts."

They jumped down from the jeep, and in their crackling new bush clothing, wide-brimmed hats, and jungle boots, posed dutifully for the cameraman. "Heap big hunter," Marty grunted, swelling his chest, but Shad punched him and he deflated again. "Sorry, Champ, lost my head there for a minute. You know how it is with us unsung heroes of the moom-pitcher world. Some cat points a camera and—"

"Where's everybody else who lives here?" Gloria was saying to the major. "I don't see any women or children."

"You will, Mrs. Smith. Later. The chief will make a signal, and then you will see them all."

And so they did—a frighteningly curious mob of shrilling, plucking natives who surrounded them the instant after they had been presented to the chief, and as a signal of his welcome, he had squatted down on his black stool.

Food appeared then—great, steaming, black iron pots, mounds of what looked to be mush lying on huge washed fronds. As they had been instructed, Shad and Marty and Gloria squatted on the ground, tasting everything that was offered. Occasionally Marty paled a bit, but he kept smiling and swallowing, nodding to Shad and Gloria as they took choked down mysterious and sometimes foul-tasting bites of the proffered feast.

The problem of a bathroom presented itself in due time, but this—according to the major—had been solved already by the general. Mrs. Smith would be taken by two of the chief's wives to a private place. Shad and Marty would be escorted similarly by the chief's eldest son—a tall, unbelievably homely young savage with a grotesque pattern of scars carved on his cheeks and bare chest.

"I'm not about to tell you my sad, embarrassing story," Gloria reported later. "But I know now what the French queens went through every time they had a baby with the whole French court in attendance as witnesses."

"Our guide," Marty said, still marveling, "turned out to be a graduate of Cambridge yet."

"Not the one with all the doodads embroidered on his face—"

"The same," said Shad. "Africa. What a country!"

The hunt was organized then, and to Gloria's delight, her joke on the steps of the hotel was realized as four villagers appeared, carrying a rough sedan chair roofed with woven matting. "How about that," she crowed. "A life's ambition, mine for the taking." Climbing in, she settled back cross-legged, haughtily ignoring Marty and Shad who made hitchhiker's thumbs as she passed by.

But that was the last of the gags—for the rest was the stuff of which bad dreams are made: an endless trek across the savannah-like country toward low hills of some shaling stone, barren of life, baking hot. On the other side was a sea of yellowed grass as high, they found, as the tallest head.

"You mean we're going through *that?*" Marty complained. "We could get jumped by an elephant and never know what hit us."

"You have hunted before, Mr. Browm?" the major asked.

Not liking his tone, Marty toughened his own. "I've hunted, yeah—where I had a chance of bagging something before it got me."

"I don't like it either," Gloria said. "This is supposed to be fun, isn't it? How can we have any fun if we can't see anything?"

"If you will be patient, Mr. Browm, Mrs. Smith, there is very fine hunting on the other side. A water hole also. I can assure you of the most plentiful game. Very tasty for the table. Excellent trophies also to be taken."

They had a choice, Shad supposed later—but what alternative might they have faced instead? They didn't know yet how far they could push their luck. At least hunting, he thought, you had a clear chance, and maybe if they refused they wouldn't next time—if there was a next chance. "Well, let's give it a whirl," he said. "But before we get down into that tall corn, let's take a few practice shots—what say, buddy?"

Right on cue, Marty picked up the suggestion, and while the

major watched, they selected their target. "You think—what?" Marty whispered when they were momentarily out of earshot. "These're loaded with blanks, maybe?" He patted his rifle.

"Something's got to be." Shad drew a bead on an icicle-shaped rock two or three hundred feet away. "Five'll get you ten if I don't knock a chip off that." Then he grinned at Marty. "I reckon it's only fair to warn you, podner, I got a sharpshooter's medal while I was soldiering a while back."

"I'll take my chances. You're on, Champ."

The sharp crack resounded in the smothering stillness. Rock chips flew. There was an ugly whine as the bullet ricocheted. Shad blew out his breath. "Well, they're live anyway." He clapped Marty on the shoulder. "Maybe we'll get out of this the same way, buddy."

To his chagrin, Marty missed his first shot, but with the second one, came near where Shad's had struck. Then as if on silent signal, they both wheeled around and marched in step back to the hunting group.

The tall grass worried Gloria, the way it rustled like paper as they passed through it, the sense of movement unseen, the sudden realization that somewhere out there something might exist which, under the right circumstances—these, for instance— had the power and freedom to injure or destroy them. And the motion of the sedan chair was not as pleasing as it appeared in all those Late Late Shows in which Maria Montez or Yvonne de Carlo inevitably played the captured princess. In fact it was downright unpleasant, she decided. So was hunting. So was Africa . . . if Africa, she amended in her most private mind, was the cause of this continuing feeling of uneasiness which had begun yesterday at the airport.

Remembering all her mother's advice and admonitions about husbands wanting their cake and eating it too, Gloria savored her suspicions like a sore tooth. Had Shad really wanted to get away from her for a while? Was that what made him seem secretive to her now? He didn't want her here.

Jogging along through the breathless heat, she suffered resentment, wifely feelings of injustice for a time. Then her equable nature began to reassert itself, humor and the reasonableness which her cool-headed father had done his best to instill in her. Oh hell, she thought, so I've pulled a boob, why make a federal case out of it? I can hop a boat tomorrow, can't I? Let him play his bachelor game if that's what he wants . . . But her decision did not quite soothe the deep unease, the shadow of something going on behind her back.

Watching her bearer's black legs scissoring patiently ahead of her on each side of the carrying pole, she thought, My slaves, appreciating her own irony, for of course her own ancestors had been chattel, too. Despite her efforts to distract herself, dismay began again to rise in her. Wondering about the others in the party, she peered back, spying Shad. Ahead she glimpsed Marty plodding along, fending off the whipping grasses. The hunters from the village seemed to have disappeared. The major, too, was making himself scarce . . . "Listen, aren't you beginning to feel a little spooky?" she called back to Shad finally.

"What about?" He moved up beside her carrying chair. "What's the matter, baby—you getting cold feet?"

"Maybe. Shad, can't we stop for a while and just talk about this safari?" Invisible in the grass, creatures scuttled away from them—little ones so far, nothing big, thank God. "Please, Shad," she plead. "I'm getting the funniest feeling. I mean—well, for one thing—where *is* everybody?"

"What do you want, baby—four more guys to carry you like the Queen of Sheba?"

Marty dropped back on the other side of the carrying chair as it jogged along, borne by the four patiently striding natives. He bent down, peering at Gloria. Beyond her he could see a portion of Shad as he walked along, pushing at the dry slashing grasses. "What's up, doll?"

"Queenie's got a case of cold feet."

"Who hasn't?" Marty mopped his flaming face. "For God's sake, I can't see anything up there unless it's right under my nose. How much longer, you suppose, before we get there?"

"Ask Big Chief Smith." Fanning herself with her hat, Gloria peeped out at her husband, but he didn't notice. To Marty, she said, "Now I know why the general decided to hang back and powwow with the chief. Shade and a floor show—what's he got to lose? Anyway, I don't think he ever meant to come along. He didn't even have a hat, did you notice?"

Over the roof of the chair, Shad and Marty exchanged a look as she went on: "Why don't you two yell at the major? We ought to stop anyway, shouldn't we? These poor boys toting me are probably ready to drop."

"Not a bad idea," Marty said.

"I'm with you. Let's take a break." Shad signaled to the chair carriers, but they continued on, not understanding. He took the nearest one by the arm, pointing to the ground. "Stop—you dig? Take five, fellas."

"Hey!" Gloria cried as first one, then another, set the chair down, throwing her from side to side. "Keep that up, and I'll get seasick, I promise you."

The carriers stood impassively, staring into space, seeming to listen for something. But there was nothing to hear, only the dry creaking of the grasses before the gentle wind which blew back toward the rocky hills, the distant whirring of locusts ahead of them.

"Hey, Major!" Shad yelled, his voice absorbed into the vast stillness. "How about a rest stop?"

"Where *is* he?" Gloria whispered. "I mean it, Shad—where is everybody?"

In the endless sky, vultures sailed serenely around and around, looking for the dead or dying below. The tall grass rustled, closing about them like a golden tide.

"He probably stopped along the way," Shad said after a moment. "Now, come on, Glory, don't start getting in a snit. For God's sake, there must be thirty guys in this party. One of them is—Hey," he said as the first of the chair carriers disappeared into the grass. "Don't forget to come back, fella." The second, then the third, melted away as they watched. After an instant's hesitation, the fourth left also, gone with the swiftness of a snake into the waving grass. "Hey," Shad kept saying. "Don't forget to come back, you guys."

"Shad—?"

"Take it easy, Gloria," Marty soothed. "The poor guys have probably got to see a man about a dog."

They waited then, but no one caught up with them. No one, missing them, fell back to check. The hunting party was no more, it seemed. Like Gloria's chair carriers, it had evaporated.

"Listen," Gloria said finally, peering out at them from under the woven canopy of her chair. "Will somebody please tell me what's going on? Are we lost? What's happening—?"

As she crawled out of the chair, she shrieked as something rodent-like darted from under her feet. And as if wakened from a spell, both Shad and Marty began to reassure her. They must have branched off the trail through the grass somehow. There was nothing to be scared of, all they had to do was sit tight, the trackers would find them again.

Then they saw it—a sudden puff of smoke in the direction they were headed. Another appeared, and another—widely spaced across the white-hot sky.

"Looks like a signal," Marty said. "Let me see if I can get up on that thing and have a look. Gimme a hand up, Champ."

Making a stirrup with his hands, Shad boosted Marty up. Clinging, sprawled on the sagging roof of the carrying chair, he looked across the vast expanse of golden grass. "Sweet suffering Christ," he breathed. Oh, mama, mama, what am I *doing* here, a good little Yiddish boy so far from the city? "Let me down," he said shakily.

Shad let him slide so he landed on his feet.

"Marty, what is it?" Gloria whispered. "You look like you saw—"

"A brush fire. A big one. And Shad—the wind—it's blowing this—"

"Come on." Shad grabbed Gloria by the hand and pulled hard. "Run, baby, and I mean *fast*. Run like you never ran before!"

15

Behind them great sheets of flame leaped into the sky. Smoke billowed—yellow, gray, brown—carried on the wind in acrid streamers which grew thicker and thicker as they ran, panting. Around them the tall dry grasses clattered with the unseen rush of panicked animals. Dark shadows of birds sailed over them, silent and ominous as evil omens. Gloria shrieked as an enormous snake slid by, veering around them, disappearing with a flick which hardly parted the grass. Groaning and gasping, their lungs seared, they raced back along the swath cut by their own passage, Shad dragging Gloria, Marty following, their skins through their clothing already burning in the steady puffing wind that carried now the dry heat of the fire which rapidly narrowed the horizon behind them.

Then Gloria fell, dragging Shad with her. Stumbling over them, Marty sprawled also. At root level momentarily, his streaming eyes took in the Lilliputian nightmare all around them, as rodents and snakes and insects raced by—a slithering, crawling, hopping, leaping horror of apocalypse on a minute scale.

As they scrambled up, all three turned to look behind them, but the sky was gone, distance blotted out by choking clouds of yellowish smoke rent now and then by great gouts of flame which seemed to burn of itself in the burning air.

"We're never going to make it," Marty gasped, coughing. "Here—gimme a leg up again—"

His chest heaving, Shad started to argue, then gave it up, too winded to speak as he looked at his wife who lay groaning in the grass, her mouth wide open, gasping for air.

"One—two—three—" Marty bounced on one foot like an apprentice tumbler and, heaved up by Shad's cupped hands, stood balanced for a moment on one leg, high above the level of the grass. Peering through the smoke for something, anything, which might look like sanctuary, he teetered. Then as he started to topple, he saw it. "There!" And as he fell, he was pointing. "Over that way!"

"What is it?" Shad panted.

"Trees." Marty gulped. "Doesn't that mean—?"

"Come on!"

Yanking Gloria up by main force, they left their trail, bearing at a right angle from it.

"I can't," Gloria kept gasping. "I—can't—run—"

But they dragged her between them, forcing her to run—three frail creatures cutting across the path of all the others, large and small, which fled the firestorm raging across the grassy plain. Cats too swift to identify leaped out of the grass before them, graceful deerlike animals, great lumbering warthogs, gigantic lizards like prehistoric ghosts—all delivered up out of the smoke and tall grass with the suddenness of some cosmic creative madness spewing and spawning in its death throes.

Even before they reached the trees they could hear the roaring of the fire. In the blazing wind before it, the copse of what looked to be cottonwoods bent as if in a great storm, the leaves curling and drying, blowing free in the choking smoke. Then they saw the water—a brown, reedy pond roiling with the life which had already taken refuge there. Snakes shot like arrows across the surface, small lizardlike creatures. A family of baboons sat chattering in the shallows, the babies clinging squalling to their mothers, for all the world like toddlers caught in a mob scene.

"Get in as deep as you can!" Marty yelled, wading in.

"The snakes," Gloria cried.

But Shad waded in, dragging her behind him. And when they were waist deep, he stripped off her bush coat, wetting it, throwing it over her head, then did the same with his own.

"Yeah!" Marty shouted through the smoke billowing above the surface, "that's the stuff!" And wriggling out of his coat, he did the same, joining them in a huddle, splashing wildly to keep the snakes away.

Slimy and soft the bottom sucked and pulled at their safari boots. Brand new, Gloria mourned briefly between panic and horror at the snakes. At nose level, buried in their coats, they breathed smoke—choking and coughing—and the fetid saving dampness rising from the pond. Things slid by them, felt but unseen. Waves lapped at their heat-glazed faces as more and more animals plunged into the water, roaring, snorting, squealing in panic.

As the heat increased, the water temperature rose also. They kept ducking down to keep their coats sopping, gagging in the smoke, spewing muddy foul water, blinded—as the fire drew closer and closer—to the hellish crucible around them. Shad took one last look into the inferno roaring out of the pall of smoke, then ducked down again, cooling eyeballs seared by heat and the horror of burning animal flesh plunging half-alive into the muddy water. With one arm around Gloria, the other around Marty, he pushed them down under the surface of the pool. Both struggled against him, bobbing up again, but he kept ducking them in a swift piston-like rhythm which scarcely gave them time for a breath as the fire approached. Their coats steamed and sizzled when sparks struck. All around them the pond seethed with fallen bits of flaming ash blown on the swirling firestorm wind. Then the cottonwoods went up one by one like cannonshots—one second alive, the next charred remains in a smoking graveyard—and the fire passed by.

Everything that was able to outrun the fire had done so; everything else lay cooked before them, smoking still, dead or dying. Only one baboon was left alive in the pond, they saw as they waded out, the others had drowned or suffocated. A few limply wriggling snakes survived. The hides of their backs seared and blistered, a few of the animals staggered from the pond also, heads hanging, silent in their suffering.

"Oh God," Gloria whispered, "it's like the end of the world. Just look at the poor things—"

"No." Shad pulled her away. "There isn't anything we can do. Come on, baby. We've got a long, long way to go."

The golden sea had been opened by the fire, transformed into a blackened plain, still smoldering here and there, pale spirals of smoke rising. The air smelled burned and spent and ashy, harsh in the nostrils, thick on the tongue. Nothing seemed to have survived the fire except the three of them. Shad coughed and retched and wished he were blind. With his arm around his wife, followed by Marty, he hurried away from the pond, hoping his memory would be merciful enough to blot out this terrible scene.

Far ahead they could see where the fire was dying at the foot of the shale hills. Patches of flames still flared up here and there, columns of yellow-brown smoke rose straight up in the stilled air. The sky behind them was already clearing, the sun, saffron-hued, behind the thinning smoke which would climb and climb until it disappeared into the upper air. They felt the beginnings of the soft dry wind on their backs again as they plodded across the burned-out plain. The "harmattan," the major had called it, a Sahara wind which in certain seasons blew all across West Africa.

"I'm dying of thirst," Gloria complained. She smiled at Shad wanly. "Couldn't we stop at the next drive-in and get a coke?"

"You know what they call that."

"Yeah," said Marty. "Sadism."

"Lots of ice," she continued. "And two straws, plea—" she stopped. "What's that?"

"What?"

"Some kind of light." She pointed toward the hills.

Marty squinted at the flashes far distant. "Looks like a signal."

"No, it's reflections," Shad said before he thought, his voice bitter. "No signals, buddy. Those are reflections from binoculars and newsmen's cameras."

They looked at each other. "Complete coverage," Marty said finally. "Yanks Survive Bush Fire. Make great copy for the soul brothers to read tomorrow."

"Soul brothers—where?" Shad made a fist. "You say Porto Saba, baby, and I'll give you five of my best in your teeth."

"What's this all about?" Looking from one to the other baffled and exhausted, Gloria asked plaintively: "Can't we let them know we're all right? I mean signal or something?" She groaned.

"My feet are roasted! Shad, maybe they could get that English-type jeep close enough—"

"Don't worry, they'll see us soon enough. Believe me, baby, those mothers are looking."

Peering at him, her muddy, ash-stained face like a tired urchin's, Gloria appeared uncomprehending. "Shad," she said hesitantly, "are you—?"

"Come on. We've got a long way to walk. The cokes are over thataway, baby."

The sun burned down and the blackened earth absorbed it, steaming up through their soaked boots. They had lost their hats running, and all wore their bush coats as head wrappings. Even so, under the coating of mud and ash, Marty's face turned pink, then red, then purple. "Jesus," he kept muttering, "I'm frying alive. Why wasn't I born one of those *dark* Jews?"

When they stopped to rest, Shad kept watching the hills in the distance. The smoke had cleared, there were no longer any flashes. By focusing, shading his eyes, he though he could see what looked like a train of white ants trailing across the blackened plain toward them. "Looks like the s.b.'s coming to meet us," he said finally when he was sure. "Soul brothers, that is. If I still had that rifle, I'd bag me a few."

"Why?" his wife asked quietly.

"Come on," Marty muttered, "cool it, Champ."

"No, don't." Looking from one to the other, Gloria waited. "Shad? Marty? Listen, before they get here, I want—" Then her voice rose, hoarse from breathing smoke, and shrill. "Listen, you two, will you quit *looking* at each other that way? I know something's been going on. I've known it ever since I saw you at the airport yesterday!"

Marty made Yiddish hands: what can you do?

"Okay," said Shad wearily, "I guess after today she's got a right to know."

16

For once in his life, Marty was glad to be a spectator. In fact, for preference, he could have missed this bit entirely. Poor chick, she kept shaking her head as Shad told her—not flipping out as Marty himself had done—just looking more and more bewildered as he kept trying to explain.

"But Shad," she kept saying, "why did you do it? That's what I don't understand. Why you—"

"Look, somebody had to. And you're missing the whole point, baby—"

The hell she is, Marty thought.

"—That's a rocket base out there. Ask Marty, he saw it, too."

"I don't care what he saw! What I care about is why—" but instead of listening, she covered her ears, turning away, standing huddled and beaten-looking with her back to them. "I don't know you, Shad," she wailed. "I just don't know you at all!"

"Look, will you try to understand? If I'd known it was going to be a scene like this—" and Shad reached for her.

But Marty stopped him. "You better cool it, man."

"What're you talking about? I've got to make her listen, for chrissake!"

"So wait awhile. Let her get used to it, why don't you, Hero?" Scorched, furious, Marty glared at his client. "You think it's so easy to swallow in one gulp her husband's a tin hero some crazy bastards tried to fry alive?"

Fry, she heard, but her mind refused, *alive*. She had not caught up yet with the significance of the fire, only that Shad, at some fool's urging, had agreed to play the fool for him. All around her the charred land wavered—sinking, tilting under the burning sky, undulating as her eyes teared, dried, teared again. Then shock swung like a sledge hammer in her. *They* did this? Because of Shad? On her mind's unforgetting eye the pond blazed as it would forever, the drowned baboons, the shriveled beasts with hides still smoking, the limp question-mark shapes of serpents lying still upon the murky surface. Dead, she instructed herself. Fried alive. As she and Shad and Marty were meant to be. Because of Shad.

"I'm sorry," she heard him saying behind her. "Baby, believe me, I never figured—"

"Famous last heroic words," Marty sneered. "Let me take those down, will you, pal?"

"Look, take yourself a walk, why don't you?"

"Where to—New York maybe? I'm ready, Hero, any time you are."

"Oh, stop it!" she screamed, whirling on them. "Stop it!" And in the silence that followed they stared at her, diminished by the empty landscape, their seared faces blank, unknowable. "You clowns," she said softly. "Oh, you silly—" Then she began to cry hard, her sense of outrage like a violent sickness at the root of her being.

"Baby, don't." Shad reached for her. "Don't cry—"

But she jerked from him and began to run.

"Hey," he called after her. "Glory? Hey, wait—"

He caught up with her finally, and against the blackened land around them, under the incandescent, unending sky, they looked to Marty like the last people left on the face of the earth. A new Adam. A new Eve. This time for their Eden they had the bottom of hell to get out of . . .

"Then—it's true," Gloria was saying as he joined them, peering up blinking into her husband's stony brown face. "Shad, tell me."

"Ah, God, baby." He appeared suddenly ready to weep with her, alive with misery. "If I'd known what a bad scene this was going to be—"

"Answer me!" she cried. "Is it true what Marty said? That they—they—" and she swung one arm wide, taking in the desolation—"did this. Deliberately did this?" And when he nodded, she closed her eyes, leaning heavily against him. "Oh, God. Oh,

my Lord, what kind of a world is this?" Then her eyes snapped
open. "What kind of people are they? Shad, what kind of a
crazy man are you—?"

"Glory, if you'd only listen—"

"To what? What, Shad? How you—you, a man with everything to lose—"

"Listen, you think I expected this? Or that you'd be here?"

"What difference does that make? Oh, don't you see?" she
cried furiously. "It doesn't make it any worse that I'm here, for
God's sake. What's so awful is your getting into this stupid mess
in the first place. Shad, have you forgotten what real life—?"

"Hey," Marty butted in, stopping it there. Never talk to an
actor about real life. "Listen, guys," he went on compassionately,
"we've got a lot of talking to do, you dig? Much rapping before
those cats get back here. I mean—" and here he looked vaguely
embarrassed—"maybe, you know, we won't get the chance
again."

From somewhere she summoned calm then, courage, and
Shad told her about the message they had received—the scrap
of sheet music—and his instructions to go upriver. "I don't know
what it is, baby—who, or where—nothing about it," he finished.
"All I know is there's somebody to help us, and he'll know we
need it."

"But, if they did this—"

"Look," Marty interrupted, "whatever they try, it's got to be
an accident, see? Mucho trouble if they knock off celebs. So all
we got to do is stick together and keep our eyes open till we can
split or get help . . ."

The simple problem of staying alive in a closed, cut-off, alien
land. A land which was a prison. Nazi Germany couldn't have
been more so. They agreed to keep watch on each other, to be
separated for no reason, and to try, each, to find some way out.
There was no airfield available any longer, thanks to the general's timely repairs, but there was a harbor, after all, the chance
of a boat. Shad would keep insisting they must report by phone,
using for leverage the fact that if they didn't, somebody would
be sure to follow up.

It was whistling in the dark and all three understood this, but as they watched the party from the hills approach, they planned as imaginatively as they were able, stirring hope from the ashes around them.

"The most important thing now is that riverboat," Shad said as they waved to the oncoming party, as if to rescuers. "If we can talk them into letting us go upriver."

"We won't have to, will we?" Gloria asked coolly. "Talk them into it, I mean."

"What're you getting at?" This from Marty.

"They tried this excursion, didn't they?" She eyed the two men. "Stands to reason they'll try another."

What moxie, Marty thought. For two cents he'd fall in love with her—if he stayed alive long enough, that is.

By this time they could hear the shouting, the joyous charade of their rescue party—white-robed villagers whose beaming faces seemed like evil tribal masks, grave hunters with bare scarred warriors' chests heaving—and Major Belelondres, the general's aide. "What a miracle," he kept murmuring as he shook all their hands, his handsome face dripping, anxious, a veritable picture of the relieved rescuer. "These terrible fires. No warning whatsoever. Oh, what a tragedy! We sent runners immediately, of course. The general himself—" then he stopped. "But you must have water, shelter." In angry gutturals, he gave orders, and water in a gourd was produced, wide plaited hats, light very clean robes to cover them from the terrible beating sun.

Then as they wearily started back toward the low shaley hills, he explained elaborately about the general's personal investigation. "You must be assured that the villagers who abandoned you will be sufficiently punished. It is a matter of the greatest shame to the chief," he assured them, "that his people should have run like dogs, leaving their guests to burn."

"What happened to you, Major?" Gloria asked. "The last time I saw you, you were ahead of us."

"Ah, but that was an hour or more before I first saw the smoke."

"You were behind us, then?"

"I regret to say, yes. Far behind the party, Mrs. Smith. I had dropped back perhaps two miles or more to make sure that our supply of water was adequate." He held up helpless apologetic palms to the sky. "There was not time to warn you personally."

"Like New York," Marty said. "When it happens, man, it's every guy for himself."

"No, you must not believe that, Mr. Browm!"

"Forget it," Shad said. "It was an accident. The same as our finding that water hole was an accident."

"Such a happy one, that last," the major agreed. "A most unfortunate gathering of circumstances which happily ended well."

"I suppose those handy newspaper photographers got great pictures," Marty commented.

"Cool it," said Shad. "Let's not waste our breath."

And presently they began to climb the low shale hills, pausing at the top to look back at the desolate plain which had nearly become their graveyard.

"My one and only safari," Gloria said, smiling sweetly at the major. "Like they say—an unforgettable experience?"

Then they started down the other side of the hills, hearing already the dull pulsing of the drum of B'akou across the wide savannah.

The washboard roads seemed smoothed by the general's heavy air-conditioned limousine, the savannah narrower, the jungle small, the mangrove swamp only a glimpse through the windows. Riding in the front seat, turned back toward his guests, General Okefe kept up a mild-voiced running commentary of the punishments he had meted out in the village of B'akou: For all directly concerned in the hunt, lashing, of course, and tribal isolation. For their women and children, silence until the moon had waxed and waned twice over. For the entire village, tobacco forbidden—

"I'd really rather not know," Gloria said finally.

"But you must." The general smiled. "I would not wish you to believe that this near tragedy should not be paid for."

"We picked up the tab," Marty said. "Why not let it go at that?"

"Mr. Smith?" Mild and steady, the general's eyes fixed on Shad. "You have no comment also? No plea for mercy to be shown to these cowards who abandoned you?"

Little Brother of the Knife, Marty thought. And how he loved to twist that blade!

"You said it yourself, General." Shad shrugged as he replied, looking indifferently out the window as they sped along, trailing a cloud of dust. "There's no way for your people but violence."

"I believe I said kill. There is no way for us except to kill." Again the general smiled. "Is it possible," he added gently, "that you think these punishments less than deserved?"

"Not for patsies, no."

"I am afraid I do not—"

"That's old-timey slang," Marty filled in hastily. "Patsy. Means —uh—something like nebbish. That's Yiddish—"

"And untranslatable," Gloria added. "Take it from one who knows." She spied the city far ahead, and beyond it, the long curve of the sea horizon. Experiencing a false sense of relief, of safety, she realized the danger ahead in being lulled by comfort, urban surroundings, the sure knowledge that the general must, to some degree, play along with them. The city could be more dangerous, she thought, than the jungle . . . "I want a long bath," she said, "and a nap, and a marvelous dinner." She smiled invitingly at the general. "How would it be if you were *our* guest this evening, General Okefe? I've never had the chance to entertain a real live head of state before."

For an instant surprised, the small man gazed at them, his eyes flicking from one to the other. "But after such a harrowing experience," he murmured. "Surely—"

"Oh, no." She giggled. "We're tougher than you think, Your Excellency. And we've got to make the most of this marvelous experience—" then she stopped and turned to Shad. "Honey, I've only got another day or two at the most, you know that." And she turned back to the general. "It's my father's birthday, you see. If I'm not back, he'll probably call the President and get him to send the whole U.S. Marines after me."

"Believe me, the Republic of Danju would be honored." Okefe seemed amused now. "But if you are serious—surely if your father were concerned for you, he would contact Mr. Brom's person. What was that name? Ah, yes, Golden. I am sure a very valuable contact."

"But he doesn't know I'm here. Nobody at home," Gloria faltered, "does."

"Our telephone service is unreliable," the general suggested. "But a cablegram perhaps?" Again he looked from one to the other, clearly the master of this situation. "In any case, I recall that Mr. Smith mentioned a desire to cruise our river. It would be a great pity, Mrs. Smith, if you should miss such an interesting voyage."

Gloria pretended to think. "Well, if I knew I could fly out. But with the airport closed, that cuts down on my time."

"There is no problem, Mrs. Smith. In three days' time, a Greek cruise ship will visit our harbor." He waited, seeming to savor a sense of their silent secret communication with each other. "It will stay until sundown, then sail on to Nigeria. I am sure you—and if they wish, of course, Mr. Smith and Mr. Brom—will be able to make that short voyage to Lagos. From there you will be able to pick up an international flight. A matter of a few hours only to New York . . ."

Thus the carrot dangled, and as Marty said later—what could they do but play donkey?

17

The river steamer looked like a squashed oversized tugboat—wide in the beam, low in the water, its peeling white superstructure high and ungainly. "*This* is a boat?" Marty scoffed as they climbed out of the limousine the following morning and started across the wharf where it was moored. "I wouldn't even trust that scow in a bathtub."

★

"You will find the *Leolo* very—what is the word?" the major asked. "Ah, yes—seaworthy."

"River-worthy," Marty kidded. "We're not going to do any wrong-way stuff and end up outside that harbor, are we?"

"Indeed not, Mr. Browm." The major bowed to them. "Allow me to precede you aboard. It is necessary for me to check on all arrangements." And he hurried across the wharf, taking the gangplank in four giant strides.

"Unfinished business?" Marty suggested. "Maybe they haven't got all the holes bored in the bottom yet."

"There doesn't seem to be anybody but us around," Gloria commented, nervously aware of the sunstruck silence, the musty smell of rot and mold, the gentle lap-lap of the current against the pilings.

Long, low, rickety-looking wooden sheds lined the waterside—all windowless with dark cavernous open doors. A skinny dog sniffed at a heap of refuse. There was no sign of any other humans about, not a voice to be heard in the spellbound quiet, not a small boat to be seen on the broad surface of the wide brown river.

"Maybe we're early," Shad said. "What do you do to get in a boat—make a noise like a doorbell?"

"If you're not expected you yell 'ahoy.' " Marty grinned. "That is, unless you think you might be interrupting something. Us old yachtsmen learn these things—yachtsmen being such well known—" he glanced at Gloria—"uh, lovers."

Preceded by their own long shadows, they went as far as the gangplank then stopped. Dazzled by the sun on the smoothly flowing deep brown water, they blinked at one another, waiting as if for a signal.

Shad took Gloria's hand, squeezing it tight, moved by the delicacy of bones like those of a bird. Sweet brown hand. Sweet brown girl. His arms remembered the supple softness of her body last night, and on his mouth was the burn of burning kisses still, her sad sighing murmur: Oh, Shad, I want to live to be ninety with you. In the dark he had held her and prayed it would be so . . .

"At the risk of being repetitious," Marty was saying softly, "adventure I dig, suicide no. I still say we ought to fake the next seventy-two hours, or whatever it is—and be here when that cruise ship comes in."

"*If* there's a cruise ship."

"Okay—it's a chance, isn't it, one way or the other?"

"You're dreaming, baby," Shad said. "We have to make our own chances." Squinting into the blaze of morning, he looked back at the waiting limousine. Not only a driver this morning, but an armed guard also. Both sat like images, watching them.

"Okay," Marty was shrugging, "like they say in the moom pitchers—it's your funeral."

"Will you cut that crap!"

"Shad, don't," Gloria murmured. "Marty's just trying to keep it light—aren't you, Marty?"

"Sane is what I'm trying to keep it." Gazing directly into the white-hot reflection dancing on the river, he added sourly, "I'm not guilty of this caper, *he* is. And according to the shrinks, guilty guys don't think straight."

"Oh, please," Gloria plead. "Let's not start this again."

In feverish whispers on the balcony last evening they had hashed and rehashed, argued and fought out their various ideas about their chances from now on. Marty had been all for doing nothing—if necessary faking illness so they could stay in the hotel. But Shad had stubbornly stuck with the upriver plan, certain that it was their one real chance, since someone was there to help them.

"But what if you're wrong?" Gloria had kept insisting. "What if it's someone who's helpless by now, Shad? At least here we're somewhat safe."

"You think so?" Shad had rattled the balcony railing, imagining how easily an accident could be arranged. "Look, our only chance—and I mean only!—is to go along with whatever the general's got up his sleeve. That way at least, we aren't fighting him all the time, see? Twenty-five, fifty miles upriver, he's not going to have a regiment eyeballing every move we make."

"You're a great tactician, old buddy," Marty had said. "Except for one little problem—you're still thinking like a hee-ro. Don't forget there's nobody to say 'cut—print that' at the end of this scene . . . Pour me some more of that medicinal gin, will you, baby?" Gloria had been nearest the bottled goods. Glass against glass had clinked gently in the humid dark. From the garden below had come the heady fragrance of some nightblooming plant. Gloria herself had looked like a flower in the starlight. A gorgeous dusky hibiscus, say. Nothing like a little Beefeater's to bring out the poet in a guy.

Remembering how longing for Beverly Hills had struck him then—dinner at The Bistro, kicks at The Factory or The Daisy, his own pad overlooking the Strip, a broad of his own to romance over drinks—he went on with his last night's argument, blinking in the dazzle from the river: "Okay, first His Worship gets us out of the way. This is just in case there *is* a cruise ship. Then, about fifty miles upriver, guess what? We crack up. And who's to say how it happened? A survivor or two for the records, that's all. And us three cats turn into crocodile meat." Then his voice started rising: "Okay, I shouldn't be talking this way in front of Gloria, I know that. She's scared, yeah. Well, I'm scared, too! I'm scared to death of *you*, Hero, because I think you really believe you are!"

"Why, you stupid flack," Shad began, "don't you remember what we saw back of that mountain—?" But Gloria stopped him, jerking his arm hard.

"We voted," she said quietly. "We did it all last night, Marty."

Yeah, he thought, like two against one. I mean, a woman's got to trust her man, sure, but that don't mean—then he stopped himself, took a deep mental breath. Any way you sliced it they were lousy insurance risks. And maybe that cruise ship *was* just a myth. "Okay, that was Brom's Last Pitch." He grinned at his client. "I'm your boy, Shaddie, remember? Good old Brom your ten-percent pal?"

"We get out of this—" Shad threw his arm around Marty's shoulders—"you can make that twenty percent."

"Remember, I got a witness—"

"No sale," said Gloria. "You forget you can't make a woman testify against her—"

A dark form cut the brilliant light. "Will you come aboard, Mr. and Mrs. Smith?" Belelondres asked cordially. "Mr. Browm?"

"We who are about to," Marty muttered. "You think a pocketful of lovebeads'll help us any?"

The master of the good ship *Leolo* turned out to be a squat black man dressed in badly soiled tropical whites, barefooted, an old British navy officer's cap squashed on the back of his bullet head. Captain Ngoru, his name was—instantly changed by Marty to Captain Bligh. "*Dirty* Captain Bligh, that is," he added sotto voce as they followed the major along the sun-baked deck, "the laundryman's worst enemy."

Poking her head through the deck-level door which the major was holding open for her, Gloria peered into a gloomy stuffy cubbyhole, and stepped back a pace. "*That's* it?"

Shad grinned. "That is it, baby. Welcome to your second honeymoon."

Their luggage was already arranged, the major was saying. "Mr. and Mrs. Smith's in this cabin, and Mr. Browm's—" he moved down the deck to the next narrow door—"in here."

"Brace yourself," Gloria advised Marty.

He did, and stepped into a hot fetid cabin barely large enough to turn around in. Two narrow bunks fastened to the interior bulkhead took up most of the space. In one corner sat what appeared to be an old-fashioned marbletop commode holding a ewer and basin of chipped china. Over it hung a mildewed mirror cracked at the bottom. Bathroom facilities, he saw, were in the thundermug class.

"But there's no plumbing," he heard Gloria's shocked voice through the thin partitioning between the cabins.

"True, the facilities may seem—you shall forgive me—somewhat primitive," he heard Major Belelondres reply, "but please be assured, Mrs. Smith, that there will be compensations—"

Yeah, Marty thought, like a midnight swim when we least expect it. Shuddering slightly, he bounced once on the thin hard mattress, then gave it up. Stifled by the musty heat, he stepped out on deck again.

Shad was standing at the rail, looking at the limousine sitting in the shadow of the sheds on the wharf.

"Second thoughts, Champ?"

Shad jumped as if he'd been stung.

Marty laughed. "Nervous times for heroes, right?"

"—Well, I suppose we'll have to make do," Gloria's voice floated out to them. "But several days without a bath—"

Shad groaned. "I ought to have my throat cut for getting her into this."

"You may, buddy—and mine, too." But Shad looked so miserable, Marty had to relent. "Listen, it was a bad break, forget it. Two weeks from now it'll be something for her to thrill the boys with at her beauty parlor."

"I'd like to believe that. Man, I would."

"You got to." Marty punched his arm. "Don't go losing your chutzpah *now*, baby."

They both started as the captain shouted gutturally from the wheelhouse high above them. As if by magic, a deckhand appeared, leaping lightly onto the railing, poising there for a moment, to soar like a highjumper across to the wharf. A deep rumbling began in the bowels of the riverboat, and the deck beneath their feet shuddered. As Gloria and the major appeared, the door of the limousine opened simultaneously, and the armed guard got out, trotting across the wharf, his automatic rifle glinting in the sunlight.

"—Wish you to have a pleasant voyage," the major was saying behind them, but Shad and Marty were transfixed watching the guard.

"We'll try," Gloria answered uncertainly. Taking both Marty and Shad's hands in cool fingers, she said, "What're you two so fascinated by?" Then she said *oh,* and they all watched silently as the guard bounded up the gangplank, saluted in their general direction, then squatted in the shade with his back against the superstructure.

"His Excellency felt you should have—shall we say?—extra protection," the major explained.

"Yeah," said Marty. "Like insurance maybe."

"That is it exactly, Mr. Browm. Insurance." He smiled at them, his black eyes gleaming. Then saluting, he added, "A pleasant voyage," and turning snappily, disembarked, making a signal to the deckhand waiting on the dock.

"And so they cast off and sailed away into the unknown," Marty mocked a mellifluous travelogue tone. "Will we ever see this intrepid trio again?"

"I wish you'd shut up." Gloria shivered. "You're giving me goosebumps."

"They'll see us, all right," Shad said grimly.

"I like your thinking." Marty waved to the major waiting beside the limousine. "Say aloha to the nice man, kiddies. Aloha oi vey, that is."

Then the *Leolo* commenced to move, churning the smooth, oily brown surface—and their voyage upriver had begun.

18

Where it flowed into the harbor, the Mobene River was wide, dotted with mangrove islands, lakelike, for there was no sense of current under the still brown surface. But inland where the river cut the coastal plain it began to narrow slightly, and as the steamer *Leolo* swung against the current, they could feel its engines laboring. In the wheel-house, Captain Ngoru-Bligh kept shouting periodically, and from time to time the agile deckhand passed them in their wanderings, grinning as if to mock his captain's excitable-sounding orders. The armed guard slept through the morning, his automatic rifle cradled in his arms.

By noon, when they saw ahead the beginnings of the rainforest, Shad and Marty and Gloria had prowled around the riverboat enough to get their bearings—discovering a tiny lounge which also seemed to serve as the captain's quarters, the galley where a native boy wearing only a loincloth worked feverishly in the unbearable heat, and the engine room manned by a demonic-looking half-caste with a bushy beard. No one but the captain spoke English, they found.

Later, when the deckhand beckoned them into the lounge, they saw that some effort would be made about meals—which was a relief, since by now they were all hungry and beginning to worry about the eating problem. Bligh was waiting for them. "Simple food," he said sternly, as if daring them to complain. He gestured for them to choose among the folding canvas chairs which had been set up around the wobbly table. "You wish blessing before food?"

The cabin smelled of him—a curious greasy musty odor which combined unpleasantly with that of the steaming bowls of food the drenched cook brought in from the galley.

"Blessing," the captain said impatiently, indicating the chipped china bowls steaming before them.

"We usually don't say Grace," Gloria admitted finally, only vaguely comforted to find a possible Christian aboard.

"Eat then," Bligh commanded, waving filthy hands with black nails. "All is prepared for your pleasure."

There was a kind of stew made of some strong-smelling meat and vegetables which Gloria could not identify. There were also biscuits which had evidently been fried, a bowl of something that looked like Cream of Wheat, and a plate of fresh bananas and pineapple sliced into chunks. Sweat rolled off them in rivulets as they lunched, and conversation with the captain, they found, was limited to the deliciousness and plenitude of their repast. He kept eating and eating with unbelievable rapidity, gorging himself as if he'd been starving.

"Where exactly are we headed for, Captain?" Shad asked finally when Bligh had slowed down somewhat. "Any place special upriver?"

With his head bent low over his plate, shoveling in another mouthful, the captain shrugged.

"Far as I could see on the map," Marty commented, "there isn't anything much. No towns that I could see."

Without bothering to lift his head, the captain peered at him
—looking for all the world, Marty thought, like Gargantua.
"Map? You got map?"

Marty said no, and explained about their flights over the
countryside.

The captain grunted. "Airplane map no good. I show you
plenty places. Plenty villages." His scars crinkled briefly. A
smile? They couldn't tell. "Much to see where we go. People
very simple. You comprehend? Wild, like animals." Again the
crinkle. "Visitors take many pictures with Kodak."

"Oh, then, you're used to having passengers," Gloria said,
brightening.

"No passengers for long time."

As he stared at her, she became feverishly aware of herself—
iridescent nails and lipstick, haircut by Sassoon, skin-tight Pucci
pants suit in "hot" colors—much too hot, she realized now, for
this climate.

"Visitors no like Africa so much now," he went on, never taking his eyes off her. "Not colonies now of greedy foreigners. No
boys to run when white ladies and gentlemen—" he demon-
strated, startling them—"clap hands quick-quick."

Oh dear, she thought. Should she argue the point? But he
didn't look like a man you could argue with casually. She tried
again: "Tell me, Captain, did the major explain that my husband
may make a film here in Danju?"

"Yeah, that's what we're here for," Marty said when the captain did not reply. "Looking for locations."

Obsidian eyes in the scarred face peered at Shad suspiciously.
"Black man make film? You?" And when Shad nodded, he
scowled for an instant, staring down at his plate. Then, so
abruptly they all jumped, he slammed a fist on the table. Bowls
bounced. Their plates shifted. Murky-looking tepid water in
their glasses slopped to and fro. "No!" he howled. "Haha! You
make joke!" And his bellowing resounded painfully in the small
cabin. "American black man make film, haha. Film of burning
city, yas? Haha," he laughed, and jabbed a finger in Marty's
direction. "For film you shoot him, yas? In American film, white
man always shoot black."

"Look," Marty began, "that isn't—" then stopped.

"Yas?" The captain grinned at him. "I look. I see."

"You tell him, Shad."

"Well, it's not that kind of a picture." Shad thought a second, then started again. "I mean it isn't a problem story. It's about this soul brother—me, that is. I'm the lead, the star—you dig me?"

The captain nodded, grinning grotesquely.

"Anyhow, this cat's a shrink, see. A do-good kind of stud, but not a square either. In fact, he's kind of a swinger in his own way . . ."

Watching the captain's grinning attentive face, Gloria wondered how much he understood. He kept nodding and nodding, but what did that mean? Don't confuse him with the facts probably, she decided, he'd already made up his mind. "It's really a sort of lightweight story," she said—as usual when she was nervous, blurting before she thought.

Marty and Shad both gaped at her. Lightweight? Pure heresy.

"Well, what I mean is—" she went on hastily—"it's sort of romantic rather than realistic."

"Baby, what're you talking about?" Shad cried. "What's more realistic than a guy giving up everything to serve—" he glanced at the captain—"uh, people," he finished lamely. "You know what I mean."

"But the way it's written." Gloria leaned forward earnestly, for she was a great discusser of anything in psycho-sociological terms, having majored in both fields at U.C.L.A. "I mean, the script I read, honey, just doesn't have any fabric of true realism. It's a fantasy. A romantic fantasy. I mean, you talk about realism . . ."

Like a spectator at a tennis match, the captain's head turned from one to the other, as the star and his wife carried on a critical argument he couldn't possibly understand. *Nouvelle vague* against Hollywood standards, Buñuel and Godard against Wilder and Zinneman.

Concealing his delight in the madness of it all—those two perhaps facing their doom tomorrow, reverting even so to ham actor and frau at the drop of an adjective—Marty leaned back and let the words fly by him. He'd heard them all—like how many times?—while the hambones played like resting between roles at Hamburger Hamlet's on the Strip. A sharply clear vision of the Hamlet's streetside lunchdeck came to him then, all the babyhips and teenyboppers and junior beards strolling by through the smog while the hambone elect stared down at them grandly, arguing about their art over a plate of onion rings . . . Ah God, he thought, so what's wrong with it? At least it's civilization, a dime in the slot and you can dial the fuzz . . .

By the time lunch was over, clouds had piled up on the horizon, and in a greenish light which made the river look opalescent, they steamed along jungle riverbanks so lush they seemed to threaten the river itself. The air was breathless, steamy and oppressive with the coming storm. They saw their first crocodiles, and while they were standing at the rail watching the ugly saurian bodies slithering off a mudbank into the river, the storm broke, deluging them before they could rush for the first door.

As it happened, it was Shad and Gloria's cabin they took shelter in. While the rain roared down, blotting out the river world around them, they sampled Shad's medicinal supplies.

"If I had some of that pineapple from lunch," said Gloria, who despised drinking straight liquor, "I could make us all a Passion Flower."

"Just what I need," Marty commented. "A little something to add to my frustrations."

"A gibson," Shad said. "How does that grab you?"

"Without ice?"

"Yeah, I forgot about that." He sighed, leaning back in the upper bunk. Gloria sat in the lower. Marty occupied the one canvas chair which took up the total floor space. Through the open cabin door they all watched the curtain of heavy rain moodily. Leaning over the side of the bunk, his voice barely perceptible over the thunderous rainfall and beat of the engines, Shad said, "How about it, Mart?"

"How about what?" Gloria asked.

But Marty knew. "You got hero-itis again, buddy. There's

four guys *plus* the guard. And for all we know, they're all packing iron."

"What're you talking about," Gloria cried. "Shad? You're not thinking you could—"

"Hold on, baby. Now don't get excited."

She looked at Marty, then up at her husband again, her open, expressive lovely face full of fear. "You're crazy. Both of you. You've lived in that phoney show-biz world so long you're forgotten—" but Shad's swift gesture cut her short.

As if he were an apparition, they all stared at the deckhand standing just outside the door in the pouring rain. "You want something?" Shad asked finally.

Seeming unconscious of the downpour, he grinned in at them, making no attempt to let them know his purpose.

"What's this guy," Marty said after a moment, "a voyeur or something?" Swiveling his chair around, he faced the door. "You want drink?" He waved the aluminum mug from Shad's medicinal kit. "Drinkie gin? Is that what you want?"

Still grinning, the deckhand stepped into the cabin, little streams from his clothing running across the threadbare lino flooring. As he reached under his loose-hanging sopping shirt, bringing out what looked at first to be a weapon, Marty started up out of the chair, and Gloria cried out. Shad was off the top bunk in one leap, landing like a cat in the tiny space of floor between the canvas chair and his wife's dangling feet.

But the weapon—they saw as the deckhand shook his head violently, gesturing them to wait and see—was a hollow metal tube of the sort cigars are kept in. Uncapping it, he pulled out a yellow scrap of paper rolled into a tight cylinder, and handed it to Marty.

"If that's what I think it is," Shad breathed.

And it was—the other half of the page of music which had appeared in their box at the Hotel Splendide. Across the top was scrawled in pencil: *Ebu Mission.*

Shad's gamble had paid off.

19

The storm passed as quickly as it had come, leaving the river swollen, swifter, full of dangerous-looking whirlpools and eddies. Along the banks unreeling on either side, the jungle steamed—dark, dripping, impenetrable, strangled with ropey vines as thick as the hawsers which had moored the riverboat. Brilliant-hued birds flashed in the treetops. Monkey packs chattered. Half submerged, a family of hippos bellowed at them as they steamed by, gigantic tusked mouths yawning like immense fleshy trap doors.

"What do they remind you of?" Shad asked.

"Producers at a budget meeting," Marty fired back without hesitation. "You figure out yet how we get to that mission, Champ?"

"No—but give me time." With his back to the railing, Shad leaned out looking up at the wheelhouse above them. "Think the captain might like company up there?"

"Shad, be careful," Gloria warned. "He's awfully touchy."

"Who isn't?" He grinned at them. "Duck if you see a flying object—it might be me." Then he swung himself up the metal ladder fastened to the superstructure.

Half a minute later, he poked his head in through the open wheelhouse door, unpleasantly surprised by the roughness and simplicity of the *Leolo*'s controls. Compared to the yachts he had visited, the riverboat required nothing much to run, it seemed—a huge wind-up toy with a steering wheel.

"You want sometheen, Mr. Smith?" Without taking his eyes off the river ahead, the captain scowled and spat. "Better if passengers stay below."

"Just having a look around, Captain." Shad stepped over the foot-high cabin stepboard. "We might use something like this for a scene or two." He hesitated. "I really am scouting for a picture, you know."

The captain did not bother to reply.

Leaning against the bulkhead, Shad shoved his hands in his pockets, telling himself he had to play this smooth. Cool and smooth. They had one chance and he dared not risk spoiling it. "Quite a trick navigating this thing, I guess."

"No trick, no." Ngoru glanced at him. "You worry for your safety, Mr. Smith?"

"Me? Why would I worry about that?"

The scarred face crinkled. Ngoru shrugged. "You will know better the answer than I, Mr. Smith." He pointed ahead. "Watch now. Soon river squeeze us tight." One stubby hand rolled, vividly illustrating his next words: "Big current. Fast. Wild. Sometime so bad, don't make it."

What did that mean, Shad wondered, they might sink? Turn back? At this point, either could be fatal. "What do you think our chances are today?"

Again Ngoru shrugged. "We see. River will tell us."

Tension grew in Shad, tightening like a watchspring as he considered their helplessness. With all they had to bug them, now there was Mother Nature, too? Ebu Mission. They had to get there. Beyond that, he could not think.

He peered ahead at the next curve, and the next, half-blinded by the white-hot glare from the Mobene's surface. With each turn they made, the lush debris-strewn banks moved in closer. The land began to rise, the banks growing higher and higher, torn away in great chunks here and there, exposing tree roots as bare and bleached as bloodless entrails.

The *Leolo*'s engines began to throb harder, louder, their thump-thump shuddering through the old riverboat like the pulse of a struggling faulty heart. Even so, their speed began to diminish perceptibly; it was the high muddy banks which seemed to crawl by them now, moving slower and slower. Watching the swift current, Shad kept urging the boat on silently—come on, baby, come *on*—while another part of his mind noted flotsam whirling by at express-train speed, calculating the damage to the hull if just one thing, a log say, hit them bow on. "How many times have you made this run?" he asked Ngoru, who was steering imperturbably, his black eyes seeming to see every hazard before it even appeared.

The captain grunted. "How many times, don't count. Many years. All my life go up and down river."

Opp reeber. Ebu Mission. Atop the current, a tree branch flew by, scraping the *Leolo's* side as it passed. Shad looked down on Gloria and Marty leaning over the railing to watch it. Beyond their heads streamed the deadly millrace—brownish-green here in the narrows, viscidly opaque as crankcase oil. The bank on this side looked close enough to touch now, crumbly and rain-softened. Even as Shad watched, there was a shifting of one overhanging section, and as they passed by, a huge chunk fell into the water, instantly churned up and swallowed by the current.

The engines labored, shaking the deck under his feet. What happened, he wondered, if they failed? Surely without way in this current, they must swing around, perhaps capsize . . . "How much longer does this go on, Captain?"

Far from reassuringly, Ngoru replied, "With luck, soon over."

Thanks for nothing. Ahead, Shad saw, the river curved sharply. And here it had teeth—he could see whitewater. Keerist, he thought, this is as bad as shooting the Colorado. And the wrong way yet. To make the turn, they would have to buck not only the current but the boiling churn where it turned on itself.

Bracing himself, Shad sucked in his breath, watching as Ngoru swung the wheel sharply. The *Leolo* yawed toward the opposite bank, bucking in the whitewater whirlpools. The main current hit them broadside for an instant, buffeting the old hull as it heeled over. Then the wheel swung the other way, and head on to the swing of the central flow of the river, they cut diagonally across the curve.

"Wow," Shad breathed, "that's seamanship, man!"

But the captain only grinned and pointed.

With a sigh of relief, Shad spied calmer water ahead, for the banks were beginning to draw apart again, spreading the violent flow into something like its placid beginnings.

He began to talk then, telling about himself, inquiring about the captain, expressing what he hoped was an adequate interest in the history and future of the Republic of Danju. For the most part it was a one-sided conversation, for they had language against them, custom, and the captain's indifference—a result, perhaps, of the long reaches of the New World to which Shad belonged and Ngoru did not.

Soul brothers, Shad kept thinking as he talked. *Soul* brother? The phrase here in Africa had a funny hollow sound. Had Marty felt the same when he went to Israel last year? Brother maybe way down deep, but no deeper surely than the same level where every man was every other man's kin . . . "By the way," he said to his brother under the skin, "all that jazz about a blessing at lunch got me thinking."

"Yas, Mr. Smith?"

How sharp is this bucko? There was no way of telling. "Just wondering, Captain." Shad glanced at him furtively. "Maybe you got missions in this country, too? Christian missions?"

"Why you want to know, Mr. Smith?"

"Well—" Shad offered his box of Benson and Hedges longs. The captain took two, tucking one behind his ear like a taxicab driver, allowing Shad to light the other for him as he kept talking: "I've never seen a mission, for one thing. And for another, this picture I'm going to make has a mission in it. The way I figure—" he stopped as the captain grasped the hand holding the lighter.

"Is gold, this?"

"Yeah, my wife gave it to me. Nice, hunh?" He pulled slightly, but the captain did not release his hand.

"All gold?"

"Yeah, that's right. Eighteen carat."

Through the fuming smoke of their two cigarettes, Ngoru's eyes fixed on Shad's—a chilling look as greedy and fierce and cold as a hungry animal's. Then he let go Shad's hand. As if the moment had not happened, he admitted that there was a mission upriver, but the *Leolo* only stopped there to unload a shipment, and since there was none aboard this trip—

"I'd like to have a look at it, Captain." Shad waited, watching the black scarred profile, the slow puff of cigarette smoke from between Ngoru's thick scar-puckered lips. A silent bargain was being struck, he knew, costly as all such bargains always are. The crunch between what you have to have and how dearly you must pay for it . . .

Later, on the afterdeck where Gloria and Marty sprawled under a tattered awning in rickety deck chairs, he reported that the Ebu Mission was about an hour more upriver. The captain hadn't wanted to stop, but he had managed to persuade him to. "But we'll only lay over about half an hour," he warned. "He says he wants to make some pea-picking village beyond it before dark."

"Let him make it—we're gonna be missionaries," Marty said. "Nice work, Champ, you're a real magician."

"Yeah, that's me." Shad sighed. "Now you see it, now you don't." Gazing at his wife, he held out his hand. "Anybody got a match?"

Marty didn't get it, but Gloria did. "Oh, Shaddie," she murmured sadly, "it was a present."

Flipping him a matchbook from The Bistro, Marty looked curious, but Shad didn't bother to explain. Sitting tailor-fashion on the deck near his wife, he smoked silently and watched the river go by, feeling spent and helpless, drained by the suspicion that by bribing the captain he had only managed after all to increase the hazards in this one-sided cat and mouse game.

The sun beat down with terrifying intensity, piercing the rotted awning, heating the air to a blast-oven temperature. Across the now-serene waters, the cries of jungle creatures carried eerily clear and immediate. They spied animals drinking in the shallows—a pair of wildebeests, then a leopard and her cubs dabbling on a sandspit, then a warthog as fierce and ugly, Marty said, as the wild boar he had hunted on Catalina.

"Is there any kind of sport you haven't done?" Gloria asked, fanning herself, "Or do I mean any kind of sport that hasn't done you?"

Marty laughed. "It's all in viewpoint, sweetie. Doer or done to." He squinted at Shad. "You're mighty quiet there, podner."

"It's guilt," Gloria said. "I hope." She caressed her husband's head. "Baby, stop brooding. You did the best you could—now we just have to wait and see."

But waiting and seeing was the hardest part. Shad longed for action, decision, some violent and compellingly simple solution —like that in the plane. Here, no matter what happened, he knew, they would have to deal with this savage land—the jungle, or the river, there was no other way now.

A shout from the wheelhouse made them all jump. Shortly after, the deckhand came racing back, pointing upriver, gesturing for them to come see. Shading their eyes, the sun like hammer-blows on their heads, Marty and Shad and Gloria stood at the railing, watching the spot from which a spiral of smoke rose straight into the windless sky. The riverbank rose there, they saw, becoming a dried-looking brownish wall. An earthwork manmade wall, they realized. And behind it lay their destination—Ebu Mission.

20

From the riverbank where they tied up a path led upward to the top of the promontory. Here, by the mission wall, the jungle stopped like a half-spent, solid dark green wave. But twenty yards away you could be lost in that tangle where the sun never shone from one century to the next. One rainy season of neglect,

Shad thought, two at the most, and it was obvious that this mission wall and whatever lay behind it would sink like a flooded island beneath the tidal onrush of the rainforest.

The path led a short way around the ten-foot earthen wall. Graffiti had been scratched at shoulder level, they noticed—strange geometric-looking signs, and the wavering mission-school artwork of some loyal convert: *Gesu Safes.* The solid gate was closed tight, but from within they could hear a marketplace babble, faint but unmistakably the noise of a crowd.

"So where's the brass band?" Marty asked, and as peremptorily as a man with a search warrant, banged on the timbered gate. "Hey! Open up in there!"

Silence, ominous and complete, was their answer. Then a head popped up over the wall. Terrified, a black man gaped at them, then ducked down again.

"Keerist," Shad groaned, "isn't there anybody in this whole country who isn't scared for his skin?"

"Don't look at me," Marty said. "Mine's got permanent goose-bumps an inch high."

"Oh, why didn't somebody from the boat come with us," Gloria cried. "We'll never be able to make them understand us, will we?"

"Somebody's got to." Shad blew out his breath. "Try again, Marty."

So Marty yelled again, and kicked the gate hard enough to bruise a toe. "Hey! Hey! Jesus, I just broke my—Hey, speaka English maybe? Anybody," he roared finally, "home in there?"

A scraping sounded on the other side of the gate—as if a heavy bar were being drawn aside. There was a babble of voices, then sudden silence again as the gate creaked open a bit and a ruddy face topped with curly white hair appeared.

"Good Lord," the man gasped, then disappeared. A moment later the gate swung wide open, and the tall thin old man, ruddy and white-haired, welcomed them with open arms. "By George, Americans! You are—? I'd heard, but I never dreamed you'd manage—" Laughing, he stopped, then started again: "By George, they told me, but I simply couldn't believe it. Well, you

can imagine. Haven't seen a soul from home in—well, let's see—
five years? No, four at least. But look here, I've got to stop
raving like this, haven't I?" He laughed deliriously, appearing
drunk with joy and excitement. "Come out of the sun. Follow
me." And he turned away, pushing roughly through the crowd
of jabbering white-clad natives surrounding them. "Make way
there. Step back, will you? Damned gaping idiots. Step back, I
say!"

He was straight and slender as a reed ahead of them, brittle
with age, sun-dried, his neck and face and bare short-sleeved
arms the deep ruddy brown of russet leather. Blue eyes whitened
by the sun or age kept flashing back at them so frequently they
wondered how he could see where he was going. A smile like a
child's made them welcome ten times over.

"Back!" he kept shouting as they crossed a large compound of
bare, sunbaked beaten earth. All around it were mud and wattle
huts. At the farthest end was a mud-walled house with a
thatched roof and raised porch. Beyond this stood a chapel, also
made of mud, with a peaked conical thatched roof crowned by
a white-painted cross.

"Come in, come in," the old man cried, beckoning them up
the steps to the porch of his house. Huge flies buzzed wildly
around his head, but he didn't seem to notice them. Holding a
screened door open, he welcomed them into a dim, musty-smell-
ing room. For a moment they stood bunched just inside the door
as the screen slammed to behind them, their eyes blinded by the
abrupt change of light.

"By George, this is something," the old man was saying. "Now
isn't this something? I ask you. Three fellow countrymen—" he
stopped again. "Dear me, I must quit this babbling. Will you
stop me from babbling, please?" And he laughed. "We'll never
get anything said if I go on and on like this, will we?"

"My name's Marty Brom," Marty said quickly before the old
man could draw breath. "This is Gloria and Shad Smith.
We're—"

"I know," the missionary interrupted gently. "Do believe that
I know, Mr. Brom. Almost everything about you. And," he added
softly, "everything that's happened." Then he bowed jerkily,

making a little joke of introducing himself. "I'm Dr. Collins. Thomas Collins at your service. Though, what service I can be—" the shadow of some unhappiness crossed his face, then he smiled again. "Ah, well, times change. Times do change. We must expect the bad as well as the good, mustn't we? Cope as best we can. But I'm neglecting my hospitality. Do sit down, all. I'll see what I can do about something to refresh—"

"Dr. Collins, we haven't got much time," Shad said.

"Oh? Well, I'm sorry to hear that."

"Can we talk? I mean—is it safe?"

The old man sagged against a table, his joy gone, his age now cruelly revealed. "Safe," he said quietly, "Such a civilized word. One learns to do without it these days." Then he smiled again, straightening. "However! Do sit down. Let me tell you you're safe—but don't count on it—you understand?"

The room was smallish, stifling, crowded with chairs and settees made of hides stretched over rough frames. The long table the missionary leaned against was of some dark rough-hewn wood bound with iron bands. On it sat an inkstand, three pens, a stack of paper, a large leatherbound Bible, a long narrow box, and a kerosene lantern. Overhead swung another larger lantern of brass. The floor was bare, rough, and dusty. There was only one small screened window to be seen.

"I'm afraid we're rather primitive here," Collins apologized as if he read their minds. "But our chapel is somewhat more attractive. And our dispensary certainly cleaner. They don't understand about cleaning, you see. A very clean people personally, but as to housekeeping—" he made a gesture of futility. "And it's useless anyway—" laughing—"without soap, wax—all those ordinary luxuries of civilization."

"Can't you get things sent up by the riverboat?" Gloria asked.

"Once upon a time, yes." The old missionary smiled wryly. "Now I'm afraid we're here on sufferance. We must take what they wish to bring us—which, at present, seems to be nothing."

"You mean they refuse to deliver you anything?" Indignantly, Gloria looked at her husband, forgetting their purpose here. "If only we'd known—"

"Now, now, please don't worry," Collins said comfortingly.

"I'm an old hand at doing without. Every missionary learns that as a first lesson." He smiled at her. "You must forgive me for not asking before, Mrs. Smith. Will you want to lie down for a bit?" For of course he belonged to a slower gentler time of the world when women were fragile creatures, much in need, when they traveled, of rest, and repose. He looked surprised when Gloria said no. "Well, as you wish, Mrs. Smith. But please do say if you get to feeling a bit tired—"

"We got your message," Shad interrupted. "The deck—"

"Easy!" The old man cried. Then stealthily, seeming to mock with his exaggerated attitude the very seriousness of his purpose, he tiptoed toward a curtain strung across an inner doorway. Twitching it back, he revealed a fat native boy wearing wash-worn white ducks. The boy grinned. "You see?" the doctor asked. Then rapidly, he spoke to the boy in a native tongue which clicked like castanets. "He says he's waiting my pleasure. My pleasure!" The old man laughed harshly. "As if my pleasure had changed after thirty years. I am *his* servant, not he mine." He motioned the boy away, and when he had gone, said quietly: "You see what happens in trying times. The first loss is innocence." He shook his head sadly, as if mourning some secret failure in himself. "Well, no matter now. We must speak quickly, please. No, hear me first. Let me say that I should have no part in this. But in times like these, one's choices—" he made a limp gesture. "Evil against good. Right against wrong. Hopeless for a simple man—" His voice died away, and they all watched a shadow move across the screen door, stay for a second, then melt away. "By George, I must show you my piano!" the old man cried loudly. "How much time have you? Time enough for a little concert perhaps?"

Piano, Marty thought, dizzy with disappointment—like where, for instance? A little concert, for chrissake. This old geezer's got a hole in his head. Our last chance, and he's a nut of some kind. Looking at Shad, Marty tried desperately to catch his eye. But Shad was watching Collins intently. Gloria sat as if stunned in her chair, radiantly colored and out of place in this room as a butterfly in a nest of spiders.

"Believe it or not," the old man was saying as he lifted the lid off the long narrow box on the table, "*this* is my piano. You'll forgive the joke?" Blankly they looked at the keyboard lying there—all eighty-eight black and white keys connected to nothing. "This climate would ruin a piano in no time, you see. And the freighting. Well, impossible. But all the same I have my music every evening." He peered at Shad. "They said you were an entertainer, Mr. Smith. I do hope that means you play the piano."

They said. Who said? Wondering what they had got themselves into here, Shad rose and went to the keyboard. Without thinking, he struck middle C to test the tone—but of course there was none. Yet his mind heard it. Suddenly his heart began to beat faster. The old man pulled up a chair, and while Shad watched closely, began to play.

"You recognize this, Mr. Smith?"

For chrissake, Marty thought, is he kidding? The scene had a lunatic quality which gave him the shivers. That batty old coot and Shad. Hairs on his neck prickled as they both began to hum, then sing, "God Bless America"—for all the world as if they were accompanied.

The old man segued into another tune which Shad recognized as "Come Josephine in My Flying Machine." Playing with a gusto which the silent keyboard made eerie, Collins was saying: "Question and answer. Music is always this, isn't it? One way or another."

"Listen, we're short on time," Marty began, but Gloria shook her head, silencing him.

"I have stacks of sheet music," Collins was saying as he thumped the mute keys. "All old songs, of course. The new things—the chording and all that—are quite beyond me. Syncopation will never be my long suit. Do you know this one, too?"

The melody was familiar, but Shad racked his mind for words to go with it. And words had to. His throat felt thick. An old song. English maybe. Folk? Question and answer. He'd got the first one—but what did this signify?

Then suddenly the words popped into his mind. Do ye ken

John Peel. Do ye ken. Do you know. *Did you see?* Fondness for this clever, kooky, brave old Christian doctor flooded him, and he pressed his shoulder briefly. I ken. Collins nodded and smiled, winding up with a music hall flourish. "My turn now?" Shad asked.

"Jesus," Marty muttered. "Of all the cockamamey—"

"Hush, you're disturbing the concert," Gloria stage-whispered.

Shad had drawn another blank. The questions had been asked and he knew the answers, but how, musically, to convey them? What could he play that would say what he wanted and still be within the old man's corny musical grasp? Trying a few bars of an old Ella Fitzgerald number, he played very simply—no beat of any kind or this old boy might miss it. The old man began to hum behind him. "I'm Beginning to See the Light."

"Yeah man, I *saw* it," Shad murmured.

"It's the rhythm that quite escaped me on that one," Collins said, "but not the tune or the sense, you see."

Grinning at him, thinking what a great old guy he was, Shad segued into "It's a Long Way to Tipperary." It's a long way back home, yeah man. A moment later they were both singing it. And across the room, Marty gaped at them, too astonished even to grumble any longer.

Over their voices—Shad's smooth, trained, long used to projection, and the old man's thin and clear but wavering—came a hollow hooting sound. The riverboat. Both their voices trailed away, leaving a curious ringing quiet in the room.

"Well, I suppose—" Collins faltered, his old seamy face crumbling briefly. "I suppose you must go now?"

Shad nodded.

Collins cleared his throat. "Tell you what," he said briskly, "you're going upriver, are you?"

"That's right," Marty answered before Shad could do more than nod.

"Tell you what you do then," Collins went on. "You have them drop you by again tomorrow, eh? Could you arrange that, do you think? Then I'll be able to show you around a bit." He smiled drily. "Pride goeth before the fall, I know—but I am very proud of my work here. And the people do trust me. Most of them, that is. They'll do anything I ask—you understand?" He clapped Shad on the shoulder. "Be sure you come back, you'll be glad you did, eh? You're a grand piano player, I want to hear you again. Much better on this old keyboard than I could ever hope to be. But even so, there are a few tricks I might be able to teach you."

"I'm counting on it, Doctor." Shad rose.

"Tomorrow then."

It was a promise, Shad knew as they walked across the baking hot compound to the gate of Ebu Mission. Taking Gloria's hand, he started down the path, followed by a baffled Marty. The gate banged shut behind them. Below, on the river, the *Leolo* waited. But Thomas Collins would save them. Tomorrow was the day they left Danju for good.

21

The "pea-picking" village the captain had wanted to make by nightfall was another twisting ten miles or more upriver. The village stood on what looked to be a sandspit—a cluster of huts built on stilts, each with a canoe-like skiff tied at the bottom of a woven vine ladder. Beyond these, a rickety-looking dock thrust out into the still water cupped by the sandspit. In a clearing onshore, they could see a mud house surrounded by a veranda, two sheds, and a flagpole. In the windless hot evening air, the flag of the Republic of Danju hung like a rag.

With a great bustle and much shouting by the captain the *Leolo* was tied up at the wharf where three men in slovenly uniforms awaited them. The engines quit suddenly, leaving a void of silence. Then the gangplank was lowered with a bang. Captain Ngoru climbed down from his wheelhouse, and without a word to his passengers, disembarked, huddling clandestinely with the three men on the dock.

"More brass bands," Marty commented glumly as they watched the conference. "What d'you suppose those birds're cooking up?"

"That's a briefing session, man," Shad said. "Give 'em five minutes, they'll roll out the red carpet."

"I'd rather they didn't." Shuddering, Gloria rubbed her arms. "I don't like this place."

Now that the engines were stilled they could hear the rumbling of the river somewhere far off, screeching in the jungle nearby, a rising hubbub from across the small pond where natives gathered in their skiffs, paddling by twos and threes toward the riverboat.

"Dig the neighbors," Marty said as they circled the deck and looked down into blank black faces caked with dried mud. "Friend or foe—take your choice."

"Ugh, they look like cannibals!" Gloria whispered.

"Don't knock 'em," Shad said, "They might just be kinfolks."

Then the captain and one of the uniformed men came aboard.

"This one Sergeant Ubondi," Ngoru said by way of introduction. "River patrol here." The sergeant beamed and bobbed his head. "He say people have bad thoughts. Best you stay aboard this night."

"Like I was saying—" Marty murmured.

"If they're unfriendly," Gloria interrupted, "shouldn't we go back to the mission, Captain?"

"Too late." Raising his scarred face, Ngoru studied the flaming sky reflected like a sheet of fire on the river. "Cannot go back before dark now." His eyes rested on her, opaque, unreadable. "Not to worry, Mrs. Smith. Guard will keep watch—" he gestured toward the two on the wharf, and the soldier who had accompanied them upriver. "Plenty safe. Not to worry."

"Your men are armed, I hope?" Shad asked the sergeant, who kept grinning and nodding.

"Has no English," Ngoru explained. "But I will speak. You stay here on *Leolo*. Eat. Sleep. Tomorrow we will see."

"What d'you mean we'll see?" Marty asked pugnaciously. "We're going back down the river, aren't we?"

"If that is what you wish, yes."

Shad opened his mouth to say they wanted to stop at the mission again, then decided against it. Tomorrow was soon enough to hassle that one out. "You'll post a watch all night then, Captain?"

Ngoru grinned. "Mr. Smith worry all the time. Yes, I will watch. He will watch—" pointing to their guard and the men on the dock as he had before. "They will watch. Now we eat." Gutturally he said something to the sergeant, who nodded and went down the gangplank. "Come, please. Food is waiting."

As the melodramatic sunset light faded from the river, they ate again the smelly stew, flat grainy mush, and the fruit they had had for lunch. Only the biscuits were fresh—rank and rancid with hot grease. Then excusing himself, the captain went ashore. And as darkness fell swiftly, accompanied by an increasing clamor from the jungle closeby, Shad and Gloria and Marty sat on the afterdeck, chatting nervously about everything but their worries.

Their guard stood at the top of the gangplank, lounging against the rail. On the dock the half-caste from the engine room fished desultorily, yawning and scratching himself, his movements carried to them clearly on the still night air. Insects hummed, but protected by the spray repellent which Gloria had foresightedly purchased before leaving New York, they were fairly comfortable sitting out. In the house onshore yellowish lamplight shone, and they heard laughter, talking, the occasional blare of a wireless set going full blast.

"From the sound of things," Marty said at last, "neither one of those cats is going to be in very great shape tomorrow."

"I just hope it's only the two of them," Gloria added. "Can you see anybody on the dock still?"

Shad tried, but by now it was full dark, too early yet for moonrise. A match flared at the end of the dock. The engineer? He wished now he had tried to talk to him. All their eggs, he thought, were in one basket—Ebu Mission. Pretending to yawn, he stood up after a time, stretching. "Time for a walk."

"Me, too." Gloria started to rise, but he stopped her.

"This is for the pause that refreshes, baby." He grinned at Marty in the dark. "You too, buddy?"

"Better over the side," Marty said, "than in that pot I call my plumbing." His chair creaked as he rose. In the dark, he felt for Gloria's hand and squeezed it. "Sweet dreams, honey chile." He was going to add that everything would be all right, but didn't have the heart for it. Following the shadow which was Shad, he made his way to the bow of the riverboat.

Two streams splashed below. From somewhere came a coughing roar, and the high howling laughter of a hyena. "Sounds like a goddam sound track," Marty muttered. "Man-oh-Manischevitz, how I wish it was!"

"Amen, brother." Shad cleared his throat. "Listen, you still got that flashlight?"

"Yeah, here." Marty handed it over.

"I'm going to keep my own watch tonight."

"Like who isn't?"

"Yeah, well, I don't want to bug Gloria with it."

"What makes you think she'll sleep?" Marty reached toward him and found an arm, grasping it tight. "You think that old kook back there can help us, Shad?"

"He said he would. We've got to believe him."

"But all that campy piano bit—"

"Cool it, man. All God's children got big ears here in Africa."

"Okay. But I just hope you're right. I just hope to Christ, you're right, buddy!" Then he was gone, fumbling along the forepart of the superstructure toward the lantern which hung between their cabin doors, glowing like a firefly in the pitch blackness.

In the upper bunk where Shad had insisted she sleep, Gloria dozed fitfully, waking in the stifling dark as nightbirds hooted and called along the river. Her skin crawled and her head ached fiercely. She was certain there were fleas or ants in her bed. "Shad?" she whispered. "You awake, honey?"

"Yeah, baby."

"Can't I come down there with you? I hate it up here."

"Not enough room. Go to sleep, baby."

She heard him turn, sigh, and guessed he had not slept as yet. Their goodnight kiss seemed hours ago, a lifetime away . . . " 'No two-bit song-and-dance man is going to marry my daughter,' " she whispered, and felt rather than heard his laughter below her. "Little did he know—my poor old Daddy—what a versatile ham his son-in-law would turn out—"

A faint scraping concussion traveled along the deck boards. As Shad sat up in his bunk, he heard Marty stirring next door. "Don't move," he breathed. "Whatever happens, stay here—you promise? Right where you are."

"I—" she drew in a breath. "All right, I promise."

A rising moon glowed behind the black line of the jungle bank across the river. In its faint light, Shad could see Marty peering out his doorway. Clouds of mosquitoes whirled before his eyes. He blinked twice to clear his sight, but intensely as he might peer toward the gangplank, he could not see their guard. Or the gangplank. After a shocked instant, Shad realized it had been raised.

"Hey," Marty whispered.

Moving silently on his bare feet, crouching below the line of the railing so he could not be seen easily from the dock, Shad joined him. "You see the guard anyplace?"

"Uh-uh." Marty poked him. "Dig the gangplank. And while you're at it, take a look at the party."

Onshore, the glow of lantern light still shone from the open door and glazed windows of the house by the flagpole. But it was silent now. And on the dock, the two soldiers could no longer be seen.

"Come on," Shad breathed. "Let's have a look on the other side."

They crept along the deck to the forepart of the superstructure. Here Shad stopped, peering around the corner. By now the moon had slid up over the black line of jungle—an incandescent half-circle. Across the path it threw on the surface of the river, they saw a shadow pass, and another, and another.

"Keerist," Shad breathed, "aren't those native boats?"

Marty looked at him, his face pasty in the moonlight. "Fishing, I hope."

"Could be." Shad sucked his teeth. "But why so quiet?"

"And no guards." Marty grabbed his arm tight. "You still got that flashlight?"

Shad nodded. "I dig you—let's go."

From stern to bow they prowled the *Leolo*, inside and out, finding no one. The cook was gone, the deckhand who had brought them the message, the half-caste engineer, the guard and the captain. There was no one aboard but themselves.

22

The moon burned like a coin of acid, its dead light killing the life in their faces. What to do now? They had no options. Two frozen shadows, they stared at each other—dreamers suffering the same nightmare.

"You think—" Marty's whisper became a rasp and he started again. "You think it's all of 'em splitting? Like we're marooned or something?"

"No—they wouldn't leave this boat behind."

"A tub like this—why not?" But Marty didn't believe it either. "Maybe it was just the neighbors," he went on hopefully. "The rest of the cats are over there—" pointing to the house—"stoned out of their minds and sleeping it off."

"Could be." Shad drew a deep shuddering breath. "Maybe they figured as long as the gangplank wasn't down—"

Marty grabbed his arm. "So if they're all over there, how'd

it get raised?" He shook Shad's arm. "You got to pull it up from on board, Shad. See what I mean?"

"Jesus. That means whoever raised it—"

"Yeah. Hopped in one of those canoes. Had to." Marty swallowed noisily. "But, it don't make sense. I mean—leaving us here with this tub?"

"Does if there really will be a cruise ship in port. All they need is forty-eight hours—"

"Yeah, and then what?" Marty shook his head. "They're gonna cut our throats anyway—so why bother with this kind of crap?"

"I don't know." Shad closed his eyes, trying to think. "Unless maybe—" his voice quickened—"there's somebody on that cruise ship. Somebody who might get to us. Like reporters—"

They both jumped, tense nerves lacerated by a screeching from the nearby jungle. Something plopped in the river. From somewhere far distant came a mindless howling—a loon perhaps.

"Newspapermen," Marty breathed. "No flight in, so anybody that wants a look-see has to grab the first boat." He snapped his fingers. "Listen, I think you got something there, baby! I mean, come on," he cried, "Shad Smith disappears in Darkest Africa without even a stringer to follow up? Of *course* there's gonna be a newspaperman on that boat," and he laughed excitedly. "Just goes to show you—"

"Come on, I got to get back to the cabin. Gloria won't be able to hack it much longer wondering what's going on out here."

"Newspapermen," Marty kept babbling as they made their way back along the deck. "You know I almost forgot there was such an animal? Talk about alienation—"

It made sense, even Gloria admitted it did. There had to be a cruise ship. Had to be newsmen. In the trembling lamplight, her face altered magically, its sudden radiance striking a blow on Shad's heart. And what if he were wrong, he kept thinking. The idea began to obsess him instantly. To be wrong here was the same as being dead. God. Lord. Don't let me be wrong. "Listen," he finally interrupted their happy speculations, "Okay, it sounds good. The greatest. The old man'll get us down the river, and the next thing you know we're in Lisbon again.

Sounds good, sure—but maybe only because we want it to."

"Are you kidding, man?" Marty glared at him angrily. "Look, what're you now, the nevermore raven or something? All we got to do is—" he stopped, his face going blank. He sighed wearily. "I forgot that little matter about getting back to the mission."

"But surely if we don't get there, he'll come looking for us. Dr. Collins will."

Shad rubbed his forehead. "Maybe he won't be able to. Didn't look to me like they even went outside that wall."

"So," Marty said impatiently, "we borrow a boat from the neighbors. Can 'ou canoe—you know."

"Either borrow," said Gloria gloomily, "or get eaten for trying."

"So funny she is."

"Will you two cool it?" Shad cried. "I'm trying to think!" And as if spellbound, both stared at him, the measure of their fear the lack of wisecracking about the idea of his thinking. "Whatever happens—whatever we're gonna do," he went on haltingly —"we can't do it now, right? We've got to wait till we can see. Till daylight." Again he rubbed his head, blinking rapidly. "We better take watches, Marty. Just in case—" he glanced at Gloria, swallowing the words *we're wrong*. "Well, just in case. I'll take the first watch. Two hours, okay? Marty, you get some sack time while you can."

"How about me?" Gloria asked. "I can watch, too."

"No, baby, you got to sleep."

"But—"

"Just say 'aye-aye-sir' like a good girl," Marty advised. "Remember you promised to love, honor, and obey . . ."

If any of them slept, none would admit it. Nevertheless, the first faint freshness of dawn came as a surprise to all, the subtle lightening of the sky in the east, the slow emergence of the world around them. Shad was on watch again, slumped against the bulkhead facing the bow of the riverboat. It seemed to him that he blinked once, and suddenly his eyesight cleared. He saw the faint outlines of the sandspit, the village materializing. The paling sky was filled with fowl swooping up into the new light. In heavy ectoplasmic shapes, mist swirled over the river.

Shad stretched and yawned and rubbed his eyes. Then abruptly rigid, he rubbed his eyes again, peering into the low-lying undulating mist, perceiving ghostly shapes within it. A moment later he saw the first boat, the slow movements of the paddlers. Another followed it, then another and another. He didn't wait to see any more, didn't need to.

Moving silently along the deck, he crept around the bulkhead and down the door of his own cabin to Marty's. "Rise and shine, buddy," he hissed, "they're here."

Later they realized that the captain must have known they had seen the arrival—perhaps even knew they had spotted the party's departure last night. But the matter was not mentioned that morning: Even assassins, it seems, have their proprieties, too.

Playing possum in their cabins, they heard and felt the bumping of a native boat against the *Leolo*'s hull, a scraping as someone climbed the rope ladder which dangled over the side. Then the gangplank was lowered; feet clumped on it hollowly; they all heard the metallic click as their guard set his weapon on safety.

In the brief seconds they had had before separating to play possum in their cabins, Shad and Marty had decided to jump this guard. Whoever survived would have the automatic rifle they hoped, and from then on was responsible for Gloria. "Whatever you do," Shad had whispered desperately, "don't leave her to those mugs to tear apart. You dig me, Marty? Swear you won't." And when Marty nodded, he had gone on hastily: "Let's lay low as long as we can, though. See what happens first. Maybe—" he'd rasped here. "Maybe we can get to the mission after all." Then he'd made a half-salute, and slid away. Like a ghost, Marty thought, in the gray dawn.

But then the daylight spooks were heard from. "Good morning, all people!" Ngoru boomed. "No sleep now. Eat in short time!"

The galley boy brought them pitchers of tepid water, his eyes cast down as if he dreaded the sight of them. And before they had washed, the engines were going; once more the *Leolo*'s decks shuddered under their feet.

"Sleep good?" Ngoru inquired cordially as they filed into the tiny lounge where the table was set up. His hands were clean, they saw, as was his clothing. His wide scar-faced grin struck a chill into all their hearts. "Sit!" he boomed. "Eat! All is prepared for your pleasure." Then he dived into his plate, gobbling as if he had not eaten for days.

The pineapple was mildly fermented by now, but new bananas had been peeled, they noticed. Chicory coffee as bitter as lye steamed in white chipped-china galley mugs. All three gulped it gratefully, braced for whatever the captain held in store for them this morning.

"You wish to go upriver to falls?" he asked finally when he had stuffed himself full. "Very tall water there. Very beautiful. Many passengers take picture with Kodak."

"Sounds great," Shad said, "but not what we're looking for this trip."

"Ah?" Guileless as a surfeited carnivore, the captain glanced from one to the other. "Not this trip, then—what? You say, Mr. Smith. What you look for?"

"We call them locations," Shad explained. "What they are is—well, scenes we might use for the film. Backgrounds."

"Ah, the film, yes."

"That mission, for instance. Ebu Mission." Fixing the captain as if in rifle sights, Shad said calmly: "We'd like to go back, have another look around. You didn't give us much time yesterday."

"True." Ngoru seemed to study the problem, staring down at his plate. Then his face crinkled. "Very good," he said amiably. "Ebu Mission. We will leave now."

So great was the release of tension that they all felt deflated, and like drugged people, filed back and sprawled on the afterdeck. There was no need for any of them to express their gratitude. Not even Marty—usually so ebullient—mentioned the fact that they were saved.

Their boots and heavy sun-proof clothing were stifling in the morning sun. Knowing their escape with Collins might possibly be through the jungle, they had all changed during the night, agreeing to suffer in their long-sleeved bush jackets, sun-proof shirts and twill pants rather than take the chance on trying to smuggle them off the boat.

Gloria finally broke their silence: "You know who I haven't noticed? The amateur ballet dancer."

"The who?" Marty grinned. "Oh, yeah, I get it. You mean Lightfoot. Our friend with the message."

"He probably took French leave last night," Gloria said.

Shad nodded. "If he's a smart boy, he did."

Then destroyed by distraction, the pall of fatigue, their talk died again. It was enough to just sit here and wait to be helped.

By now the brilliant sunrise sky had turned into the limitless, pale hot blue to which they had become accustomed in Africa. The river shone white ahead of them. In the jungle along the banks they could see occasional flickers of color in the dense shadows, the swift silent passage of a big cat, the parting of reeds along the waterside as a crocodile nosed into the river. Fisher-birds darted around the boat, plunging like projectiles into the water after their prey. Monkeys howled. Birds screeched. But there was silence now and then too, when their own heart-beats seemed to blend with the pulse pounding through the riverboat.

Gloria dozed and daydreamed their flight into New York. She was hungry now, she found, and stirred by her pangs, saw menus on her closed eyelids, chafing dishes full of succulent foods. Dozing also, Marty dreamed of home too. But home was girls, not food, to him. Savoring his list of darlings both used and tantalizingly not so, he planned his first evening in elaborate detail, smiling unconsciously as the Mobene flowed by.

Only Shad watched the banks, trying to calculate their speed, to figure roughly when they would arrive at the mission. Every noise on the boat sent alarms through him, and remembered habits of soldiering made him tense, ready for whatever the next second might bring.

What he was not ready for, and could never have been, was what the next hour brought—a harsh hooting whistle from the riverboat as they rounded a bend, pillars of smoke rising from the promontory ahead. As they had for fifty years the mud walls of the mission stood steadfast against the jungle. But the graffito *Gesu Safes* was a mockery now, they found, invalid. For the gates stood open and within them lay chaos. Whatever was flammable had been burned to the ground, and whatever had been living lay dead or dying.

23

Bloated bodies fixed in strange postures told them unsparingly of sudden death in the mission compound. Panting, breathless, their mouths and hearts shriveling in horror, they ran like lunatics from body to body, unaware of their own hoarse cries. Gloria began to sob hysterically when they found the deckhand who had brought them the message. "He was so graceful . . . so graceful . . ." Shad pulled her away and they stumbled across the compound after Marty.

In the smoldering ruins of native huts lay charred children and their butchered mothers. In the gutted clinic sprawled the sickly, now dead. But in the doctor's house was nothing, no one. Dreading what they knew they must find there, they looked at last in the chapel.

He lay at the foot of the simple altar, his head split open, his body partially burned. Thomas Collins, medical missionary. An old man who had only done good. In death he looked his age yet somehow also young—bland and blank, no longer troubled by the choices he should not have had to make.

Transfixed, they stood there for a time. Finally Marty covered the upper part of the body with his bush jacket. Still holding Gloria, Shad picked his way through the rubble of the burned roof which had fallen in, into the compound again. In the utter silence, both retched noisily.

His face greenish, Marty staggered out after them, and heaved also. Then weak in the knees, he leaned against the bullet-pocked mud wall of the chapel. Clouds of flies began to buzz around them, iridescent in the blazing sunlight. Batting at them feebly, he said: "We got to do something. Listen—" and his voice rose hoarsely: "Come on, will you? We got to *do* something!"

As if wakened from a feverish dream, Shad blinked rapidly and rubbed his face. "Yeah—" dully—"yeah, we do." Taking Gloria by the shoulders, he stared into her face anxiously. "You all right, baby?"

She nodded mutely.

"Don't look any more. Promise me. Don't look at anything, hear?"

Again she nodded.

"Okay," Shad said to Marty, "let's go." And taking Gloria's hand, he began to walk rapidly across the compound to the gate.

Marty followed. As they stepped out, a squatting figure rose out of the deep shadow cast by the mission walls—their guard from the riverboat.

Gloria gasped. Pushing her behind him, Shad said calmly, "That was quite some picnic you boys had for yourselves last night."

Clicking the safety off, the guard leveled his automatic rifle at waist height, gesturing to the path down the riverbank.

"You think he'll use that cannon?" Marty asked, moving closer.

"Maybe—if he has to."

Angrily, the guard gestured again. Sweat was rolling down his black shiny face. To Shad he looked nervous but plenty tough. Nobody, he thought, to fool with.

Bending down as if to fix a shoelace, he said, "I think he's got orders not to shoot unless he has to. They want us dead, sure, but no problems about it. They've got to have bodies that can stand inspection."

"Yeah—like three more that got caught in the massacre? I hope you're right and I'm wrong, buddy."

Muttering now, the guard again pointed down the path, grimacing savagely.

"He means it," Gloria breathed. "Shad—?"

"Ladies first, baby. Go nice and slow."

As she started off down the path, the guard's eyes fixed on her long enough for Shad to palm a fist-sized rock. He stood up, stamping his boot as if settling his foot into it. The guard's eyes swiveled around to him, black and dull as lava pebbles. Shad grinned. "Nervous, friend?" Then he said to Marty: "You next. And when you hear the tone it'll be time to duck—you dig me?"

Marty started slowly after Gloria, careful of his footing, for once they'd left the mission promontory, the path was steep. From this view, the jungle seemed to fester around them—live, shimmering, mottled green—like an algae-covered sump. Below the river glistened in the morning sun. Smoke twined from the riverboat stack. He could see the captain—a tiny figure—standing in the door of the wheelhouse watching them. Then the path curved and the jungle shut out their view of the river.

Holding the rock tight against the front of his body, Shad listened to the guard behind him. Booted feet sliding like their own on the steeply pitched, packed ground. And the guard couldn't watch his footing, didn't dare with three of them in front of him. It came at last: scraping as a boot slipped, a muttered imprecation. Like a top, Shad whirled, flinging the rock, shouting: "Duck!"

Off balance, the guard staggered as the rock struck his shoulder a glancing blow. A burst from the automatic rifle whined wide into the jungle undergrowth. Shad scrambled back up the path, but he was too far away, and instead of fighting for his footing, the guard began to lurch, half running downhill toward him. As the rifle barrel swung unsteadily, an instant off target, Shad launched himself in a flying tackle, and they hit with a crack that shook every bone in his body. In a rolling tangle, they went down, the guard tumbling over Shad, Shad hanging desperately onto the man's thrashing legs—all he could reach in his wild lunge.

His eyes glued on the rifle which the guard clung to, trying to use it as a club, Marty bolted up the path in jackrabbit leaps. Grappled like lunatic wrestlers on a greased slide, they hit him hard as he leaped for the gun. His breath knocked out of him in a groaning grunt, Marty clung to the arm holding the rifle. Sweaty black flesh slipped greasily under his fingers. The barrel swung wildly this way and that, and deafening at this point-blank range, came another burst of fire.

His ears ringing, coughing from cordite fumes, Marty wrenched the guard's wrist savagely, prising the rifle free. Then he lost it again as a fist smacked him hard in the face, and he flew backward. The rifle bounced away out of his hands, flying like a live thing as it hit a rock and disappeared into the dense undergrowth which lined the path.

Only a minute or two had passed, yet everything was changed forever. Shrieking, a jagged rock held high over her head, Gloria scrambled up to them. Then she just stood there, her wild cries dying away as she stared at the guard lying unconscious on the path. Marty nursed his bruised face, gasping for breath. Shad lay huddled in the dirt near the undergrowth, his chest heaving, lungs seared. The rock Gloria held seemed monstrously noisy as it fell clattering down the path. In the silence, they heard the captain's distant shouting.

Shad scrambled to his feet. "Where's the rifle?"

"Somewhere—" Marty gasped, pointing into the jungle—"in there."

"In—" Shad groaned. "For chrissake, couldn't you hang onto it?"

Without bothering to argue the point, Marty began thrashing around in the green tangle so thick it obscured even the earth from which it sprang. A snake slid hissing an inch from his hands. Great sticky fronds, rasping as tiger tongues, scraped his bruised flesh. He could hear Shad beating the bush behind him, his breath wheezing like a bellows.

"I can hear them," Gloria kept calling, out of sight now. "Shad, they're coming after us!"

"Okay, baby, just hang on."

"Jesus," Marty muttered, "where is it? Where could it be,

for chrissake. That goddam effing—it's gotta be here someplace!"

Shad tugged his arm. Breathless and sweating in the shadowed, humid smothering green they stared at each other. "We can't wait to look."

"But we—"

"I know, but we don't have time."

"What'll we do without it?"

"Run—what else?"

"In this?" They both looked into the seemingly impenetrable lush green thicket.

"We got to, Marty. There's three of them, and they'll all be armed."

Marty opened his mouth to protest, then did not. Shad nodded, and thrashed back through the clinging tangle to the path where Gloria stood staring at the fallen guard.

"I think he's coming to."

"Okay, you take off up the path. We'll be right after you."

"Shad, what're we—"

"Go, baby. Will you please *go?*" He gave her a little shove. "We'll be tailing you."

She started off reluctantly, then after a look back over her shoulder, began to scramble as fast as she could up the steep dirt path trod smooth by fifty years of mission travel.

24

Almost immediately they found a small clearing where two generations of the carriers who had packed everything for the mission on their backs must have rested. Dried human excrement dotted the perimeters of the trampled ground. A broken gourd lay abandoned under a bush. Scouting for a minute while they caught their breath and listened to their pursuers laboring up the trail, Shad found a place where the undergrowth seemed thinned. Beckoning to Gloria and Marty, he plunged in, and pulling at the leafy vines after them, covered their tracks as well as he could.

Then leading the way, he pushed through a path for them, parting nets of creepers hanging like draperies, trampling underbrush as thorny as barbed wire. When they had gone a way, he stopped again. Bunching closely behind him, Gloria and Marty breathed softly also, listening so intently their mouths hung open.

Almost to the minute, Shad had guessed when their pursuers might reach the spot where the guard lay. And when the shout came, he looked at Marty, then both stared hard at the ground.

Gloria saw the look, and remembering the weight and texture of the rock she had grabbed up for a weapon, closed her eyes, sickened for them all. For she had seen Shad hefting it as she had gone up the path, looking back over her shoulder. Like Lot's wife, she thought, punished for having done so. Turned to salt, the taste of tears. Turned to acid, the taste of horror. His fingers on her arm made her open her eyes again. As she looked up into her husband's still, shadowed face, Gloria knew if they lived by some miracle to be ninety, as she had wished, this would be the secret they kept from each other. For she would never ask, and he would never tell her. There are some things even lovers cannot say.

"We've got about five minutes before they're here," Shad whispered. "Can't chance them hearing us now."

Marty nodded, also whispering. "Let's lay low, yeah. And for God's sake, pray! If they come looking—"

"Separate. Make a run—" Appearing hypnotized by his wife's face, Shad stopped. Then gulping, he tore his eyes from hers and went on: "Run like hell. Head downhill for the river. We'll try to meet—"

Cutting him off with a fierce silencing gesture, Marty pointed toward the trail. They could hear boots scuffing now, closer and closer, a grunting mutter which sounded like the captain.

Like a child playing a scary twilight game, Gloria sank down, covering her face with her hands. Standing over her, Shad listened so intently he forgot to breathe. His heart pounded. His flesh turned cold. All of his body became an instrument to hear with.

The men had found the clearing and stopped there—to rest evidently—for their voices were quiet, and did not move on. No search was made, which puzzled Shad. A long discussion was all he heard—glottal and excited, yet carefully muffled. Baffled, he listened and tried to figure what they might be saying. One down, why risk our hides? We either risk them now or get skinned in Porto Saba.

Why were they so cautious? Then suddenly he knew the answer. The rifle, of course. Elated, he signaled to Marty, making a silent hand-play of machine-gun fire, then mouthing and pointing: *They* think *we've* got it.

For an instant Marty frowned, bewildered. Then his mouth opened wide in a silent *Oh,* and in the greenish half-light which pervaded the jungle, his sunburned freckled face split into a huge grin.

There was a dim chance now, dim but perceivable. Stifling their sighs of relief, both men crouched on either side of Gloria, trying to convey silently their sense of renewed hope.

The captain must have figured—as they did—that their only chance of escape was the river. After a long discussion—quiet and unintelligible—they could hear their pursuers leaving, going not upward, but back down the steep trail again. But Ngoru was not a man for subtle games, they discovered, no patient hunter to wait for his prey without crowing over his power. From somewhere on the trail below—perhaps beside the guard they had left behind—he roared: "I get you! We wait, and I get you!" Then several pistol shots reverberated, echoing in the silence after his voice died out. They felt that a duel had begun— and they were right.

"Okay, so now what?" Marty whispered. "You think that's a ploy?"

"Could be." Distractedly, Shad caressed Gloria's trembling

arm. Then holding her tight, he made her stand up beside him. "One thing we can't do is go back to that trail."

"That's what I meant. He's probably got that galley cat sitting under a bush somewhere with a butcher knife."

"Two things for sure," Shad scowled, rubbing his head. "He figures we've got the rifle, and that we'll try for the boat."

"So we haven't got it, and we won't try—so then what?"

The jungle, which had been silent, had begun to stir again around them. They sensed movement everywhere, a subtle rustling as the wind rose high in the trees overhead. From far distant came screeching cries, a raucous calling from treetop to treetop as birds and monkeys warned each other. The sky they could see only indirectly began to darken. And even as they stood there, still waiting indecisively, thunder began to rumble far off.

"I got an idea," Shad said finally.

"Me too," said Marty. "It's going to pour soon."

"Hope it does, man, 'cause it'll help us maybe." Shad hugged his wife. "Think you'll melt, sugar-baby, if it rains on you?" Forcing a smile, she shook her head no, and he hugged her again. "That's my girl. Where's your purse, baby?"

"I didn't carry one. All my stuff's in my pockets."

"Like what, for instance? Let's take a look."

As wind sighed eerily in the tall trees far above them, Gloria emptied her pockets, producing a lipstick, a tiny gold compact, a cigarette case and matches, a diamond-dust nail file, a tiny bottle of clear nail hardener, and two neatly-folded Kleenex tissues.

Poking in the frivolous heap of her belongings, Shad took the nail file and returned the rest to her pockets. Then it was Marty's turn. The result was equally meager—a wallet, a credit card case, a pen, the flashlight Abby Golden had given him, cigarettes and matches, a Kennedy half-dollar key chain, and a small gold pocket knife.

Shad took the penknife. "Now me," he said, sighing. "Jesus, I'd sell my old second-class nigger soul for that Boy Scout toad-stabber I used to carry!"

"Listen," Marty hissed, "if you're thinking about jumping those studs with a nail file and a pen knife—" but Shad stopped him.

"We're not jumping anybody. Because that's what they expect. They know we can't get out except down there on the river." Shad blew out his breath. "And they're right. We'll never make it tramping this jungle."

"So they're right—"

"Shad." Gloria shook his arm. "If you've thought of something, for God's sake tell us this minute!"

"Okay. Are you ready for this?" He grinned. "We're going to make a raft."

"A *raft!*" Marty clawed his sweat-sodden, Sebring-cut straw-colored hair. "Are you out of your mind, a raft? They'll pick us off like a shooting gallery."

"Not on this raft. Look, the Indians used to do it all the time," Shad said eagerly. "I bet when I was a kid I must've read fifty stories about—"

"Indians! Stories!" His eyes round and bulging as marbles, Marty glared at him. "You've blown your mind. You know that? You—have blown—your entire—mind!"

"Wait a minute, Marty." Gloria patted his cheek. "Listen, hunh, baby? What's the harm? And we can take a vote—"

"Yeah, vote, schmote. I know all about your two-to-one votes." But he listened anyway, and as Shad explained, began to nod—hesitantly at first, and then enthusiastically. It takes one genius to recognize another.

The idea was one thing, but making it tangible was unbelievably arduously another. And to even start it, they had to reach the riverbank. Which meant fighting the jungle without implements to do so; fighting also their urban horror of its inhabitants, imagined and real. Every branch and vine looked like a snake to Gloria; she kept seeing the deadly mamba the major had pointed out on the way to the hunt, the giant serpent they had seen fleeing the fire. Too many terrors had been burned into her mind these last two days, and although she tried, she could not stifle the shrieks which welled like bubbles in her throat.

Shad and Marty took turns breaking a trail, each concealing

from the other his dread of what he might encounter. To make it worse, every branch, every vine, every frond seemed malevolently alive, for by now the wind had risen in velocity, sweeping the jungle like a minor hurricane. The false dusk of the storm deepened and they fumbled through greenish half-dark, feeling drowned in the humid, hot swirling air. Then lightning began to crackle, moving closer and closer until the jungle blazed around them, bleached out by the phosphorescent million-volt flares, battered by bomblike concussions of thunder. Minds reeling, flesh revolting against the will to move on, Shad and Gloria and Marty finally stopped, crouching together like savages waiting out the wrath of their gods. When the rain came, it was like a waterfall, saturating the air so they seemed to breathe spray, a flood from which there was no protection. Then the storm rolled on like a juggernaut across the heavens eastward, and in the dripping aftermath they moved on, clothing plastered to their bodies, boots squelching with every step, gasping for breath as steam rose all around them, re-creating the shape of their terrors.

Downhill they slid and wrestled their way, half strangled by vines as thick as ropes, torn at by creepers laden with brilliant blossoms which concealed thorns as cruel as spurs. Things that looked like leaves took flight as they approached, and things that writhed with life turned inanimate as they passed. Giant ferns rained streams of water on them, surrealist-looking fronds holding quarts, gallons, lakes, drenched them again and again as they crept underneath, tunneling for passage like lost miners.

By the time they finally spotted the river ahead, they were exhausted, disheartened by their weariness, verging on hopelessness. "We can't do it," Gloria wept bitterly. "You want a miracle, Shad, and we just can't do it!"

"I agree," Marty muttered, and slumped down moaning. "Count me out till I rest awhile."

"There isn't time." Shad stifled a groan. "Look, I'm as tired—" then he stopped himself, stopped pitying them all, including himself. "On your feet, Jew-boy," he said in a cruel, quiet, cutting tone. "You too, nigger-baby. Time you two leeches did something honest for your keep."

"Why, you—" Marty lunged for him and missed by a yard.

Speechless with outrage, Gloria scrambled to her feet, both hands full of mud which she pitched at him wildly.

"See?" Shad said cheerfully. "All you needed was a little encouragement. Come on, gang, let's get rolling." And as they watched dumbfounded, he began his part of the work they had planned—a search for the fallen logs with which they would fashion their raft.

25

Because he believed they had the rifle, they figured, the last thing the captain would anticipate was the very thing they had planned. "He'll expect us to rush him after dark," Shad said during a rest period. "They're probably keeping under cover till sunset, then they'll push off and cruise up and down."

"There's a jolly idea," Marty said glumly. "What makes you think we can get by them?"

"We've got to."

"Yeah—miracle number two."

"Maybe they'll give up," Gloria suggested hopefully. "Mightn't they just take off and leave us here?"

"Dreamer." Marty groaned. "Not a chance, sweetie. Little Brother of the Knife'll cut their throats if they go back without us."

"But if they think we have the gun—"

"That's only one ace in the poker game." Shad rubbed his chin, imagining himself in Ngoru's shoes. "For one thing the captain knows we can't make it in this jungle. We've got to come to him to survive. So all he has to do is wait, see? Play it cool till we get desperate. Sooner or later he knows we'll show."

"Hey, you think maybe he might make a deal?"

"Marty!" Gloria looked horrified.

"Okay, okay, it's just habit, I guess." Marty grinned sheepishly. "Why have a war, I always say, if you can do business instead?"

"If we *had* the rifle—" Shad shrugged. "No use talking about it," and he rose, moaning—a scarecrow figure, as they all were now, in his muddy brush-torn clothing. "Come on, let's go. We've only got till sunset."

"Then what?" Marty dragged himself to his feet. "So maybe we do a couple of miracles and get down that river—what if there isn't any cruise ship?"

"We'll worry about that when we get there." Shad held out his hand to Gloria. "Alley-oop, baby. Time to go to work." She staggered against him and he held her tight for a second, then let her go. "Come on, Tiger," he said to Marty, "I got a little weight-lifting chore for you."

Behind a screen of undergrowth at the river's edge they had trampled a space in which to work. Marty had sawed down vines with the penknife and nail file, stripping the leaves, leaving long wirey cords which Gloria was plaiting with the dreary patience of a prison inmate. Her fingers had blistered and were bleeding as she worked, but dulled by exhaustion, she had ceased to feel the pain. Only horror remained like a residue in her, a sickening fear of every tiny noise or movement in the mat of greenery surrounding them.

When Marty disappeared following Shad, she sat rigid, only her eyes moving. Things seemed to watch her, unseen, malevolent. From behind her came a subtle rustling, and she dared not cry out. All her life she had been terrified of snakes, spiders, insects—whatever slithered or crept or crawled. And this was their world, here they proliferated in the nightmarish multitudes of a dipsomaniac dream. Pressing both hands to her mouth to keep herself from crying out, she looked over her shoulder. But nothing was there. See? she told herself. Then, as she began to twist the vines again, braiding them into a rough rope, she spied something through a rip in her pants leg—a shiny blot of mud that seemed to pulse.

The task of finding logs had turned out to be more complicated than Shad had expected, for as well as locating the fallen trees, size was a problem. Any raft they could handle had to be small, he knew. And there was no way to cut the logs he found, so long ones had to be left.

"I've got some matches left," Marty said as they reluctantly stumbled by one fallen tree after another. "Some of 'em still dry. Couldn't we burn the logs to the right length?"

"Great idea, but what about the smoke?"

Marty sighed, plodding after him. "I should've known an old Indian scout like you would've thought of the angles."

"Here's one." Shad pointed to a creeper-covered log only slightly longer than he was. "Watch where you grab it. We don't want any snake bite problems."

As they began to heave at either end, trying to break the log free of the vines holding it, Marty asked panting: "Hey, how come you're such a big woodsman, Champ? I thought you-all was a city slicker like me."

"Reading, man." Shad gulped for breath. "Jesus, this thing might as well be nailed to the ground!" He heaved mightily, gasping: "Part of the country I grew—uh!—up in, you had two choices where to go to keep warm. The pool hall or the public library . . . There it comes, the bastard!"

The log broke free, sending them both staggering. His face pasty, Marty gasped at the hissing nest underneath. "Christamighty, will you *look* at that? There must be a million—"

"Snake nursery." Shad shuddered. "Looks like green spaghetti, don't it? Come on, let's go before momma comes back from the supermarket."

They were almost to the clearing they had made when they heard Gloria's stifled cry. Dropping the log, both thrashed back over the trail, finding her crouched where they had left her, staring at her leg.

"Look," she moaned. "That slimy thing—" and covering her mouth again, she began to shriek softly.

It was a leech, Shad realized, sickened for her. "Gimme a

match," he said to Marty, snapping his fingers. "Come on, man, move!"

"What is it?" His freckles darker against the underlying pallor of his sunburn, Marty stared at the thing as Shad ripped the cloth away from his wife's brown shapely calf. "Hey, what're you doing? You're going to burn her!"

Without speaking, Shad held the match flame against the leech which swelled like a small balloon off her skin. "Just hold still," he said to his wife. "Let it fall off."

After a moment it did, leaving a small bleeding wound on her skin which Gloria stared at, horrified. "It was drinking my—"

"You can take ticks off that way, too," Shad said. "But turpentine's better." Then he took her by the shoulders, shaking her gently. "Okay, baby? Okay?"

She nodded mutely.

Shad hugged her. "That's my girl." And grunting he stood up again. "You better stay here for a while, Marty. I'll go drag that mother back here."

"No, you stick around." Marty swallowed hard, remembering the writhing nest of snakes. "I'll get it."

Staring up at them in the greenish shadow—filthy, torn, sweat-soaked—Gloria experienced a kind of surging of the spirit which was almost like courage. And horror died in her at last, recollection sank. She knew from now on she would be all right. "Go on, blow, you two," she said in a tough sidewalk twang, enjoying their startled faces. "Lift dem trees, men. Tote dem logs. I got my own knitting to tend to here."

They lost track of time in their struggle against the jungle, against time itself. And the heat grew. Their hunger grew. Fatigue made of every smallest effort a mythical Sisyphus-like terrible strain. Truly they were rolling the stone up the mountain, and truly it would crush them if they stopped for a moment.

To spur them on from time to time they heard shots from the riverboat—reminders of the duel. And later, as the sun began to slant across the river instead of standing overhead, a white glare on the water, they heard the engines thudding, the *Leolo*'s hoarse hooting whistle across the jungle as she cast off.

Another swift storm blew out of the west—brief and torrential as the earlier one—but they kept working feverishly, Marty cutting at underbrush with the silly little blade of his gold penknife, Gloria still plaiting, Shad in a wild plunging search for the fourth log to complete their raft.

By the time he found it, the light filtering through the trees overhead was already fading. In the dripping jungle dusk had already fallen. Grunting like an animal, his effort squeezing the last strength from aching muscles, Shad dragged the log along the path he had made, only to find his way blocked by a huge lizard.

Saurian eyes as cold and yellowish as agates gleamed at him. Two purplish pouches on either side of the creature's spiny head puffed in and out like exposed lungs. Panting, Shad watched it, wondering what to do. He'd read that wild things wouldn't attack you if you were still. But on the other hand, how long could it stand there? His inside knotting in apprehension, Shad slowly pulled the log forward hand over hand, inching it toward the lizard.

But the creature did not move. "Out of my way, you mother," he whispered. The exposed lungs puffed in and out, horrible and obscene. Finally, in desperation, Shad gave a great heave and the log slid like a battering ram at the lizard. With a flick more like the movement of a shadow than anything tangible, it was gone without a sound. Dragging the log as fast as he could, Shad staggered by the spot where the lizard had disappeared, his skin prickling with the acid sweat of his atavistic horror.

As he crashed into the clearing, Gloria and Marty both shushed him, pointing toward the river. Dropping the log, Shad stooped low, peeking from behind their riverside screen of underbrush. The *Leolo* drifted by, looking peaceful, a sanctuary. There was no one to be seen in the wheelhouse, however. Then Shad realized that the windows were screened—Ngoru must have erected a shield for himself.

"They keep shooting every so often," Marty whispered behind him. "Every ten minutes or so, one of 'em takes a potshot at the bank."

"I heard it. Anything come close?"

Marty shook his head. "Trying to scare us, I guess." In the dimness, he grinned. "So what else is new?" And he patted Shad's shoulder. "Onward and upward, sweetheart. Let's get this show of yours on the road."

Before moonrise, they knew, the raft must be launched. Their whole ruse depended on darkness. And it was nearly sunset. Only an hour of light left to them, Shad guessed, then they would no longer be able to see to work.

With Marty's help, he dragged the four logs as close to the river as he could, pointing them at the water's edge. Then they all began to lash them together, weaving the viney ropes Gloria had made in and out for greater strength. The sun was gone, the sky blazing with its afterglow when they had used up the last of the rope. The raft looked too narrow and flimsy to hold them. But it was done—except for the covering which would come last. "Try it," Shad said, instructing them to lie flat on their stomachs, facing toward the river. Then he began to heap on them the brush which Marty had cut. Both complained, but he would not let them up until they were only faintly visible through the branches and foliage which covered them.

Marty's pale skin showed, but mud would take care of that. To his mental list of things to be done before they got away, Shad added mudbaths for all. Then crawling back to the jungle side of their tiny clearing, he stood up, inspecting the raft. Just big enough for two, a squeeze for three. Good thing they were friends. But did it look like flotsam? God help us if it doesn't. "Okay," he whispered, and crawling back, pulled off the covering brush. "R-and-R time, buddies. Rest and relaxation. All we got to do now is wait for dark."

26

Using the river for a mirror of true darkness, they waited long after the jungle around them became black, impenetrable, before they began to launch the raft. Starlight gleamed on the water surface. Like a pale massive ghost in the dark, the riverboat stood off from the shore just above them, its engines thudding like the pulse of a giant over the screeching, squawking din from the rainforest.

"Jesus, *look!*" Marty muttered as a beam of light shot suddenly from the bows. "Where the hell did that come from?"

Shad could not repress a groan. Why hadn't he noticed a searchlight on the *Leolo?* "Got to be battery-powered." He tried to sound indifferent. "Means they can't use it much."

"So—once at the right time'll be enough, won't it?"

As Gloria's hand found Shad's and held tight, he silently cursed Marty for saying it aloud. "Forget it," he rasped. "The odds are on our side. He's looking for a needle in a haystack, and he knows it."

Swinging this way and that in swift arcs which scythed the darkness, the light searched the banks then went out abruptly. From time to time pistol shots reverberated across the water as they waited, sending waves of silence through the jungle behind them. "That's whistling in the dark," Marty whispered. "Those cats are as scared as—"

Shad jabbed him in the ribs. "Come on, let's get started. Time for mudbaths, gang."

"So good for our complexions," Gloria joked tremulously, and remembering the leech on her leg, shuddered.

Three shadows, they slipped through their riverside screen of underbrush, sliding down the shallow incline into the water. It was tepid and slimy. Standing hip deep in the currentless shallows, they gingerly plastered themselves with mud which smelled of rot, of decay. Then pushing Gloria up the bank, Shad breathed: "You push, we'll pull. And for God's sake, keep watching that boat! If it drifts this way—" but he didn't have to go on. They all knew they were exposed now, no way to hide until the raft was in the water.

Tugging together, wincing at every noise, Shad and Marty inched the raft forward—no easy task, for their footing was slippery. Their breath sawed in and out of their throats. Stubborn, mulish, the raft refused to move except fractionally. "Can anything this heavy really float?" Marty whispered, and for the tenth time slipped, sprawling face down on the bank, making a splash that seemed to resound like a waterfall. "Jesus!"

"Will you cool it?"

"Listen!" From the darkness above them, Gloria's whisper had a snakelike sibilance that froze them where they stood half in and half out of the tepid slimy water.

Motionless, they listened as the *Leolo's* engines thumped louder and louder. Peering through the starlit dark, they could see clearly the huge spectrally pale outline. The riverboat was headed downriver toward them.

Plunging up the bank, grappling for handholds, Shad pulled himself up. Reaching back, he yanked Marty after him by main force. "The brush," he whispered frantically. "Quick—make a camouflage!" And grabbing wildly in the dark, he pulled an armload of the undergrowth Marty had cut toward the exposed spot where the raft now nosed out in full view of the river.

Searching the darkness like a glaring cyclops the searchlight swept to and fro, probing the riverbank. Filtered by the brush as it swept by them, the light fell like a dazzling rain on Shad and Marty and Gloria as they lay flat behind their hastily-made screen, praying that its dying foliage concealed the nose of the raft. In mud-plastered faces, their eyes glistened. Shad noticed a dark shiny blob on his arm, and his skin crawled. No time now for burning off leeches. They would have to live with them from now on.

"They're coming about," Marty whispered. "Look."

Cautiously, Shad poked a peephole through the underbrush in front of him—then automatically ducked as a round of pistol shots crackled through the dark like Fourth of July fireworks.

Marty crawled closer to him. "They're either panicky," he breathed, "or loaded with ammunition."

"For chrissake, keep your head down!"

Holding Gloria tight, Shad held his breath, waiting. But there was no more shooting, only the steady pulse of the engines as the *Leolo* turned in the middle of the river, steaming slowly upriver again.

"Now?" Marty asked finally.

"Yeah, let's move—and, baby, like *fast!*"

Pushing their screen aside, they slid down the bank again, heaving at the raft until it leaned over the brow of the bank, tilting downward, beginning to slide. A moment later, splashing, it floated in the water. Ceremoniously, Marty bent and kissed it. "I christen thee magic carpet," he whispered.

Above them they heard Gloria sighing. "Thank God."

"Come on, baby." Shad held up his arms toward her shadow, and she came sliding down the bank. "You and Marty get on. Lie down like you did before. I'll go up and toss down the brush."

"But—but, Shad, who's going to cover you?"

"Get on, will you, baby? I'll cover myself." I hope, he thought. Everything from now on must go by feel, guesswork. Time now to trust to luck, and pray.

Gloria lay in the middle, Marty to one side of her, and Shad heaped brush over their prone bodies. The space that was left was a thin man's share, he saw, but he squeezed onto it, and holding to the bank, pulled the balance of the brush he had heaped there over himself. With luck, they would only need their covering for a short time, he figured. From then on they could discard most of it. If needed, more could be cut before they reached the harbor—*if* they reached it. "Curtain," he whispered when he had finished. "Everybody set?"

"I feel like a sardine traveling steerage," Marty answered. "Cast off, mate."

Feeling Gloria's fingers pressed against his side, Shad turned his head against the scratchy branches covering him and tried to kiss her. Something crawled on his neck—a leaf? He hoped so. Taking a deep breath, he said, "Here we go," and pushed hard at the muddy bank.

The raft moved out, turning sluggishly. Thinking of crocodiles and snakes, Marty and Shad stroked slowly, using their free arms as oars. Come on, current, Shad kept thinking. Jesus Christ, Marty worried, the thing don't move. Gloria stirred against them as the raft began to swing so they could see upriver. Her long sigh struck on Shad's senses like a scream in the dark, and he saw that the *Leolo* had turned again, heading back down the river toward them.

Ahead of the riverboat, writing death on the water, moved the yellowish beam from the battery searchlight. Then it turned inward, raking the shore. A voice called across the water, another answered. Then the thump-thump of the engines blotted out all other sounds as the huge shape, pallid in the dark, bore down on them.

It was luck, Shad decided later, they hadn't caught the current sooner. Three minutes later, five, and the *Leolo* would have run down the raft perhaps, or at the very least, capsized it. As it happened, they were still too close to shore for the riverboat to do more than rock them as it passed. But the searchlight found them—swept by once, then more slowly crawled back over the surface, fixing on a heap of brush and flotsam carried down by the storms.

Trapped under the wilted leafy covering which seemed too thin now, hopelessly so as the searchlight glared into it, they lay rigid on the raft, not daring to breath. Remembering his own words—*they're either panicky or loaded with ammunition*—Marty felt his flesh shrinking against his bones. His mouth opened in a silent yell. Digging his fingernails into the rotting bark of the logs, he fought his own nature with all its temptations to move, to act, to escape from this trap—to roll off the raft, swim for shore—anything but lie here and wait to be shot.

Don't move, Shad kept willing them, *don't move,* as his legs trembled, his fingers clenched tight around Gloria's with the effort to keep them both still. The taste of panic was dry on his tongue, bitter. When he closed his eyes the slum he had grown up in leaped upon his lids—a trap as ugly and inescapable as this. Patches of snow lying like dirty rags on the sidewalks. Old men huddling in doorways begging. Wind that went through you as if your body was tissue paper because after the rent man come around wasn't nothing left for anything like a coat. Ah God, he thought, Lord? I got out of that, can't I get out of this? But you put yourself here, Mr. Big. You done it, baby, not Old Man Fate.

The taste of panic was aridity, hopelessness now—for they would shoot, he knew. But with only a pistol and no marksmanship . . . He hoped he was right. Most devoutly hoped.

Against him, Gloria jumped as the first shot boomed. And she lay so still, Shad knew she must be hit. Then, in the next merciful instant, he knew she could not be, for spray from the bullet showered warm on his cheek: it had hit the water not far from his head.

Three more shots followed, then the riverboat slid by them, engines thumping, searchlight moving on. Rocking in the wake, they waited, feeling the raft begin to drift on its own now. "Hang on," Shad whispered. "One more act, then the curtain goes down, baby." He could feel Gloria nodding, trembling against him. "Marty all right?"

"Are you kidding?" came a swift answer, only slightly unsteady. Their brush covering rustled slightly. "I'm ten years older in the last two minutes."

Downriver from them, the *Leolo* swung about, engines laboring hard as it faced into the current again. By now the raft had been caught by the flow, and as Shad took a chance, lifting his head enough to look, it seemed to him that their speed was immense as raft and boat sped toward each other.

Again the searchlight probed through their covering, but this time slid by them swiftly as the *Leolo* chugged back upriver again. In its wake once more, the raft bobbed like a rocking horse, swinging wildly this way and that. Nails dug into the logs under them, Marty and Shad hung on grimly, too occupied by the struggle to stay aboard the raft to realize they'd passed the first hazard.

A ghost ship, the *Leolo* fell behind them. Thick and fibrous as a shroud, the night covered their passage. But in the sky over their near horizon, an unseen moon cast a pale glow. Paddling laboriously, Marty and Shad maneuvered the raft into the middle of the river where it moved sedately with the surface currents. After they had gone around the first bend and the riverboat was out of sight, Shad began to clear away their brushy covering. The raft rocked perilously as Gloria sat up pulling leaves from her hair. Marty carefully rolled on his back, staring at the stars, his smile a white slash in his mud-plastered face. No one spoke for a long time, then Gloria said, "I'm thirsty," and they all laughed like lunatics.

From the jungle on either side came answering howls of night prowlers, preying and preyed upon. Marty thought about the crocodiles they had seen—great gaping-mouthed beasts, some of them longer than the raft. And Gloria thought about the leeches; fearful of finding more on herself, was thankful for the darkness. Remembering the voyage upriver yesterday, Shad worried about the narrows where the Mobene raced in a torrent. "Big current," he could hear the captain saying. "Fast. Wild."

So they missed getting shot only to drown instead? Groaning inwardly, he realized he should have made some sort of rudder, for in that savage millrace—chances were—the raft wouldn't have a chance without one.

27

"We had two choices," Marty told it later, "either hang on and pray or swim and get eaten. Well, go figure it! We hung on and prayed."

Whining clouds of mosquitoes attacked them, and as the moon rose, radiant on the river, they saw other more menacing pursuers—the loglike shapes of trailing crocodiles. Lying low as it did in the water, the raft made an easy target for these marauders. All it took was one bold one.

"Keep tucked up," Shad said. "No more paddling from now on. Try the flashlight, Mart. Maybe it'll scare 'em off."

"Flashlight, he says. Like it's soaked, man!"

"So try it anyway. Maybe they're Eveready batteries. They always used to advertise in the funnies how they'd work even underwater."

"What a dreamer." Marty grinned at Gloria. "You know this guy's so literary he scares me? First Indian stories, now funny papers." But he tried the flashlight doubtfully, and as the beam shot forth, thin and wavering, they all cheered.

And it worked, too. Every time the beam hit them, the crocs sheered off bellowing.

"Hey, it's better than a ray-gun!" Marty shouted gleefully, stabbing into the dark like a swordsman. "Take that, Ugly. Down, you monsters. Hey, looka me, Ma, I'm king of the crocs!"

"If you spot anything that looks like it won't bite, grab it," Shad advised. "We need something to steer with." Then as unalarmingly as possible, he reminded them of the rapids ahead.

Perhaps an hour or so later, they spied a small limb torn from a tree, and hauled it aboard, leaving the foliage dragging behind the raft. Trying it as a steering oar, Marty the yachtsman shrugged. "A little answer maybe, but that's all. Nothing like we need. So we hit that rough water—" again he shrugged. "We got to spin like a top, that's all we can do."

Shad blew out his breath. "Okay, then, we'll tie ourselves on."

"With what?"

"And what if we sink?" Gloria added, trying to make a joke of it. "I'd rather be a rat and desert ship."

"Not in that giant-sized Jacuzzi," Marty said. "I saw that spot. You wouldn't last two minutes swimming."

"Oh." Gloria stared down at her muddy hands. In the moonlight they looked black instead of brown. Black is the color of my true love's hands. She felt hollow inside, sick and afraid. As she raised her head, she saw the two men watching her, their faces in the moonlight anxious, curiously tender. "I have an idea," she said quietly. "Our belts. They're woven, aren't they? They're bound to be strong enough to hold us."

"Tarzan and his Jane." Marty shook his head admiringly. "The unbeatable twosome. I hereby nominate you two cats for The Couple I'd Like Most To Be Marooned With."

Unfastening their belts, they threaded them through the tough viney plaiting which fastened the logs together. Sink or swim, they would be one with the raft now, their lives utterly dependent upon it.

Like time in a nightmare, the hours passed, unmeasurable and hazardous, stitched up by terrors both real and imagined. They talked about the riverboat, the chance it might follow them. They spoke of the cruise ship, then wished they hadn't. For fear is like an edifice built brick by brick in the imagination. And the walls were growing. In the dark ahead, they seemed to tower insurmountably.

"One thing at a time," Shad kept saying. "For chrissake, let's take each thing as it comes!" But the construction went on in his own mind, too. There seemed no end to the hurdles they must leap. And each time into the unknown.

"Even if we make it," Gloria murmured as if she'd read his

mind. "To Porto Saba, I mean. It'll be daylight, won't it? They're bound to—"

"Stop it, baby. Will you please stop?"

"If there's anything I hate, it's a broad who thinks." Marty patted her arm. "Don't make me hate you, hunh?"

Then they heard it. A distant rumbling—not thunder but water. Tons of water careening through a gap.

"We're making good time," Shad said over-casually. "Everybody got their seat belt fastened?"

The rumbling grew, deep and resonant as the riverbanks rose and the moon rode high, throwing a sheet-silver glare on the mild waters which somewhere ahead became a raging torrent. Shad checked the belts, then lying flat like the others, buckled his own around him until it cut deep into his flesh. The raft began to stir and swing in the current. Then dead ahead the banks drove in on them, rising higher and higher until the sky seemed shut out.

Now all around them the water boiled, roaring like a surf against the high banks. Pitching this way and that, the raft bobbed weightless as a leaf now, driven faster and faster by the accelerating current. Nose down, they took waves dashed from either bank, then whirling, pressed down by the force of the swirls, spun to and fro as Marty had predicted. Tugging against the restraining belts, their bodies answered the centrifugal forces, dashed this way and that, battered and bruised. Spitting and gagging, Shad tried to get his bearings as the raft leaped like a bucking horse, sidewinding, fishtailing, spinning dizzily in tighter and tighter circles. He had glimpses of the gorge, then ahead the curve where, coming upriver, he'd seen the worst of the rapids. Here the current fought itself into waves, whirlpools, vicious swirls which had shaken even the riverboat. Lord, he prayed inchoately, Lord? Then the water smashed at them, drowning the raft, lifting it high, then drowning it once more.

Shad felt the woven belt giving, stretched by the soaking. And he heard a gargled screaming—his own perhaps, and Gloria's— then a wild shout from Marty. Goners, he thought, they would never make it. And under the green-brown racing water, he groaned, consumed with sadness for all they would miss of life. But even so, he fought—fingers cut by the plaiting as he hung on, one arm flailing wildly, reaching out to grab Gloria.

Then the raft bobbed free, and swinging into the main current, raced beyond the curve and down the gorge. Half of him off the raft, tugged at by the current, Marty hung on grimly, gasping for breath. Gloria had slipped almost through her belt, he saw, and hung from it limply, eyes closed, mouth open spewing what seemed to be gallons of river water. Beyond her, Shad lay coughing helplessly, his long legs dragging over the side.

"Okay?" He gasped. "Okay?" But in the rush of the river they could not hear Shad. He tugged at Gloria but she lay inert, her fingers frozen around the wet woven belt which had slipped now up to her armpits. "Marty," he yelled, choking, "help me!" But she began to slide as the raft swung wildly to and fro, the loose belt forcing her arms up, the current dragging heavier and heavier on the two thirds of her body which now floated help-lessly behind the raft. Shad grabbed her hair, Marty her arm, and they hung on as the river pulled at her.

Later they decided she must have acted like a rudder, for the raft began to settle on a steady course as the river widened and the current slowed. Scrambling, Marty and Shad both pulled themselves back on the raft, then each holding an arm, pinned Gloria tight until they had purchase enough to drag her aboard. "It's stretched," she gasped furiously when she could finally speak. "That damn belt—it *stretched* on me!"

Huddled together against the unexpected chill, they dozed and shifted and drifted silently, dazed with exhaustion. Layers of cold, fetid mist floated ghostily around the raft. They passed like a primitive funeral barge out of reach of the moon as it slipped in the sky, pulling them into night everlasting.

Suspended between sleep and wakefulness, Shad's mind spun around the lunatic violence he had plunged them into, and a kind of muteness veiled his thoughts; he could not find his own dimension in this nightmare of his making. For a time, merci-fully, sleep overcame him, and when he wakened again the darkness had thinned, leached away by the coming dawn.

The river turned pewter-colored, reflecting the sky. Then suddenly, in flaming streamers, sunlight pierced the drifting mist. There was no heralding screech of jungle fowl this time, however, no howling of monkeys, for they were passing through the low coastal plain, they saw—only a short distance from Porto Saba and the harbor.

Arab-rigged native boats sailed serenely across the Mobene delta. From riverbank settlements, smoke from cookfires rose straight into the calm luminous sky. Lying prone on the raft, Marty and Shad and Gloria watched in every direction now, fearful for the first discovering shout. "Time to jump ship maybe?" Marty asked finally. "I hope you're loaded with bright ideas, buddy."

"If we could tease one of those boats over." Shad sighed. "Well —come on. Let's start paddling." He raised his head cautiously, pointing. "There's a sandbar, let's head for that."

Through clumps of what looked like water hyacinth, they slowly paddled the sluggish raft. The banks looked deserted where they were headed, reedy and marshy, full of small dark-colored waterfowl feeding. When they were close in, Shad slipped over the side and found himself only waist deep in the tepid water. Marty followed him, then Gloria. With a reluctance they had never expected, they pushed off the raft and made their way up the marshy shore.

"Let's stop and powwow," Shad said, squatting in the reeds. "We probably won't have another chance to."

Sinking down beside him, Gloria groaned. "If only we weren't so filthy. I feel as if I'd been soaked in a cesspool overnight."

"Marinated—that's the word you want." Marty chuckled. "I don't figure any of us can pass the underarm test this morning."

"Look, the first thing we've got to do is get some clothes," Shad said. "Native stuff, I mean."

"Great idea. Where's the nearest Sears and Roebuck?" Marty looked from one to the other. "Native! Listen, how am *I* gonna pass—" and stopped as Shad grinned. "Yeah, I get it, sweetheart. Like the tables are turned? Haha. Just happens I'm serious, though. How the hell am I gonna look like some cockamamey native?"

Shad stopped him with a swift slicing gesture. They all sat rigid, listening to a squeak-sqawk like that of a rusty gate, carrying on the still air. Beckoning them to follow, Shad began to inch forward through the reeds. They had crawled perhaps fifty feet when he stopped again abruptly, turning to them. "There's a house," he whispered. "That's a pump or something we heard. I can see somebody toting water in a bucket."

Marty took a look. "Hey, that's an Arab broad, isn't it? Looks like an animated ragbag."

Gloria saw the idea in Shad's face long before Marty got it, and a kind of thrill went through her, fearful yet exciting. "Shad, you aren't—?"

"Yeah," he breathed. "Listen, how do I look?"

"Lousy," Marty answered. "Look, if you're thinking about hitting her up for some breakfast—"

"I'm thinking about threads, sweetheart."

"Something simple," Gloria murmured, "yet appropriate."

"Hey." Marty gaped at them. "Hey, you don't mean for *me!*"

"You two stay here," Shad said. "And keep your fingers crossed her old man's not home." Then he stood up and started strolling idly toward the mud-walled house.

28

On the dial of Marty's shock-proof, waterproof, self-winding chronometer, they watched five minutes drag by, seven, ten. A thin shriek tore the still misty air, distant but unmistakably human. Marty glanced at Gloria then away again guiltily. "Oh God," she whispered, "he won't have to hurt her, will he?" And when he didn't answer, she grasped his arm tight. "Marty? Tell me!"

He patted her hand. "Relax, baby, it'll be all right."

"Will it?" She shook his arm. "*Will* it, Marty? We're like Typhoid Marys, you know we are. Every place we've gone, something or somebody has had to die because of us. People have suffered and *died* because of us!"

She was right, of course. In a way, he amended, and gulping, fumbled for the right words. "Look, it's the breaks, Glory. Like war, see? I mean, innocent people die in wars, too, don't they?" Her fingers seemed frozen, stiff on his arm. He was afraid to look at what her face must show him. "Okay," he went on, "I don't know what to say. You figure it! I mean, it just happened, that's all. Like a landslide we couldn't do anything about."

"And how about that guard?" He could scarcely hear her. "How about that man on the mission path, Marty?" Her nails dug into him and he winced. "Was he some more of our land-slide?"

"What're you talking about?"

"You killed him, didn't you? You and Shad."

"Killed him!" He groaned. "Jesus, what a bloodthirsty broad. Listen, will you please pull in your claws?" He massaged his arm where she'd dug into it. "All we did was mash the guy a little. His foot, see, so he couldn't come running after us."

"His—oh." She sagged against him. "Oh, thank God. I thought—"

"Hey, look!" Peering through the reeds, Marty squinted, shielding his eyes against the sharp glare of the rising sun. "Isn't that our boy? Look, he's waving to us! Come on." Marty grabbed her hand, pulling her up into a staggering run which took them rapidly across the sandy marsh to the mud-walled Arab house.

In a filthy undergarment like a shift, the woman sat rigid in one corner, fat wrists and ankles bound, gagged by Shad's muddy handkerchief. In her swarthy seamy face, her eyes burned at them fiercely. "Fought like a wildcat," Shad said ruefully. "Kinda had to get rough with her—"

"You think anybody else lives here?" Marty asked.

"Husband, I suppose. Kids too, maybe. They must be off some-place, maybe farming," and he jerked a thumb toward the door. "Take a whiff. They got to own a horse or a donkey. And it isn't here."

The house was one room—a windowless dirt-floored stable-like place which smelled strongly of fowl and animal droppings. Just outside was a lean-to shed. Woven reed baskets in various stages of completion were stacked against one wall.

"The way I got it figured," Shad said, "she's getting these ready for market while the old man does his plow-jockey bit." He indicated the baskets. "We'll just borrow a few to make you look kosher," and he tossed a bundle of dark clothing at Marty. "Here, climb into these, Fatima. You're about to become an Arab business lady on her way to market."

Four rolled up pallets lay stacked against one wall. For a stove, there was a charcoal brazier in the middle of the room. The only other bit of furnishing seemed to be a rusty tin trunk. As Shad bent over it, the woman gave a muffled cry and fought against her bonds wildly, glaring at him as he opened the lid. "Hey, look." Shad grinned. "Something for everybody maybe?"

They all peered down at the feast-day finery within—round embroidered caps, pale clean cotton robes, Arab slippers of cheap tooled leather. Pulling the garments out one by one, Shad tried them for size against Gloria. "You got to cover those pants for sure, baby. African ladies just don't dig 'em."

Gloria sniffed one of the robes. "At least they're clean—sort of."

"That's more," came Marty's muffled comment, "than I can say about these." Then his head popped out of the voluminous folds of the fat woman's rust-black everyday clothing. "How do I look in drag?"

They washed sketchily, and ignoring the flies, the pervasive odor of filth in the mud house, crammed their mouths full of the mealy flat-tasting cakes which sat, still warm, on the grate over the brazier. Lynx-eyed, the Arab woman watched every bite, but she no longer struggled against her bonds.

It was twenty-four hours since they had eaten, nearly twice

that since they'd slept, and in the momentary relaxation of temporary safety, shelter, they all squatted over the meager food, stunned with fatigue, silent as sleepwalkers still caught in their dreams. One thought now dominated all their minds— the cruise ship. Was it myth? Reality? There was no way of knowing until they reached the city lying distant across the plain, an impossible-seeming goal.

Licking crumbs from his fingers, Shad said: "Great hors d'oeuvres—now when do we eat?" And rising, he groaned as his aching muscles creaked. Holding out his hand to Gloria, he pulled her to her feet, twirling her as if she were a model. "Very chick-chick. Real soul sister threads. What do you say, Fatima, old buddy, isn't she too much?"

But Marty only grunted behind his heavy veiling.

"This is probably all wrong in the costume department," Gloria predicted gloomily, adjusting her turban-like headdress. "I mean, what if these are her husband's clothes?"

"Then you're in drag, too." Shad kissed her. "Relax, baby. It's almost over."

"Oh—" she leaned against him—"how I wish I could believe that!"

They left some money for the Arab woman, and apologizing for their thievery, set out from the house, following a footpath to a dusty road perhaps half a mile away. As the only man in the transformed group, Shad led the way, African style, striding along in a billowing white cotton robe too short for him, a round embroidered cap on his head.

Since they wore their own clothing under the native robes, all suffered from the increased heat, panting along the dusty road, complaining about their ill-fitting Islamic slippers. No one passed them either way for an hour or more as they plodded across the broad coastal plain. Far ahead they could see Porto Saba like a dream city emerging as the morning mist dispelled and the sun beat down ferociously. Dust whirled in spirals around their feet. In the distance they watched miniature cyclones spinning this way and that. Then a large one began to worry Shad. A vehicle of some sort made it, he decided—and in Danju only the military had wheels.

Something like a jeep, painted a mottled green and brown camouflage, the car careened toward them, pulling up with a squeal of brakes. A cloud of dust descended on them. Through it, Shad saw a driver and two others in the car—too many to think about jumping them. A rifleman got out first, then after him what had to be a sergeant. The world over, they must all be the same.

Remembering to be humble, he waited as the sergeant looked them over, then said something—a question, Shad guessed. With his eyes downcast, he tried shaking his head no. The wrong answer obviously, for the sergeant barked an order. They heard a click as the rifleman leveled his weapon at them. And from behind him, Shad heard a strangled sound that chilled his blood.

Gloria had succumbed to panic, he thought at first, his heart beating like a runaway metronome. Her eyes rolled and she made desperate gargling sounds, pointing to her mouth. Then Shad got it. His breath felt like a balloon swelling in his lungs. Laughton playing Quasimodo hadn't done muteness any better —or hammier. But would the sergeant buy it?

Scowling, the noncom pointed to Shad and said something in a sneering tone. And taking his cue from his wife, Shad nodded wildly, opening his mouth wide, remembering too late his expensive dentistry. But the sergeant didn't notice. His inside quivering with the effort of seeming only slightly alarmed, meek, helpless, Shad poked a finger in one ear also, hoping the sarge would get it that he was deaf, too.

Looking irritated, the sergeant hesitated. Then with a guttural command, he jerked his head toward the jeep. *They* must get in? Shad held his breath until the guard slung his rifle over his shoulder and ambled back to the jeep, climbing into his seat again. With his hands on his hips, the sergeant stared at them scowling. Shad fixed his eyes on the ground, not acting any more, *being* a helpless humble peasant. He hoped to God Gloria was doing the same.

The sergeant's feet shifted in the dust. His boots, Shad saw, had been cut here and there to make room for his toes. Then the feet did an abrupt about-face. Letting out his breath, Shad shuffled onward, not daring to look as the jeep started up, spurting dust in their faces.

"Jesus," Marty hissed behind his veil, "talk about close ones!"

They all watched the jeep as it disappeared behind a cloud of dust.

"I think," said Gloria, "I have to sit down for a minute—"

Shad grinned. "That was the best little ad-lib shtick I've ever seen, baby. Ever hope to see," and he hugged her. "*You* are the *great*est!"

"I was kind of good, wasn't I?"

"Real Oscar stuff," said Marty. "Jesus, I'd give my left—uh, arm for a cigarette, any brand!"

Squatting in the dust with their robes tucked up, Marty red-faced with his veil thrown back, they shared a moment's respite. Then Gloria said: "What I want to know is what happens when we get to the city."

"Head for the harbor," Shad replied, "that's all we can do."

"And what if there's no cruise boat?"

"Who cares," Marty grumbled. "At least we can throw ourselves in the drink and get cool for a change."

"Look." Shad took a deep breath. "All we can do now is hang loose, play it by ear. We don't know anything from now on. How soon that Arab momma'll get found. How soon the riverboat'll get back—"

"I say grab anything that floats and cut out," Marty suggested. "A few hours sailing either way and we'll be safe."

"That means lying low till dark." Shad shook his head. "By then they'll be tearing the joint apart looking for us. We won't have a chance."

"But if there isn't a cruise boat," Gloria stopped. "Well, if there isn't, we're sort of sunk, aren't we?"

"Don't you believe it, baby. We're not sunk till we sink." Groaning, Shad rose. "Come on, ladies, let's split."

The sun stood high and it was noon or after when they finally passed through the outskirts of the city, the teeming section called Old Town. After the silence of the plain, the din of the settlement smote them like hammer blows—the harsh cries of beggars, the shrieks of children and peddlers, the bray-ing and howling of emaciated animals casually abused by in-different owners. Playing their game of muteness, the three ignored the hucksters and importuning beggars springing up like evil spirits in their path. Shad kept thinking about the Akabane shack on Shepherd's Lane, wondering if they should try after all to take shelter there till nightfall. Too risky, he decided, for a number of reasons, not the least of which was having to trust strangers. They dared not chance it, had to keep going. He plodded on, consumed by the heat—a tall sweating African in feast-day robes, followed by womenfolk.

Then ahead lay the beginnings of the broad avenue down which they had ridden in state only two days ago. Shad and Gloria and Marty halted, bemused by palms lining the street with patches of shade, shining store windows. Even the cars they could see—government or military vehicles—seemed benevolent, evidence of a world they could cope with. "Here's where we really have to be careful," Shad muttered. "Keep your heads down. Don't look at anybody—" then aware of the stares of passers-by, he moved off slowly, stopping again when he could. "String out now so we won't look like a trio." A beggar grabbed at him and he stepped aside, making a menacing ges-ture. "But don't get separated. You dig me, Marty? Whatever happens, we got to stay together."

Through the heavy stifling veil which he had pulled over his eyes, Marty watched them walking slowly ahead of him. Mr. and Mrs. Africa with the afternoon off. When the distance be-tween them had widened sufficiently, he trailed them, worrying about the curiosity he seemed to arouse in the few Arab ladies passing by. Their eyes were not covered, but his had to be. He longed for the dark glasses the more prosperous ones seemed to wear.

Marty had forgotten the baskets he carried on his back tied in a bundle, and when a swarthy couple in rumpled white clothing stopped him, obviously inquiring the price, he couldn't think what to do about it. "Combien," the woman kept saying. "Quantos?" Till her piratical-looking mustachioed husband gave her a shove, saying something in a language Marty couldn't guess.

Relieved, he watched them stroll off—the husband with his camera, the woman with her string shopping bag—then he trudged on, suffering the hot pavements—until it dawned on him who the couple might be. As fast as he dared, Marty began to hurry then, praying that ESP really did work, because he had a bombshell of a message for Shad and Gloria.

29

"I tell you, they were tourists! Greek tourists. The guy was dark, see, with a mustache. Well, come to think of it," Marty laughed excitedly, "his wife had one, too, only not so pretty." He grabbed Shad's arm. "Look, the guy was carrying a camera. That's a tourist, ain't it? And his wife had this—Well, didn't the general say it was a *Greek* cruise ship? Shad, I swear to God these were Greek tourists!"

Watching the mouth of the alley for any sign of interest from passers-by on the street, Shad resisted hope in order to keep his head. Marty's voice was too loud in the quiet narrow alley, his excitement dangerously infectious. Like a spotlight, the sun drenched them, throwing back-doorways into deep shadow. What if one opened? Heaps of refuse towered precariously. They should duck, he thought vaguely, noticing that at the other end from the street, the alley seemed to run into another like it . . .

"Oh, maybe it's really there," Gloria was saying. "Shad, maybe there really *is* a cruise ship in the harbor—"

"Yeah, and maybe there isn't, too." His throat tightened. Even in Danju life couldn't be that cruel, could it? Exasperated, he stared at them, moved by their stubbornly hopeful tired faces, feeling their exhaustion as he felt his own. He tried to think, but his brain was numbed. Shad dared not think what might happen if Marty were wrong. "Listen," he cried softly, "we can't loosen up now, get careless. We've got the whole city to walk through. And even if the cruise ship's there—"

"It's gotta be." Marty sucked in his breath. "Look, there's bound to be more of 'em. Tourists around town—"

"I know where they are." Gloria smiled as they gaped at her. "In the marketplace. That native bazaar." She took Shad's arm, pressing it to her. "Remember I told you when I first got here how the major took me to see it? It's about a mile beyond the hotel—toward the harbor."

"For chrissake, the hotel," Marty protested. "That's the one place in this city we can't even go near!"

But Shad and Gloria overruled him, deciding that boldness was their best chance—they would keep to the busy avenue which cut through Porto Saba from Old Town to the harbor.

Leaving the alley first, Shad and Gloria strolled at the stately unhurried pace which seemed characteristic of all Africans. After two minutes had passed, Marty followed them, shuffling along in his voluminous Arab robes, the bundle of reed baskets bumping his back.

Luck seemed to be with them, an end to the nightmare dimly perceivable as they made their way into the heart of the city. Passing the park where they had turned toward the gates of the Premier's Palace that first day, Shad saw over the tops of trees, the wall, the colonial tower with its huge flag hanging limp in the blazing windless heat. Somewhere inside sat General Okefe like a spider. Did he know yet they had escaped his web?

A pace behind her husband—African style—Gloria eyed herself in shop windows, amazed by the transformation in her appearance. A very black man in a Western-style suit passed by, smiling at her cheekily. Two women in shifts and high-heeled sandals stared indifferently through her. City chicks, she thought, and remembered to look meek—a country girl visiting the metropolis.

Bicyclists whizzed by on the sizzling pavements, buses laden with factory workers headed out toward the industrial section. A few Indians in their own native dress were sprinkled among the pedestrians, an occasional Arab. But for the most part, the crowd was indigenous—clerks and merchants and petty bureaucrats in badly cut suits, women in mail-order style frocks, many like themselves in the flowing white robes which Gloria had admired that first day.

Then ahead they saw the block-long garden, and rising over it like a white stucco liner, the elaborate façade of the Hotel Splendide. Gloria hesitated only a moment when they passed the gates, briefly longing for the claw-legged tub, the mammoth bed, the chic wardrobe she knew she would never see again. But the pedestrian traffic was not heavy here; they dared not linger and call attention to themselves. "I'm sure the marketplace is straight ahead," she said. "Can you see Marty?"

Turning like an idler gaping at all the sights, Shad stared behind them, trying to pick out the scruffy black-robed figure.

Gloria saw it first and sighed with relief, then giggled. "If only we could get a snapshot. Wouldn't he just die if Abby Golden saw him in that Halloween get-up?"

Breathlessly they gazed at each other, sharing not only hope but belief in it now. A jeep cruised by, silencing whatever they might have said. Watching as it proceeded slowly down the shimmering street, nervously aware of the uniforms, the stares of the occupants as it had passed slowly, Shad said: "Let's get started before those cats decide to turn around for another look."

"Shouldn't we wait for Marty to catch up some?"

"Look, for all we know, there *is* something wrong with the way we're wearing these threads. Marty can see us, let's split."

They crossed the broad avenue in front of the hotel, continued a block, then again paused to see if Marty were following. He was. Forcing themselves not to hurry, they strolled on.

In this part of Porto Saba, the city's colonial past could be guessed—a busy port growing back from the harbor in blocks of buildings two and three stories high, factor's warehouses, grids of street laid down by European planners. A network of alleys seemed to connect the district—a fact which Shad noticed and filed away for future reference he hoped they wouldn't need. Pushcarts and cyclists crowded the narrow mercantile cross-streets they passed, a few trucks loading local goods for shipment. Patrols were less frequent in this area, and the life of the city seemed more natural, unoppressed. You could forget here that General Okefe existed. But they dared not forget for a moment that he did.

Ahead the street opened, seemed to stop at a long oblong plaza jammed with stalls, peddlers, hawkers crying their wares —the native market.

"Look!" Gloria whispered.

Their fatigue forgotten, they stopped in the shade of an alley entrance, counting the Europeans among the Africans in the marketplace—women in flowered dresses and wide hats, men in light suits with cameras slung around their necks. At the end of the plaza sat a bus with a hand-lettered sign propped against the windshield: S.S. *Kyprios.*

Puffing behind his heavy veil, Marty joined them, and pretending to haggle over a reed basket, they pointed out the bus to him. Gloria couldn't stop smiling. Suddenly a flack man again, Marty chortled, rubbing his hands together. "Gimme five minutes with one of those cats—anybody who talks Ammurican—and we'll be on that ship so fast!" He looked down at himself. "I gotta get rid of these rags, though. Nobody but nobody's gonna listen to me in this kinky outfit." Then suddenly aware of their unresponding expressions, he said: "What's with you two? Listen, I can—"

"Oh, Marty," Gloria moaned. "You didn't see yourself before you put on that outfit."

"So?"

"You look like a panhandler," Shad said. "Beard, sweat, dirt and all. Nobody's going to believe you're a tourist, so forget it. You take off that outfit and we'll be scooped up by the fuzz like—"

"Hey," Marty breathed. "You hear what I hear?"

They listened to a raucous hoohaw klaxon of the sort which meant Special Forces in Paris, and to another generation, SS stormtroopers. It grew louder and louder rapidly, frighteningly, and down the avenue they had just traversed came a column of mottled green and brown vehicles. Automatic rifles glinted in the sun. At the corner, trucks full of soldiers peeled off to left and right, only the first two entering the plaza.

"Jesus," Marty whispered, "what's this—a raid?"

"Whatever it is, we better miss it." Shad swiftly inspected the alley behind them, seeing that it connected with another about twenty yards off. "Don't anybody run, but let's move, and I mean fast." He led the way.

Marty and Gloria followed him down the silent baking hot tunnel. Around the corner in the connecting alley, they found a deeply recessed warehouse doorway barred shut from the inside. Empty fiberboard containers stenciled with the name of a London shipper blocked the doorway. Frantically Shad began to stack them, creating a hiding place.

"Get in," he said to Gloria. "You too, Marty."

"What're you—?"

"Come on, man, move!" They crawled into the cave he had made, and Shad shoved a stack of containers after them. "I'll find out what's going on. You two stick here, no matter what—you dig me?" Then he ran down the alley and spying an exterior drainpipe on a two-story building, shinnied up it grunting with the effort.

The rooftop was blistering hot, gravel over tar which squashed like syrup at every step. Stooping low, Shad crossed to the front of the building. From here he could see the façades across the plaza—one hung with a huge banner painted with a gigantic likeness of General Okefe. Ole Black Massa.

Below Shad the marketplace had become a prison, for every entrance had been sealed off by now, blocked by soldiers, their trucks behind them. In the tourists' bus sat a driver honking the horn monotonously. By twos and threes, the Europeans were heading for it, urged on by what looked to be an officer from the ship. Peddlers gathered up their pitiful goods with loud lamentations. Hawkers rushed after the departing tourists, desperately shrieking their wares. Over the din of their frantic huckstering the bus horn bayed like a monster trapped in a deep pit.

Maybe this is usual, Shad kept thinking. The weekly roundup to keep the folks in line? Panting in the unbearable heat, he persuaded himself this must be so, all they had to do was lie low for a while. And what better place—if they could stand the heat—than this rooftop above the show? Squinting in the glare, he inspected the block of buildings around him—all two-storied—an expanse of roofs to what appeared, on his left, to be a narrow street.

Bending double, he swiftly crossed to the end of the block, peering down on the crowded cross-street which ran at right angles to the plaza. Men in grimy undershirts and baggy trousers pushed carts laden with bolts of textiles and rugs, making the only traffic on the narrow gummy asphalt pavement. A few cyclists threaded among them, arrogantly ringing handle-bar bells for right of way. The sidewalks were packed with men in Western clothing, Arab robes, Hindu attire, carrying on a brisk trade at the top of their voices. The military vehicle sitting at the end of the street seemed to take up no one's attention.

Scrambling back across the roofs, Shad went as far as he could in the opposite direction—to the alley they had slipped into when the military arrived. Peeping cautiously over the edge of the roof, he looked down on a lone trooper stationed there. Then sliding back carefully, he returned to his vantage point for another look at the marketplace.

By now the tourists were almost all aboard their bus. A black limousine was circling the square, slowing as it approached the bus. Inside, in the back, sat an officer. Shad could see braid on a sleeve and white gloves. Glued to the blistering roof, a sinking haunted sensation taking hold of him, he watched until the limousine stopped. Watched as the door opened and the passenger emerged.

He had wondered if the spider knew they'd escaped his web. Well, here was his answer. For the white-gloved officer was Major Belelondres, the general's aide—of all people in Danju, the one who would never fail to recognize them.

So time had run out, Shad reported back to Marty and Gloria, their luck also. Their chances, they knew now, were suicidally narrowed. And their disguises were useless, their plan to make the harbor. They dared not move until night now—but by night-fall the cruise ship would be gone.

"Ole Black Massas's Boy Friday has got us cold. And he knows it," Shad groaned. "Sure he does. All he's got to do is keep his eyes open. Screen everybody who gets on that ship. Keep us holed up. Any way we play it now, he's got us."

"But surely there must be—" Gloria stopped, her eyes glisten-ing, dangerously near tears. "Shad, you said reporters. There might be reporters on board. Wouldn't they be trying to get in touch with us?"

"Yeah, that's right," Marty picked up the idea. "Maybe if we could get back to the hotel—"

"Forget it."

"The hell you say! Listen, how many days now nobody hears from us? Come on, man, there's gotta be some action there!"

"Forget it," Shad said again harshly. "You think a smart cookie like Okefe wouldn't cover himself? The wire services are prob-ably saturated with daily bulletins about Smith and Company in Darkest Danju."

As their faces fell, he hated himself violently, appalled by what he had done to them. And Gloria. He could not bear her face. Think, he commanded himself. For chrissake, Brain, *make* with something!

But her weary sadness worked like poison in him. Clown, she had called him. So where's the laugh-track? None needed. Not for this show. Because the gods are laughing fit to kill. Another Mr. Big makes his ritual pratfall. Only this Mr. Big takes his for good. And to make it even better, takes everybody with him.

With lunatic persistence a contractual phrase kept dinning in Shad's head. Time is of the essence. Time is of . . . His mind felt asleep, stunned by the loss of the luck he had counted on for so long. White gloves, he kept thinking, all that braid—isn't *he* the clown? Belelondres snazzy as some Fifth Avenue door-man. Not a clown, man, a clown is funny. He's the cat with his mice in the trap . . .

"Listen," Marty was saying stubbornly, "there's got to be some gag we can pull on these squares. I mean, come *on*, Champ—with that ship sitting out there just waiting for us?" Exasperated by Shad's unresponsiveness—what's this guy, all of a sudden paralyzed or something?—Marty pulled off the stifling veil, wildly scratching his matted hair totally unrecognizable now as the latest Sebring do. "Look, the trouble with you two—" he went on shrewdly—"I mean, love is swell and all that jazz—but you're so busy sitting there worrying about each other, you've gone blanksville when it comes to worrying about yourselves. Not—you should forgive a guy mentioning it—to mention *my* skin." Then, with a stiff finger, he prodded Shad's chest. "So okay, you crawl up on that roof and you see George Gorgeous in his white gloves and gold braid. You see a guard in the alley where we duck in here. So come on, pal think—what *else* did you see? Anything at all we might—?" stopping as he saw some idea beginning to work behind the blank brown face.

"Shad," Gloria breathed, watching him. "*Is* there something?"

There was suddenly. But it was tenuous at first, cautious and experimental now that he was luckless. The beginning of an idea spinning like a thread. A wild idea. He smiled to himself, thinking: Love is swell and all that jazz. And his mind sprang to life. With nothing to lose you can afford to be wild. Hastily, talking fast, he began to strip.

30

Imitating the shuffle of the idlers he had seen, Shad moved slowly down the alley, stopping at the mouth where it bisected the narrow mercantile street he had seen from the rooftop. He yawned like a man with no place to go. Cyclists passed, ignoring him, merchants either anxious looking or busy with the competition. Feeling miraculously invisible in his filthy undershirt and baggy torn pants, Shad savored his anonymity, tested it as long as he could bear to wait, then assured by the indifference of all passers-by, stepped out onto the street.

But what had seemed simple back there in their hiding place did not here. He watched pushcarts go by, and dodging an occasional cyclist, wandered in the opposite direction from the marketplace. People bumped him, a loafer in a dream. Over the heads of the crowd, he spied a patrol approaching, and tempted to slide away, take cover, forced himself instead to squat in a doorway, staring blanky into space.

Leather squeaked. Gear rattled. Boots crunched by him near enough to touch. Then a whistle blew, shrilly imperative, dulling the beehive buzz of the street. Two men had been stopped by the patrol, Shad saw. Both were wearing long white robes.

Prodded by their captors, protesting at every step, the two were marched past Shad back toward the marketplace. The din of the crowded street resumed. Shad rose and continued on.

He had one chance and one only. Like opening night without a rehearsal. Idling along with his hands in his pockets, he searched the street from one end to the other, anxiety swelling like a sore in him. Time was passing and time was of the essence. Marty and Gloria were probably wild by now.

Then he saw it—a four-wheeled pushcart piled so high with rugs that the pusher could not see over them. Instead, the man peered around the side of the cart, uttering hoarse cries of warning to anything in his path. A thin man black as coal. A toothless man who only gaped as Shad moved in beside him grinning, taking a place at the pushing bar.

In the alley was no sound, no sense of what was happening, and as they waited and waited, silence made fear in them, time refined it, blindness and discomfort transmuted it into dread. Once they heard faintly what sounded like shots. And a while later a shout echoed along the alley system making them both jump. Without looking at each other, not daring any longer, Gloria and Marty contained their growing tension, congealing in alarm as the minutes and quarter hours passed.

Finally they heard the sound of footsteps. Her face suddenly alight, Gloria started up. Marty grabbed her, holding her still, for this was not Shad, but two men, laughing, scuffing their feet. There was a metallic rattle. A rifle, Marty thought. Water splashed very close by, and as the glottal African voices slowly faded, the acrid stench of fresh urine strangled them.

Gloria began to shiver and couldn't stop. Helpless to comfort her, Marty stroked her arm. Should they go looking for Shad? His inside shook. If they've grabbed my boy . . . Stop thinking, he told himself. Stop already. One down still leaves two to go. "Look," he whispered, "here's what we'll do. I mean in case— well, you know what I mean." Her drained face made his heart turn over. "We'll wait half an hour more, then we got to beat it. You dig me, sweetheart? We got to face it they got him."

She seemed not to hear, but he persisted anyway, whispering as hard and fast as he could: "We got to make that ship. It's our only chance, see, to get hold of somebody. I mean somebody who can put the screws on this Danju ratpack." He hesitated, staring at her. She looked asleep with her eyes open, drugged. "Listen, use your head, baby. Even if they've got him, they're not gonna blow it all now putting a bullet through his head. Not after all the capers they've pulled. So he's safe for now—dig me?" Grasping her shoulder, he shook her ungently. "And they haven't got us yet. That's the kicker, see? Without us they're still hanging by the thumbs same as before."

Her indifference stifled him, the utter limpness of her body under his hand. Wanting to kiss her, hit her, waken her somehow from this nightmare, Marty stared at her helplessly. But the nightmare was real, and he himself a party to it—co-creator of whatever doom befell them. "Come on, baby," he whispered pleadingly. "All I'm talking about is just in case . . ."

He was a frail half-starved man, and no match for Shad when he leaned on the cart, forcing it off the street into the next alley. "Sorry," Shad said, "but I got to do this," and in the middle of the man's argument, punched him once behind the ear, catching him before he fell.

Gently easing his victim to the ground, sitting him like a drunk against the scaling wall, Shad surveyed the street. No one had looked in the alley and seen. And the cart was his. As hastily as he dared, he returned to the street, pushing the cart back the way they had come. Only a block more to go, then he could run with it. One block, that was all.

The rattling hit the alley like the sound of a barrage. Iron wheels bumping along the cracked littered pavement. A native vehicle of some sort. Shad? he prayed. Could be a patrol, too. Or, God help them, somebody coming to pick up these cartons that made their hiding place. Feeling Gloria trembling against him, Marty shifted soundlessly, fishing under his robes for his pocket. Not, he thought, that a penknife would help. But in the hands of a guy as scared as he was—

The noise stopped, and in the ominous silence as the echoes died away, Marty thought he heard movement. A soft scraping. Could that be *breathing* he heard? Forcing himself to be utterly still, he waited, his pounding pulses tapping off the seconds. Then eerie as birdsong from a desert ghost town came a soft sweet whistling. Thin and high it was, melodious and—after an instant—familiar. The theme of the Shad Smith Show. Gloria made a stifled sound, and as one body, they burst out of their hiding place.

Everything depended now on luck and timing. They had to

move, and fast, or they would never make it. Bundling their robes together, they hid them in one of the empty containers stenciled with the name of a London shipper. Then swiftly and silently they unloaded the cart of the top two layers of rolled-up rugs, stacking them neatly in the recessed doorway. Making a stirrup with his cupped hands, Shad whispered: "Allez-allez," and boosted Marty and Gloria into the cart. With the largest of the rugs he'd unrolled, he covered their prone bodies in the cart. "Okay, gang—here we go."

The first of the hazards, but essential to their plan, was the lone guard Shad had seen posted where the alley system ran into the marketplace. Trundling the cart away from their hiding place, he held his breath as it rattled around the corner. His view was cut off by the high slatted side. The noise of the iron wheels seemed deafening. Willing fortune as he had willed his own performances, Shad made himself keep going blindly until he was almost at the plaza. Then slowing the cart, his face an innocent blank, he peered around the side.

Praise de Lawd. The guard was still there.

Stifled under the dusty rug, Marty held back sneezes and waited tensely. Beside him Gloria lay absolutely still, her breathing so shallow he worried for her. Spartan tales of suffering occurred to him—some lamebrain cluck letting a fox eat out his heart. So we ride through the city and end up smothering? Trapped now, he could clearly see what a cockamamey idea Shad had conned them into.

A voice called something, muffled and foreign-sounding. The guard. Shad replied with a moaning meant to convey his muteness. Even to Marty it sounded convincing. Then the cart shook. Marty held his breath. Here's where the men and boys get separated.

Booted heels rang on the pavement. The foreign voice was close now, angry-sounding. As Marty gathered himself, full of congratulation how the idea was working, the cart swung ponderously. According to plan, it must conceal what they did next from the marketplace.

The trooper kept talking. Typical fuzz. And Shad kept grunting like a guy with a bellyache. Then the signal came—three sharp raps on the side of the cart—and with a wild surge, Marty reared up, lunging half over the side of the cart which now faced the alley.

The struggle was brief, silent except for the trooper's wheezing as he flailed pinned against the cart, fighting to break Marty's grip around his throat. He grunted twice as Shad hit him. And as he sagged, a deadweight, Marty held him upright while Shad retrieved his rifle and sidearm.

Tugging and heaving, they dumped their victim into the cart. And while Shad trundled them back down the alley to their hiding place around the corner in the connecting passageway, Gloria and Marty stripped off the trooper's webbed belt and bootlaces. Trussed like a fowl—his arms strapped tight to his sides with the belt, his ankles tied with the bootlaces—the trooper was rolled into a carpet.

"So far so good," Shad whispered elatedly.

"Working like a charm," Marty agreed.

Gloria looked anxious. "I hope somebody finds him."

"They will, baby, they will."

"But not too soon," said Marty. "I hope."

Then grinning like lunatics, he and Shad heaved their victim onto the heap of rolled-up carpets in the doorway. Marty climbed back into the cart, flopping beside Gloria. "Harbor, James," he hissed, "and don't for godsakes spare them horses!"

Shad covered them with the rug again, then the cart began to roll at a lively pace, rattling like a tumbril down the alley once more—this time in the other direction.

Figuring it was safer to chance the narrow mercantile street rather than the marketplace, Shad continued sedately, hoping no one had discovered the cart's original pusher. And what if the owner of these rugs saw him? The list of hazards grew longer and longer.

He must turn left, giving the plaza a wide berth, he decided. Later on, he could cut back again to the wide main street which traversed the city from Old Town to the harbor. Imitating the other pushcart laborers, he leaned rather than pushed his, using his whole body to keep the cart moving. Sweat rolled in streams down him. He kept his head bent, his shoulders hunched, limping slightly as the thin coal-black man had done. Between the slatted sides of the cart, he watched the covering rug for any tell-tale sagging into a human form, any sign of movement, but there was none. Marty and Gloria were following instructions to the letter, lying still as corpses, sweltering under their heavy covering.

The narrow noisy street quit eventually, coming to a dead end at a quieter avenue. Turning right, Shad continued on, keeping his pace steady as a patrol jeep slowly cruised by. For sure the dragnet was out in this town. But they were still looking for an Arab lady and two fake natives in white robes. No one noticed him. He hoped it would last. And hoped, too, that elsewhere in the city a man with a pushcart wouldn't attract attention.

Through a chink of light where the rug that covered him had folded slightly at the end, Marty could see confetti-sized pieces of the passing scene—bits of vehicles, bits of the streets and people passing by, a newspaper kiosk ahead. Would Shad remember to stay off the sidewalks? Marty's immigrant grandfather had begun life in America with a pushcart, and he could remember as a boy hearing how the cops pinched you if you got on the sidewalk, and how the gentiles would never step one side. Dust sifting from the rugs tickled his nose. The odor of his own body seemed overpoweringly bad. Feeling sorry for Gloria lying sealed in the same chrysalis next to him, he shifted his head slowly, trying to get a look at her, but she was out of range of his peripheral vision. And the cart stopped. Marty held his breath, listening to a car motor grinding by in a low gear. What had happened? His heartbeat deafened him. An endless time seemed to drag by, then the cart jerked and began to roll again. Shad did something with the covering carpet near his feet, but Marty didn't dare move to see what.

The wheels grated and clanked along the pavement. They passed by what looked to be tenement apartments, then ratty houses; the tone of the streets was definitely run-down the nearer they got to the harbor. Shad could smell now the salty sump odor of tidal flats, the oily fishy presence of creosoted pilings, barnacled docks, rotting boats and their refuse. Another quarter mile, maybe less to go. Dock cranes reared up ahead like the skeletons of dinosaurs. From somewhere distant came a hoarse hooting—a tug perhaps. Drugged with fatigue, he kept pushing and hoping, pushing and thinking, his mind dizzy from the last seventy-two hours, stunned by the events which he had touched off—innocent match to the train of powder.

Anger seeped through him, a dull dismay he knew he'd never forget, not as long as he lived. Count 'em up, Colonel, he kept thinking bitterly. Look at the dead, was it worth it? But he knew the answer. Sure, he did. All us old soldiers know the score. That's why we keep singing God Bless America. God Bless Television. God Bless the Film Industry. God Bless My Bank Account. But never—God help us—God Bless Living and Breathing. There aren't any anthems for what really matters . . .

There was a slight rise in the pavement now, and Shad groaned with the added weight of the cart. Under the glaring sun the street shimmered ahead, ugly, wavering, an undersea dump. Then the avenue turned and sloped downward. Ahead lay the port, the sea beyond, and above it all, towering into the limitless sky, black ranges of storm clouds sweeping in like a flying continent. Under them, white as a gull on the sheet-silver surface of the harbor lay their destination—the Grecian cruise ship *Kyprios*. Smoke was pouring from the stacks.

31

Warehouses empty of goods loomed hollowly around the wharf. Planking muffled the noise of the cart wheels. The dock area seemed deserted except for the long wide stone jetty where, at the end, the tourist bus jockeyed and turned, its passengers aboard a small white launch already halfway out to their ship. A military jeep sat nearby the bus. Dismayed, Shad searched for a third vehicle, but there was none to be seen.

They had gambled heavily on a single guess—that Belelondres' sole concern now would be to keep them from the ship or any contact with its passengers. The major would relax, they figured, when the bus load from the marketplace had boarded the launch. What they counted on was the second contingent—the strays such as the couple Marty had seen, for whom another launch trip would be necessary. Shad had been certain, Marty nearly so, that Belelondres must wait to scrutinize each one as these laggards returned to their waiting ship.

Stopping the cart by what looked to be an abandoned watchman's hut, Shad leaned heavily on the pushbar, catching his breath. The silence bothered him, worked on his nerves. And tobacco hunger assailed him suddenly, an interior chill: Had they guessed wrong?

Then he heard a click—unmistakably a weapon. A guard appeared, another and another—perhaps fifteen in all—materializing from places of concealment in the warehouses around them. But they kept their distance, Shad saw. Where was Belelondres? A motor started up, rumbling hollowly. And out of a warehouse nearest the jetty eased the black limousine. Shad began to breathe again.

The car stopped perhaps ten feet from the pushcart, and from behind the bullet-proof glass window, Major Belelondres gazed broodingly at Shad. All was still again. Overhead the clouds swept in, spreading a false twilight over the harbor. At last Belelondres lowered the window. "Mr. Smith?"

Shad did not answer or move. He began to pray fervently.

"Come, Mr. Smith—I have worried sufficiently about you." He waited, but Shad did not move or speak, and as if pushed beyond caution or patience, Belelondres opened the door, sliding out swiftly as wind in sharp puffs brought the first plump drops of rain down on them. Brushing the globules from his sleeves, he strolled around the cart, inspecting it elaborately. "Ingenious, Mr. Smith. You shall forgive me, please, but this—" he gestured toward the cart—"was your idea?"

Shad did not reply, but this time his silence seemed to amuse the major.

"And your charming wife? Your friend?" he asked, letting his eyes slide over the lumpy carpet in the cart. "Come, Mr. Smith. I am fascinated by the idea of seeing them again. Most particularly in such a peculiar conveyance."

Leaning against the cart, Shad watched him as he came closer —and when he was close enough, rapped softly three times on the slat side. From the corner of his eye, he saw a stirring under the carpet.

"The unveiling, Mr. Smith—please." Belelondres sighed. "Very well, then. If you insist on playing out your foolish drama—" and reaching over the edge of the cart, he caught hold of one corner of the rug.

But instead of jerking it back, revealing Marty and Gloria, he kept staring as if something in the cart fascinated him. Then straightening without moving his feet so much as an inch forward or backward, he said very gently: "What is it you would like me to do, Mr. Smith? I am—as I have just discovered— entirely at your disposal."

As carefully as if Shad could understand his orders, the major dismissed his guards and instructed the driver of his limousine to wait. The troopers took shelter in the warehouses;

the driver of the car shut off the motor. Shad nodded and they started off, the major keeping to the exact position where Shad told him to stay beside the cart—no more than a foot from that concealed rifle Marty pointed at his middle.

By now thunder boomed across the harbor, great sheets of lightning flared against the slowly approaching rain. But the downpour did not begin until they were halfway out the long jetty. "How stupid of me not to have guessed that this cart would be a decoy as well as the means of your escape," Belelondres commented before it began. "One should have remembered your profession, Mr. Smith. A soldier would not have taken such a chance."

"He would if it was all the chances he had."

"Possibly. But a military man would have considered his next position before taking the first, Mr. Smith. This—you shall forgive me—you have not done. If you had, you would see it as quite impossible." He smiled. "You know, I presume, that I shall be able to demand your surrender from the captain of the cruise ship?"

"Can he do that?" Gloria's voice came muffled from the cart.

"He does," said Marty, "and I'll blow off some of that gold braid he's wearing."

"That ship lies in our waters, Mr. Smith," Belelondres went on. "Under the jurisdiction of the Danju Republic."

"Will you shut that guy up?" came Marty's muffled cry. "What's he trying to do, get his throat cut?"

But Belelondres kept on, obviously aware that he had scored on them: "Perhaps you have counted on being recognized, Mr. Smith." He looked pleased with himself as Shad remained silent. "Pity. Because I myself have checked the passenger list. All European, Mr. Smith. Not a soul on board who will know your name. And in any case, no one, surely, who could possibly recognize the poor indigenous-looking Negro you have become."

"Shad?" Gloria's voice was piercing. The rug heaved. "Shad, is he—?"

"Get down!" he yelled, "and for chrissake, stop listening!"

"Good advice," the major said serenely, "but hardly useful any longer, Mr. Smith. Come," he urged, "be sensible. If you return with me, I can promise you—" Then the downpour began, drowning him out. Oblivious of it, he paced steadily beside the cart. And without waiting to be told as they approached the jeep stationed at the end of the jetty, he roared at the three men huddled under the flimsy canvas covering.

They all gaped at him, then as one man leaped out, coming to ludicrous attention in the blinding rain. A minute later, in the jeep again, they moved off, soon lost behind the storm which obscured the wharf by now.

Marty and Gloria climbed out of the pushcart. Belelondres smiled at them with chilling cordiality. "So now, in spite of the inclemency of the atmosphere, we may talk?" he asked. "I have been explaining to Mr. Smith the problem of leaping—as the saying goes—without looking." He peeled off his sodden white gloves, and with a disdainful gesture, threw them into the roiling harbor. "You have no more chance than that, you see. Not without passports. Or had you forgotten? You are stateless persons, nameless, citizens of nowhere without identification. Surely you must realize that it would be inconceivable for any responsible ship master to take the word of three such obviously derelict persons against mine, an official of the Danju government—"

"What makes you think you're going out to that ship with us?" Marty asked.

"You will kill me, then? But what good will that do?" Again he smiled, rather pityingly this time. "There will still be the problem of obtaining passage," and he sighed. "Quite impossible —quite hopeless, I am afraid, without identification."

Marty and Gloria both looked at Shad, their dripping faces reflecting their despair. But Shad ignored them. And there was no time to talk, for they began to feel a vibration along the rough asphalt paving which covered the top of the stone jetty. "Must be the bus again," Shad said. "Which means the launch'll be back any minute." Pulling out the pistol which Gloria had handed over as if it were a snake, he added: "Major, you're on thin ice from now on—you dig me? One wiggy move and I'll blast you with this cannon."

The rain stopped abruptly, and from under the carpet, Shad pulled a folded fresh newspaper which he draped inside-out over his hand and wrist, concealing the pistol.

Belelondres looked amused. "This is a gangster's trick, Mr. Smith? At any rate, be assured I have no desire to become your target. There is no need, you see—"

Shad cut him off, instructing Marty to dump the rifle in the cart and cover it.

"Listen, if you think I'm gonna let go of this—"

By now the atmosphere had cleared, they could see the bus slowly traveling along the jetty toward them. "Make it pronto, will you, man?" Shad snapped. "Let's not scare anybody we don't have to."

Hopeless now, Marty obeyed him, for it was too late to argue. By the time the rifle was hidden, the bus had pulled up and the driver opened the door. What looked to be an officer from the ship—swarthy-faced, starchy in whites—peered out at them. Shad stepped forward, but the major shouldered him aside, swiftly boarding the bus.

"Belelondres," he cried arrogantly, clicking his heels. "Aide to General Okefe, Chief of State! I must talk to your captain. The matter is most urgent."

Grabbing Shad's arm, Marty whispered: "Why didn't you *stop* him? Listen, are you—?" He stopped. "Look, what're we gonna do? All I can see now is cold-cocking that stud when we get on the launch. It's our only chance now."

But Shad shook his head no, and as the passengers filed out of the bus, he smiled at them all like a welcoming committee. Jesus, Marty thought, he's flipped out. He looked at Gloria, and seeing her fear and bewilderment, knew just how badly they had gone wrong . . .

Through the drizzling tail end of the storm, the launch hooted, bouncing across the choppy harbor like a child's bathtub toy. Old tires chained to the stone side of the jetty protected its fragile hull against the surge of the storm-whipped harbor as it slowed and came about. A Greek sailor in sopping whites jumped from the gunwales to the jetty, holding the launch steady as the passengers boarded. There was plenty of room for the major and his three companions. Graciously, as if the launch were his, he urged them to board ahead of him.

"Shad," Gloria whispered, "what're we going to *do*? *Look* at him! He knows we can't—"

"Hush, baby." He pressed her shoulder. "He may just be talking."

"Yeah," said Marty, "like a guy with four aces up his sleeve. You think he'd go aboard if he wasn't *sure*?"

With the pistol in his lap, hidden by the newspaper, Shad watched Belelondres as he boarded, staggering slightly with the launch's pitching, and settled in a stern seat near the officer from the bus. They talked softly all the way out to the cruise ship. "But I do not have this authority!" Shad heard the officer saying once, his voice raised excitably. Belelondres murmured something soothing, and from then on the Greek kept glancing at them warily—as if he knew now what lay under Shad's innocuous-looking newspaper.

A great rainbow arched over the harbor and the city as they boarded the cruise ship *Kyprios*. Passengers leaned against the railings, watching them curiously. One or two off the bus stopped to spread the news, and by the time they had climbed the several deck levels to the captain's cabin, a buzzing crowd had gathered to watch.

They stepped through the doorway in the bulkhead, finding themselves in a tunnel-like corridor. Shad noticed a seaman standing guard at the end. Another who had followed them took a position just outside on the deck.

"Must wait, please," the officer from the bus said, and knocked on an interior door. As he slid through it, Belelondres followed him.

Desperately, Marty and Gloria turned to Shad, both whispering at once. He only shook his head, indicating their guards. "For chrissake," Marty hissed, "at least ditch that cannon! He's probably in there right now selling us as hired killers—"

"Cool it. Let's wait and see what happens." Feigning a calm he by no means felt, Shad leaned against the bulkhead, cradling the pistol in the newspaper he had bought at a kiosk.

The door opened, and the Greek officer beckoned them into the captain's cabin which was sumptuously paneled, filled with cigar smoke. From behind his desk—lean, sallow, sour-faced— the master of the *Kyprios* stared at them. Belelondres sat opposite him, puffing on a long thin cheroot, relaxed and pleased with himself. Under the overhead light, the captain's bald head glinted like polished bone as he leaned back. "Criminals?" he said to Belelondres. "You did not say, sir, that one was a female. Nor did you mention that one was European—"

"Listen, we're all Americans," Marty began, but Shad poked him.

"You are political criminals, I am told," the captain went on sourly. "Assassins," and he sighed gustily, turning again to Belelondres. "Which is the one you say is armed?"

Using the cheroot, Belelondres pointed. The officer from the bus moved warily toward Shad as the captain gazed at him, letting his eyes slide to the folded newspaper.

Carefully Shad opened the folds, letting the pistol lie there harmlessly. The officer from the bus snatched it away, placing it before the captain on his desk.

"Good. Very wise. And now," he snapped his fingers, "passports, please?"

"They have none," Belelondres said.

"None." Resting his elbows on the desk, the captain leaned his chin on his hands, inspecting Shad, then Gloria, then Marty. Dyspeptically he belched. When he spoke finally, he sounded weary and disgusted: "This official has demanded your surrender. Since we are in the territorial waters of his country— and since you are without proof of identity, I have no choice—"

"But we have proof." Shad stepped forward, spreading the Danju newspaper on the desk. On the front page was a four-column cut of the three of them in their Abercrombie and Fitch threads—the shot the newsman had taken by the Land Rover. Not the best picture any of them had ever seen of themselves, but still it was as good as any passport photo.

A lot of things happened simultaneously then. Gloria sagged with a kind of sigh. Marty caught her, and with Shad's help, got her to a chair. The major sat very still, watching the *Kyprios'* captain as he studied the newsprint. Then the cigar between his fingers snapped in two. Belelondres jumped to his feet. "This is a lie!" he shouted. "I demand—"

"Lie?" The captain's voice overrode his. "Are you saying, sir, that your own newspaper has falsified the identity of these persons?"

There was a lot more hubbub which Shad missed, but Marty was in the middle of, talking fast, looking feverish with excitement. Something about the captain radioing Piraeus if necessary, and Marty threatening to contact Washington. Belelondres departed soon after, gray-faced, escorted by the officer from the bus. And still looking sour, the captain gave orders for the purser to be summoned. Did Mrs. Smith require the services of the ship's doctor? No? Well then, if they would excuse him, please, he must be present on his bridge for the *Kyprios'* departure to Lagos. Let him know, please, if there was anything they required. No, he did not care to hear what had happened to cause them such distress in Danju; it is not necessary for a man to know everything in this life, only the essentials, was that not correct? The next thing they knew, they were following the purser who just happened to have a deck suite available . . .

32

"One thing you gotta say for the major," Marty said later when the ship was at last underway, "he didn't waste any time crying when he lost his game. Did you ever see a guy make a faster getaway?"

"What else could he do?" Shad grinned. "After all that jazz

he told the captain about us, there sat his hometown rag making a monkey out of him."

"Wait'll Daddy hears I've been a female assassin," Gloria giggled.

"For all of five minutes."

"Was that all it was?" She sighed deeply. "It seemed like an hour we were standing there—"

Refreshed by baths and borrowed or newly bought changes of clothing, they stood at the railing watching the coast of West Africa sliding by. "Not that I don't enjoy," Marty said finally. "God forbid I shouldn't! But will you please tell me why you didn't let us in on that cockamamey newspaper gag when you first thought of it? I mean, how come you had to leave us sweating nickels all that time while George Gorgeous played his aces?"

"You think he would've played 'em if you hadn't been sweating? Look," Shad went on, "we had to get out to this ship—right? Okay, the only way we could do it was by using the Maje as our ticket. But *he* couldn't know he was our ticket, could he? He had to keep thinking he'd be winners all the way."

"He had me convinced." Marty grimaced. "Oi, did he ever! All that business about no passports—nobody'd know us—the captain'd have to hand us over. Jesus, that was the worst half hour I ever hope to live through, listening to that stuffed-shirt clothes-horse crowing!"

Shad explained then how certain he had been that the major would somehow trick them unless he was sure he could not lose by cooperating. "He had to be sure, see. And you two turning three shades of green didn't hurt any making up his mind for him—"

"So he goes along with us," Marty said marveling, "thinking all he's got to do to save his bacon is get us out here. Once we're here, they get the cannon off you. All he has to do then is con the captain about who and what we are and *bang!* next thing we know we're all back in the launch, headed for the nearest guillotine." Then his face clouded. "But how come all that blowing off he did on the pier? He as good as showed us all the cards he was holding. He was lucky we didn't throw him in the harbor."

"He figured we'd see the light, maybe—which you two nearly did—make it easier for him by just giving up."

Although the air was humid, Gloria shivered in the new dress she had bought on credit in the *Kyprios'* tiny boutique shop. "He thought he had us either way, didn't he? Like a big cat with three mice in a corner. What do you suppose will happen to him, Shad?"

"You know how the game goes, baby. Losers tell sad stories, winners say 'let's deal.'" He took her arm, then Marty's. "Mice, what do you say to a drink and some dinner?"

"Never heard a better idea in my life!"

And without looking back, they left Africa behind them, a dark shadow on the horizon.

> *CAPETOWN (UPI)—A mysterious explosion of substantial magnitude has occurred in the interior of Danju, West Africa. Unrest is sweeping the country. UN observers were alerted yesterday to the possibility of a coup in the making . . .*

UNITED NATIONS REPORT—CONFIDENTIAL

ITEM A: Intelligence sources report from Lisbon that a black male using the name Fernando Corraia departed on a jet bound for Lagos, Nigeria. Corraia is believed to be the exiled former premier of the Republic of Danju . . .

ITEM B: In a bi-motored aircraft, the property of the Danju Republic, General Albert Okefe flew yesterday to Cairo, where he was reported to have been given a cool reception . . .

From a "Hollywood Reporter"
column: *Shad Smith's SS Pro-*
ductions announced plans for
the filming of the star's new
feature not yet titled. Locations
have been changed from West
Africa to a more ring-a-ding
spot (also explored by Burton
and Taylor) called lil ole
Puerto Vallarta in Mayhico. "So
it's a jungle picture, they got
jungle there, too," says Marty
Brom, Shad's PR faithful. "And
the action, man, is strictly
swinging. Expect us when you
see us, baby!"
Well, hasta la vista, Shad and
Co—but don't forget, baby, you
got a budget and a wife . . .

However, Gloria decided to go along, just in case—she explained enigmatically—Shad forgot to leave the adventuring
where it rightfully belonged—in his script writers' heads.

☆ CAROLYN WESTON ☆
grew up in Hollywood during the
Depression. Hollywood Boulevard was
the scene of her truancies; movie houses
one refuge, the public library another.
She spent part of World War II working
in an aircraft plant, and afterward
gypsied around the country, working at
anything and everything (Reno
gambling club, specialty wallpaper
house as decorator, New Orleans
nightclub, Prentice-Hall and Lord and
Taylor in New York, among others). All
this time she had been writing and
discarding manuscripts, until at last one
of the novels was published. Now she's
back home in California, writing full
time.